D0916896

THE SEGREGATED COVENANT

THE SEGREGATED COVENANT

Race Relations and American Catholics

WILLIAM A. OSBORNE

HERDER AND HERDER

1967
HERDER AND HERDER NEW YORK
232 Madison Avenue, New York 10016

Nihil obstat: Leo J. Steady, Censor Librorum
Imprimatur: ✠Robert F. Joyce, Bishop of Burlington
February 14, 1967

Library of Congress Catalog Card Number: 67–17623

Manufactured in the United States

TO THE YOUNGER GENERATION—PARTICULARLY
KATHLEEN, THERESE, JIM, JOHN,
MATT, MARY AND JANET

CONTENTS

ACKNOWLEDGEMENTS

THE framework of this book is to be found in a report on *The Desegregation Process in the Catholic Church* submitted to the Fund for the Republic in the spring of 1964. This report resulted from the joint efforts of Mr. Robert Reynolds, managing editor of *American Heritage,* and this writer. Hence in parts of this book his editorial skills and well-turned phrases remain in evidence; the section on the Archdiocese of Washington particularly, stands, except for revisions and updating, substantially as he wrote it in 1964.

Beyond that, the book's foundation can be traced back to the early 1950's when the author met the founders of the Catholic Interracial Movement, the late Father John LaFarge, S.J., and Mr. George Hunton. There followed hours of informal discussions, recorded biographical memoirs, and focused interviews with these pioneers of interracial justice. From all this there grew in the form of a doctoral dissertation at Columbia University an historical account of *The Race Problem in the Catholic Church: 1866–1933*. This was updated and published as a special issue of *Jubilee* in September, 1955. We likewise wish to acknowledge the crucial role played by John Cogley, now associated with the Fund for the Republic (the Center for the Study of Democratic Institutions), for expediting the subsidy granted by that organization. Without that, this work could not have been undertaken.

With respect to the sections herein on the Archdioceses of New York and Philadelphia, we are heavily indebted. Mr. Dennis Clark, formerly a housing consultant to the City of Philadelphia and executive director of the New York Catholic Interracial Council, did most of the research and writing. I wish also to acknowledge my indebtedness to Father Anthony Vader who generously allowed us to supplement our own research in Chicago by drawing on his masters thesis. His historical background of the Negro in Chicago we found particularly helpful. Mr. John McDermott, Executive Director of the Catholic Interracial Council in that same city, was also of great assistance.

Special mention is due Mr. Matthew Ahmann, executive director of the National Catholic Conference for Interracial Justice. To him, we owe much. Our debt to Mr. John Sisson, Southern Field Director of the NCCIJ, and Mr. Henry Cabirac, his predecessor in that office, is of only slightly less magnitude. To Father Albert Foley, S.J., of Spring Hill College, Alabama, we wish to say a word of thanks, for his invaluable assist on research in Alabama; and likewise to Leslie Dunbar, formerly of the Southern Regional Council.

To the host of generous men and women who played the role of interviewee or "resource person" we wish again to express our gratitude. Space forbids anything but the mention of their identifying groups or organizations: the N.C.W.C. and the Chanceries, the Josephite Fathers, the Society of the Divine Word, the Society of Jesus, the Catholic Interracial Councils, Friendship House, Human Rights Commissions, the NAACP, the National Urban League, CORE, the Cursillo, and the Christian Family Movements.

To my colleague Father Richard Thayer, C.M., and John Sevior Johnson for their research assist in St. Louis, I am grateful; and likewise to our graduate assistants, Sister Rosella McCormick and Herman James, and our secretaries Vivian Papsdorf, Betty Kelleher and Marian Duffy, who bore patiently the burdens of endless typing and other labors that go with manuscript preparation.

To no one, however, is a greater debt owed for the completion of the manuscript than to my wife, Peg. Her powers of observation and insight sharpened my own. Her patience sustained mine; and her shoulders bore the responsibilities of a father too often away or late at the office.

THE SEGREGATED COVENANT

INTRODUCTION

THROUGHOUT practically the whole history of the United States, the Catholic Church has been regarded by those outside her ranks as a monolithic organization whose members not only assent to the same creed and discipline but who hold similar views in the area of politics and economics. In a nation long dominated by a white, Anglo-Saxon, Protestant majority, Catholics were commonly considered a lately arrived minority, low on the social scale, thought-controlled by an authoritarian clergy with whom they kept a perennial watch over the ramparts of sexual morality and the parochial school system. On the other hand, no one ever seriously questioned their consent to the neat racial arrangement of white domination of the Negro.

Without going into the genesis of the change, it can be stated confidently that this stereotype is fast being reversed. The election of a clerically unfettered Catholic president, the world-wide impact of the warm, unauthoritarian personality of Pope John, and the new openness after the Vatican Council have all contributed to the shattering of the old image. Moreover, if one had been following the news coverage of the mounting racial crises through the 1950's it would have been easy for him to detect a widening crack in the Catholic consensus on the traditional racial arrangement. Most impressive of all was the 1958 statement of the hierarchy which stated that "the heart of the race question is moral and religious" and that "segregation cannot be reconciled with the Christian view of our fellow man." It further declared: "It is a matter of historical fact that segregation in our country has led to oppressive conditions and the denial of basic human rights for the Negro." Against the background of such a policy statement, the national network of

Catholic interracial councils and the list of newly discovered champions of the cause, the Church appeared grandiose indeed. Among informed Negroes its liberal reputation seemed assured.

One did not, however, have to be too sophisticated an observer to note widespread and obvious flaws in the new image. The separate Negro Catholic Church, observable in practically every major city in the United States, raised doubts in one's mind. Then too, it was only on a rare occasion, if ever, that one might come across a Negro priest. Perhaps the most glaring fact that undermined confidence in the favorable Catholic image was the rank and file of Catholic people themselves. They exhibited no distinguishable attitudes nor practices vis-à-vis civil rights and all its related problems. Statistically, one could predict a Catholic's attitude toward pornography, his Friday menu and his Sunday morning observance. But no such prediction was possible with respect to his stand on allowing a Negro family to move into a neighborhood. Nor could one assume that he had even read the 1958 statement of the American hierarchy, much less agreed with it. Furthermore, membership lists of either CORE or its more conservative older brother in the civil rights movement, the NAACP, were singularly under-representative of the Catholic population. Catholic youth were notoriously absent from the "young peoples stage" of the movement—the sit-in's and freedom rides. Such observations obviously did not harmonize with the public image or reputation of the Church. It was this incongruity that prompted the research for this book.

It seemed important to us to know how typical or representative of the hierarchy was Archbishop Joseph Rummel of New Orleans. And how representative of the laity was his opposition? We had also heard stories of Negro Catholics being refused admission to Catholic schools and even hospitals. Was it possible that the facts and the laudable reputation of the Church contradicted each other, at least in certain dioceses? Whatever the answers to these and many other questions, certain other events reminded us that we were dealing with a dynamic situation. Yesterday's facts might be true of that moment, but what did they indicate about the direction in which the Church was moving? What, for example, could one discern about the direction of change in the fact that there were several hundred priests, sisters, brothers, laymen at Selma from over 50 dioceses, while almost simultaneously nine California bishops (including Cardinal James McIntyre) chose to remain silent on the notorious "Proposition 14"?

Archbishop Thomas Toolen of the Diocese of Mobile-Birmingham deplored the intrusion of clergy and religious at Selma, declaring that they "should be home doing God's work." Contrariwise, in Milwaukee, a few months later a group of curates, sisters and lay people placed an advertisement in the Milwaukee *Journal* protesting their bishop's refusal to allow the use of parochial schools as freedom schools. In the vineyards of California during the spring of 1966, as the National Farm Workers Association attempted to organize the migrant workers, sharp lines of division appeared among the clergy and bishops as to the role of the Church. Such incidents have been occurring regularly throughout the country these past few years.

Our first step was to focus our attention on those dioceses which contained the bulk of the Negro Catholic population, and which would also be representative of the major geographical regions—the North, the South, and the border states. By focusing first on such dioceses we felt we could establish a starting point before going on to the more complex problem of the meaning of the conflicts alluded to above. It was important to establish where Negro Catholic Churches exist and why. Was it simply a function of residential distribution, custom, or pressure? What are the forces bringing about desegregation at the parish level? How well do white and Negro Catholics mix?

Are all the Church's educational institutions—from kindergarten to seminary and university—equally accessible to all applicants?

Do Catholic hospitals have hidden color bars or quotas? Are qualified Negro doctors and other professionals more readily accepted in Catholic hospitals than in others?

Three Northern dioceses—New York, Philadelphia and Chicago—were chosen for a study in depth mainly because of the relatively large number of Negroes, Negro Catholics and white Catholics they contain. But there were other considerations.

For many years, especially since the death of Baltimore's Cardinal James Gibbons just after World War I, New York has become, in effect, the nation's primatial see. Its archbishop, particularly in the person of Cardinal Francis Spellman, has been the titular leader of American Catholicism. Moreover, the city's growing status as the financial and communications center of the nation and as the site of its best-known Negro ghetto has given race relations there, and what the Church does about them, national importance.

Philadelphia is a center of another kind. It has, of course, always been conscious of its history, and the best elements of its population have been characterized by a spirit of public service and a solid respectability. In these qualities its Catholic immigrants, after a period of adjustment on both sides, eventually came to share; the Catholic Church in Philadelphia mirrors in many ways the city itself. How did such a conservative, if energetic, Church react to the influx of Negroes which began in the 1890's and continued through World War I?

In Chicago for over three decades, the Church had nurtured a spirit of innovation and lay responsibility which gave the city's Catholic life an atmosphere of freedom wholly unique in American Catholicism. More importantly, the center of the Catholic interracial movement itself is located here. Chicago is the headquarters for the National Catholic Conference for Interracial Justice, and also for the Friendship House movement. Here too the Church, under the tutelage of the late Cardinal Albert Meyer, experimented with the daring techniques of social reform designed by Saul Alinsky. At the same time, Chicago has one of the most complex racial problems of any city in America, and Catholics, as the summer of 1966 proved, are in the middle of the conflict.

Of the three major border dioceses—St. Louis, Baltimore and Washington, D.C.—the latter was chosen for the study in depth. St. Louis has a longer tradition of interracial concern on the part of the Catholic Church: parochial schools there were integrated long before the Supreme Court decision of 1954—and Archbishop Joseph Ritter took a considerable risk when he made the move. The record of the Church in Baltimore, on the other hand, has been far worse: shackled by Southern traditions, its progress was slow until the advent of Cardinal Lawrence Shehan in 1961. Washington seemed to have a medley of the characteristics of the other two. Furthermore, its status as a metropolis where Negroes outnumber whites meant that there, Catholic attitudes and performance on the race problem would be most readily discernible.

In the South two factors seemed to demand sharp focus on the diocese of Lafayette and the archdiocese of New Orleans. Between them, they hold approximately three-eighths of the Negro Catholic population of the Southern states. Lafayette, with its 78,000, ranks first in the nation, while New Orleans ranked second until recent years. But another and perhaps more important consideration is the strong Catholic cultural background of both sees. They offer, furthermore, a rich contrast for sociological analysis. Lafayette Negroes are poor farmers living in an area where change comes slowly and where the civil rights movement was, for the most part, news from the outside world. In more prosperous, more cosmopolitan New Orleans, the pace of change is quick by comparison. Its economic ties with the nation, national defense industries, and the Caribbean world are far more intimate; its political and social structures, far more complex. The opportunity for a comparative study of the ways the Church grappled with the same race problem was one that could not be passed by.

While the aforementioned six dioceses received intensive treatment, the focus of our research has been broad. The chapters which follow offer the results of our study by region: the South, the border states, the North (including the Midwest and the West Coast). And in view of the "commission" of the Ecumenical Council for Catholics to embrace the world and become engaged in its travail, the crucial question in such a study as this goes beyond the race problem within the Church, to the one on the national scene. What *is* the Catholic Church doing, through its parishes, and agencies, to help the nation in its struggle with the race-poverty syndrome? Has it harnessed its economic power, its political influence and its manpower to what the bishops themselves called "the nation's number one moral problem"?

I.

THE NEGRO AND THE AMERICAN CHURCH

AFTER the Civil War, as before it, the American Negro was an enslaved man—the victim of a Christian people. Yet, as a modern historian has written: "In a number of respects Christianity was a boon to the Negro, cut off from their country and their former tribesmen. . . . It gave them a historical tradition, a literature, a background all at once. . . . They could and did fit into the concept of God's chosen people; they, like the ancient Hebrews, were in bondage, longing for the promised land."[1] But even the granting of the solace of membership in the Church stirred controversy among Christian masters.

Before the war both Catholics and Protestants had encountered resistance to their educational efforts among Negroes. John England, the Catholic bishop of Charleston, S.C., had tried to start an elementary school for colored children, but the civil authorities closed it down and the bishop received anonymous threats that if he persisted his cathedral would be burned. For whatever education and religious training they received, the slaves were totally dependent on the inclinations of their masters. Some plantation owners took this obligation seriously. In 1845 a South Carolina planter reported: "The number of people on my place is 116 . . . Rev. J. S. Hanckel is the only minister, and my wife and myself the only teachers employed among the

1. Maurice Davie, *Negroes in American Society,* New York, 1949, p. 176.

people. I read the service and teach the catechism to all the people every Sabbath afternoon. After family prayers on Wednesday night I teach those who come voluntarily to be instructed. The children are taught constantly during the week by Mrs. M. and our sons, and know the catechism and several hymns."

But many slave-owners were not so conscientious, and since slaves were legally the property of their masters, priests and ministers could preach among them only with the master's permission. Negroes had few churches of their own. "Such organizations," a white Georgia minister wrote, "we do not deem expedient." If slaves accompanied the white family to church, they were carefully segregated, either in a gallery or in special pews; sometimes separate services were held for them after the white services were over. In Catholic churches the practice was the same. Though it was written 15 years after the war ended, Father L. A. Dutto's description of segregation in Mississippi Catholic churches holds good for pre-war times as well: "In the [Catholic] churches of whites they [Negroes] are tolerated but seldom welcomed; and they must not mingle with the congregation, but remain separate."[1]

Thus it was that at Emancipation the Catholic Church in the South was in no better position than the Protestant Churches to help the freedmen adjust to freedom. Of the 7,000,000 Negroes who lived in the United States in 1863 (including 3,000,000 in the North), only about 100,000, a little over 1 per cent, were Catholics, and the overwhelming majority of these were in traditionally Catholic Louisiana and Maryland.

The fact that Catholics accepted the color line as carefully as did Protestants was only one reason for their failure to make Negro converts before the war. In the South, throughout the 18th and 19th centuries, there was always a shortage of priests, most of whom were in cities, while the slave population was primarily rural. Moreover, Catholicism was for the most part an ill-respected religion, frequently attacked by the dominant Protestant sects; in 1867 the American Missionary Association's

1. "The Negroes in Mississippi," in *The Catholic World,* Feb., 1888, 576.

annual report expressed fear lest Catholicism's "splendors" would appeal to the colored people's "love of display," and noted that the Church, this "man of [Satan]," had already entered the colored mission field. About the same time the Methodist Episcopal Church was warning against Catholicism's "evil schemes" and urging Methodists to "save them [Negroes] from the wiles of Romanism."

In the North, where the Church was stronger and might have been expected to attract free Negroes, her appeal was blunted by the violence of the Irish who had begun to arrive around 1820. As they helped dig the canals and lay the rails that were moving westward from the sea, Irish laborers met intense job competition from freed Negroes who would work for lower wages. Every large city had its strong-arm groups made up largely of Irish workers: in Cincinnati they were called the "Iron Mongers"; in Baltimore, the "Plug Uglies"; in New York, the "Flat Heads"; in Philadelphia, the "Moyamensing Boys." Tension, beginning in a struggle for bread and butter, frequently exploded into race riots. In a three-day running battle in Cincinnati in 1829, Irish hooligans attacked Negro property and killed many freed Negroes and fugitive slaves. Almost the entire colored population of 2,000 was uprooted and moved to Canada. An 1834 riot in Philadelphia developed into a bitter pitched battle, and in New York, in 1863, mobs of Irishmen enraged by the inequalities of the Civil War draft laws—which conscripted the poor and permitted the wealthy to buy exemption—vented their bitterness by hunting down and brutalizing the city's Negroes. "Irish and Catholic were one to the Negro," says a somewhat naïve Catholic historian, "and he hated both, thoughtlessly blaming the mother for the sins of her sons."

This was the background, then, against which some 60 Catholic bishops and archbishops from all over America convened at Baltimore in 1866 for the Second Plenary Council. The War had ended only a year before; in the Council's sessions were bishops some of whose priests and people had fought for the Union, others for the Confederacy. Strangely enough, the Church had survived both the slavery controversy and the war united;

but the Baptist, Methodist and Presbyterian Churches split into Northern and Southern branches. Acrimony was absent at Baltimore as bishops from North and South took up the problems of reconstruction.

Churches, schools and other ecclesiastical property had been destroyed or damaged in many Southern dioceses, particularly Richmond and Charleston which had lain across Sherman's line of march. Bishop Patrick Lynch of Charleston, appealing for help to Archbishop Martin Spalding of Baltimore, wrote: "I find my hands full and my heart overfull. What suffering. How much to do. How little to do it with. I have not yet got a house to live in. I would also like to have a Negro church." His episcopal residence and St. Finbar's Cathedral, valued at $180,000, were in ruins. In Louisiana, where Catholics were fairly numerous, casualty figures in the local regiments had been very high. New Orleans had 1,200 war orphans, cared for by the Catholic Church and the Federal Army—hungry, ragged testimony to the large numbers of Louisiana Catholics who had died for the Confederate cause. In men, money and property the Church had suffered most where she was weakest, in the South.

Archbishop Spalding, in summoning the bishops together, had told them: "I think it is our urgent duty to discuss the future status of the Negro . . . We have a golden opportunity to reap a harvest of souls, which, neglected, may not return." And the cardinal prefect of the Congregation for the Propagation of the Faith, in naming Spalding apostolic delegate for the Council, had informed him that Rome regarded the welfare of the recently emancipated Negroes as "of the utmost necessity." Yet no concrete, practical plan for mission work among the Negroes came out of the Council. In the pastoral letter the bishops issued after adjourning they said: "Our only regret in regard to this matter is that our means and opportunity of spreading among them [Negroes] the protecting and salutary influences of our Holy Religion are so restricted." They begged diocesan priests and members of religious orders "by the bowels of the Mercy of God" to volunteer for work among the Negroes. The Church in Europe was also asked to send missioners. Outside of these appeals, the Council left the question of the freedmen living in each of the Southern dioceses to the Southern bishops, who even if they had the desire had neither the personnel nor the money to solve the problem. Little help came from Europe, except that given by an Englishman, Father (later Cardinal) Herbert Vaughan.

In 1871, in obedience to the wish of Pope Pius IX and in response to the earnest plea of the American bishops at the Second Plenary Council, Father Vaughan and four other members of his recently founded Foreign Missionary Society [Josephite Fathers] arrived in Baltimore to work among the newly freed Negroes in the United States. After being formally installed by Archbishop Spalding, Father Vaughan made a tour of Southern cities to determine the scope of his task and to raise funds. The diary he kept on the trip gives a first-hand picture of how white Southern Catholics treated their Negro co-religionists. Vaughan, who had expected the worst, was shocked. Negroes were "regarded even by priests as so many dogs," he noted. "I visited a hospital where there were a number of Negroes. Talked to many in it and in the street. All said they had no religion. Never baptized. All said either they would like to be Catholics or something to show that they were not opposed to it. Neither the priest with me nor the Sisters in the hospital do anything to instruct them. They just smile at them as if they had no souls."

Everywhere Father Vaughan went—Savannah, Vicksburg, Natchez, Memphis, Charleston, New Orleans—the situation was the same. In a Catholic cathedral he saw a Negro soldier refused Communion by a white priest. There were low, backless benches marked off "For Negroes." First Communion was administered on one day for white children and on another day for colored. Reaching St. Louis in January of 1872, he visited the archbishop, and afterward noted in his diary: "The Archbishop thought all my plans would fail; could suggest nothing for the Negroes, and refused permission to collect; and declined to give a letter of approval." Despite this unpromising beginning, the Josephites stayed. In 1893 they set up an independent

American foundation with headquarters at Baltimore; from there, for more than 70 years, they have been going out to cities, small towns and rural districts all over the South, bearing, in the words of one of their number, "the heats and burdens of a prejudiced day."

Since the Church in the South was overwhelmed by the shortage of priests and the physical tasks of rebuilding, help from the North in caring for the Southern Negro might have been expected. In 1883 an anonymous writer in *The Catholic World* had said: "There are more priests in proportion to the Catholic population now than in 1840. With some bishops we are informed that the question is, 'What shall we do with our young priests?' . . . As to the religious orders, it is hardly an exaggeration to say that their novitiates are overflowing." Whether the Northern bishops could have spared priests to help their Southern confreres is conjectural. The fact remains that they did not.

When the Third Plenary Council convened in 1884 it recognized the inability of the Southern bishops to cope with the problem the Second Plenary Council had bequeathed it. A Commission for Catholic Missions Among the Colored People and the Indians was formed to administer the proceeds from an annual collection to be taken up in all parishes on the First Sunday of Lent. There is no official record of the Council's attitude toward the plight of the Negro, but some glimpse of it is found in the sermon which Bishop W. H. Gross of Savannah delivered before a congregation of priests and laymen in the Baltimore cathedral while the Council was in session. "What is to be done with them [the Negroes]?" he asked. "There is only one thing that will do any good, and that is to elevate them morally; make them honest men, chaste women, obedient, law-abiding citizens."

To this patronizing view there were some exceptions, notably those of Archbishop John Ireland and John Boyle O'Reilly. Ireland, a former Civil War chaplain who in 1888 was consecrated archbishop of St. Paul, Minnesota, was to become in the next three decades a national figure—a fierce patriot, a champion of his fellow Irish immigrants, a leading spokesman for the liberal wing of the American hierarchy. On the race question, no bishop of his time was as far-sighted. Throughout his thirty-year tenure in the See of St. Paul, the parochial schools were integrated. "Surely it shall not be said," he remarked, "that the State schools go farther than Holy Church in the application of the great principles of the brotherhood of man and the common Fatherhood of God." In a speech delivered in 1891, three years after he became archbishop, he voiced a set of goals which today, some 75 years later, are the same ones which Negro leaders seek for themselves and their people: "I have said," he began, "that slavery has been abolished in America: the trail of the serpent, however, yet marks the ground. We do not accord to our black brothers all the rights and privileges of freedom and of a common humanity. . . . What do I claim for the black man? That which I claim for the white man, neither more nor less. I would blot out the color line. . . . It is not possible to keep up a wall of separation between whites and blacks, and the attempt to do this is a declaration of continuous war. . . . Let the Negro be our equal in the enjoyment of all political rights of the citizen. The Constitution grants him those rights; let us be loyal to the Constitution. If the education of the Negro does not fit him to be a voter and an office holder, let us for his sake and our own hurry to enlighten him. I would open to the Negro all industrial and professional avenues—the test for his advance being his ability, but never his color. I would in all public gatherings and in all public resorts, in halls and hotels, treat the black man as I treat the white. I might shun the vulgar man, whatever his color, but the gentleman, whatever his color, I would not dare push away from me."

In John Boyle O'Reilly the Negroes of Boston found an equally articulate champion. In his youth in Ireland, O'Reilly, a member of the anti-British Fenian movement, was sentenced to penal servitude in Australia. He escaped and was picked up by a New England whaling captain. In 1870, within a year after his arrival in America, O'Reilly became editor of Boston's Catholic weekly, *The Pilot* (now the official newspaper of the archdiocese), and soon rose to leadership in the Irish community.

O'Reilly was one of the first to recognize the problems posed by the newly freed slaves (whom he compared to "new metal out of the mine"), as well as the promise they held out for the enrichment of the country's life. "The destiny of the colored American is one of the big problems to be worked out in the life of this Republic," he wrote prophetically. "The day is fast coming when this man's claim cannot be answered by a jest or a sneer. The colored American of today may not be equal to his position as an enfranchised man . . . But this man's children are coming and they are receiving the same education in the same schools as the white man's children. . . ."

When O'Reilly died at 46, worn out by insomnia and overwork, Boston's Negroes placed crossed palm branches on the lid of his coffin, and Portland's Bishop James Healy, the only Negro ever to head a U.S. Catholic diocese, delivered the eulogy. A memorial to his spirit is the John Boyle O'Reilly Interracial Council of Brooklyn, in which today's Catholics of Irish descent labor for interracial justice.

But men like Ireland and O'Reilly were rare. Bishop Gross's sermon more accurately reflected the prevailing Catholic approach toward race relations at the time: it was a one-sided view, a white man's perspective. If in the white man's eyes, the Negro was illiterate, superstitious, irresponsible and immoral, it was assumed that he was that way by nature, or by reason of his African ancestry. No heed was given to the peculiar type of slavery in the United States, which had done so much to stunt its victims. Thus, except for the establishment of the Commission and the decreeing of an annual collection for the missions, the Third Plenary Council was unable to formulate any over-all plan for relieving the Negro's plight.

It is true that from the end of the Civil War to the turn of the century the bishops of the United States faced problems which were matters of life or death for the Church in America. All through those years immigrants, most of them from Catholic countries, crowded into the United States. In one decade, 1880–

1890, the Church in America gained six million members. Churches and schools had to be built, the newcomers had to be helped to adjust to American life and build American loyalties. "National churches" were set up to ease the difficulties of transition, but these, unintentionally, lent strength to nationalistic factions whose bickering nearly destroyed Church unity. Moreover, in the process of Americanizing the immigrant and proving that he could be both a good citizen and a good Catholic, leaders of the American hierarchy were charged in Rome with the "heresy" of Americanism. The anti-Catholic American Protective Association was at its peak during these years; there was a vitriolic dispute over whether religion should be taught in public schools; and Catholic workingmen were under severe pressures for and against the newly formed labor unions.

All these factors deflected the time, the attention and the resources of the bishops away from the situation of the Negro. Given their limited means—as late as 1909 some 21 U.S. dioceses were still partially subsidized by Rome—they may have been hard put to implement an ambitious plan for the Negro missions. But meanwhile the Southern Negro, who was forced into his own segregated churches after the Civil War, was becoming more devoted to Protestantism. "Wherever I go," the ex-Union general Carl Schurz reported following a trip through the South soon after the war, ". . . . I hear the [white] people talk in such a way as to indicate that they are yet unable to conceive of the Negro as possessing any rights at all. Men who are honorable in their dealings with their white neighbors will cheat a Negro without feeling a single twinge of their honor. To kill a Negro, they do not deem murder; to debauch a Negro woman, they do not think fornication; to take the property away from a Negro, they do not consider robbery. The people boast that when they get freedmen's affairs in their own hands, to use their own expression, 'the niggers will catch hell.' "

By and large, once Southern whites got courts, legislatures and elections procedures back into their own hands, Negroes did "catch hell." So swiftly and securely was the white supremacy reëstablished that within a few years after the war thousands of Negroes were migrating West and North; Governor John St. John of Kansas, where many of them sought refuge, said that in the South the freedmen were "being forced back into a condition if possible worse than the slavery of a few years ago." Those who anchored in poverty or bound by love for their homes could not or would not leave had to find ways to soften the harshness of staying. Supplementing whatever reservoirs of patience they could find within themselves was the external reality of the Negro church.

All through the slave days, Negro religious gatherings, whether held in the slave quarters or in a church, had been subject to white supervision. Now for the first time Negroes had churches which were really their own. Most were Baptist and Methodist, and all were far more than houses of worship. After services on Sunday the Negro housewife, who had no newspaper, could find out what was going on in the community; the farmhand and the artisan could find a market for their labors; a young woman could find a husband and a young man a bride.

Looked at from a mid-20th century point of view, when the problem of restoring unity to Christendom is a vital concern to so many in all churches, the establishment of separate and independent Negro churches simply added to the number of "pieces" to be reunited. In the Catholic experience, the absence of a Negro clergy plus the principle of universality, that all men belong in one church, prevented the segregated Negro church from taking that last step—independence. Yet the number of conversions to this ideally universal church in the post-war decades is hardly worth counting. The explanation is that there was no missionary enterprise worthy of the name.

But more important was the communal nature of the Negro Protestant church. Conversion from it would simply have meant obstracism from this combined social club, employment agency and community center: this was tantamount to secession from the racial community. Partly because of the strong emphasis Catholicism placed on doctrine—very few Negroes had any education, and wherever the Church did manage to set up

Catholic schools they operated under severe difficulties—and partly because the general sentiment against Catholicism, noticeable in ante-bellum days, intensified after the war, "The feeling against our holy religion is very marked," said Bishop Leo Haid of North Carolina in 1890, "stirred up and kept alive by ignorance, and sometimes, I fear, malice, especially in the country." For the Negro, dark skin itself was a heavy enough burden without his taking on the added one of membership in a maligned Church.

Separate Catholic churches for the Negroes had begun to spring up as early as the Second Plenary Council of Baltimore, either because white Catholics would not worship in the same building with Negroes or because white priests, foreseeing this difficulty, wanted to spare their colored parishioners the inevitable indignities to which they would have been subjected. But separate churches did not become numerous until World War I. In the Catholic experience the separate church has often proved a mistake: Catholic Negroes, many of whom at first wanted their own churches, soon realized that these were being founded merely because of prejudice. Though Negroes were segregated in the Methodist and Baptist communions, and though in addition their own church buildings were often shabby and the colored ministers inadequately trained, those colored congregations at least had control over parish affairs, including the power to dismiss an unpopular pastor. The Catholic Church could offer no such autonomy.

Against obstacles like these a small band of priests and nuns, all but ignored by their fellow Catholics, labored steadily in the Negro cause. In 1891 Father Vaughan's Josephites were joined by a community of nuns, the Sisters of the Blessed Sacrament for Indians and Colored People, founded by Katharine Drexel, the daughter of Philadelphia financier Francis Anthony Drexel.

Katharine Drexel built schools and missions in New Mexico, along the Colorado River in the Northwest, in the big cities and small towns of the South, and in the mill towns of New England. Perhaps the most famous institution founded and staffed by her nuns is Xavier University in New Orleans, for decades America's only Catholic Negro University.

If Katharine Drexel's is the best known among the religious communities of women working among American Negroes, it is not the only one, nor was it first in the field. In 1825 a young Frenchwoman named Josephine Alicot was debarking from a ship in New Orleans harbor when the gangplank collapsed and she fell into the Mississippi. A Negro standing on the dock dived into the water and rescued her, whereupon she vowed to devote the rest of her life to the service of the Negro race. She began by going from plantation to plantation, teaching the catechism to the slaves. In 1842 she founded the Sisters of the Holy Family, the second order of colored nuns to be started in the United States. The first, the Oblate Sisters of Providence, had been begun in 1829 by four Negro refugees who had fled the slave uprisings on the island of San Domingo and who had been parishioners of America's first Catholic colored church, St. Francis Xavier's in Baltimore. Today each of these colored communities has almost 300 professed sisters, and between them they operate nearly 70 Negro schools. Two other groups of nuns who have devoted a major share of their work to the Negro missions are the Sister-Servants of the Holy Ghost and Mary Immaculate, of San Antonio, and the Franciscan Handmaids of the Most Pure Heart of Mary.

Though all dioceses will now accept colored candidates for the priesthood, the only major seminary in the country established exclusively for them is St. Augustine's at Bay St. Louis, Mississippi, which saw its first four graduates ordained in 1934, and which has since sent out more than 30 other priests. In 1965 its rector, Father Harold Perry, S.V.D., was appointed auxiliary bishop of New Orleans, the first Negro to hold that rank in the South and the second to be consecrated in the United States. Though St. Augustine's is the most famous institution run by the Divine Word Fathers, it is by no means the only work for the Negro being done by this German community, which first came to the U.S. in 1906 and which, along with the Josephites, the Holy Ghost Fathers (1872) and the Society of the African

Missions (1907), has been prominent among the priests who minister to Catholic Negroes in America. All these communities of men and women have been trying at great sacrifice to follow the advice of Venerable Francis Libermann, the Jewish convert who founded the Holy Ghost Fathers: "Act toward them [Negroes] as servants toward their master," he told his priests. "Perfect them, sanctify them . . . and make them, slowly and surely, into a people of God."

In their efforts to do so, these Catholic missionaries to the Negro shared a common handicap: a continuing shortage of money. In addition to the Commission for Catholic Missions Among the Indians and Colored People set up by the Third Plenary Council, the hierarchy established in 1907 the Catholic Board for Mission Work Among the Colored People. Its first director general, Monsignor John Burke, wrote about a not-untypical reaction to his fund-raising efforts: a Northern pastor read to his parishioners a letter from their bishop recommending the Board's work to their charity, then casually remarked: "I do not know about this collection. . . . You will find a box down there at the door and if you wish to put anything in it, for the Negroes and Indians, you can do so." Not many did; in 1919 contributions averaged three-quarters of a cent for each Catholic in the United States.

Living an impoverished existence, forced to accept the pattern of race relations as he found them, the Catholic missionary to the Negro also had to face the scorn of white Catholics. In the 1920's a Benedictine in Kentucky stopped for lodging one night at a Catholic rectory. He was well received until he happened to mention that he worked among Negroes, whereupon the white pastor became indignant and ordered him from the house. About the same time a Josephite in Maryland reported that though he had been introduced to the seven Catholic and Protestant clergymen in the town near his mission, none of them would speak to him in public because of his association with the colored people.

Yet the work went on. In 1939, looking back on almost half a century on the Negro missions, Father Louis Pastorelli, head of the Josephites, said: "I can see the marvels that have been accomplished by the priests and sisters of yesteryear—many now sleeping in nameless graves in forgotten cemeteries of the Southland; many still straining to the yoke. Looking at them it becomes at least slightly irritating to hear so much emphasis placed upon what has *not* been done for Negroes in this country. To me the noteworthy fact is that so much has been done with so little and against so much opposition both without and within the race."

Starting with World War I, rural Negroes in the South, attracted by the prospect of high-paying jobs in war plants, began a wholesale migration toward the centers of industry both north and south of the Mason-Dixon line. The movement slowed down during the depression years, but regained momentum during World War II. American Negroes were once a rural people, but in 25 years an estimated two and a quarter million left the farm for urban areas. Today more than 73 per cent of them are city-dwellers.

In almost every imaginable way the move has meant a revolution in Negro life, and whatever benefits it has brought—a higher standard of living, fuller educational opportunities, a somewhat more complete integration into the nation's life—have been paid for in the bitter coin of knowing, after the long exodus, that the promised land is not called Birmingham or Detroit or Los Angeles. If Emancipation was an earthquake, migration has been a steady erosion in which the pace and values of city living have tended to undermine the migrant Negro's family life, shrink his moral fiber and sap his religious loyalties.

In the North, as Negroes poured into the major cities, the "race problem" became an issue for the first time. A combination of poverty, personal preference and white prejudice forced the newcomers into colored ghettoes—Harlem in New York, the South Side in Chicago—which soon acquired the characteristics of pressure chambers as overcrowding forced the Negroes to look for housing elsewhere while white homeowners, driven by fear and ignorance, tried to enforce segregation. For the most part the reaction of Northern whites to "the Negro problem" was no more creditable than that of whites in the Southern states. And as far as Irish Catholics in particular were concerned, the historical record makes for sorrowful reading. Gilbert Osofsky, an historian who wrote *Harlem: The Making of a Ghetto,* notes that "San Juan Hill," running from 60th to 64th Streets and westward from Tenth Avenue, got its name from the battles fought there between Negroes and the Irish. "The antagonism between these two peoples was undoubtedly one of the harshest inter-group hatreds in American history," states Osofsky.

What was happening in the North at large was also taking place within the Catholic Church. For the first time, segregation and discrimination began to be a local problem, as in growing numbers Negro families sought to join "white" parishes, Negro children applied for admission to parochial schools, sick and injured Negroes came for treatment to Catholic hospitals.

But the record of priests and bishops, as far as access to parish churches was concerned, has been generally good, even though the Negro press occasionally reported a number of incidents in which it was clear that membership in some churches was denied non-whites. In 1929 New York's Cardinal Patrick Hayes, pressed for a statement of policy by the National Association for the Advancement of Colored People, said: "Every Catholic church is wide open for anyone who wishes to enter for devotional purposes . . . [Segregation] does not represent the attitude nor the spirit of the Catholic Church." In a few cases churches were set aside for the exclusive use of Negroes, sometimes because of white prejudice, sometimes because Negroes themselves requested them. But apart from these the separate Church in Northern cities has not been the result of a policy of segregation; most "Negro parishes" today are products of population shifts.

The fact that Catholic priests stayed in these changing neighborhoods when other whites left was not lost upon Negroes.

This is explainable by canon law which defines the parish on a geographical rather than a congregational principle. Recently, the veteran pastor of what is now a Negro parish in Harlem recalled that at first some colored people regarded him with suspicion because he remained while white Protestant ministers —and his own white parishioners—moved away. But when they saw that service was his only motive, respect replaced doubts. Some of the priests were prejudiced. But they overcame their resentment, learned to know and love their new communicants, and were repaid with a measure of affection. Today, one of their number has said, priests in Harlem find their work so rewarding that few would leave voluntarily.

In Catholic schools and hospitals, justice and charity were less well served. Though accurate information on discriminatory practices by schools and colleges is difficult to acquire, the truth is that until recent years there were relatively few Negroes in Catholic schools. Valid reasons unconnected with race (the physical inability of the Catholic school system to admit all who applied; the financial inability of most Negro families to pay even modest tuition fees) may help to explain the fact. Yet it remains true that from its founding in 1907 until 1937, the Catholic Educational Association never once went on record as favoring integration. Father Edward Kramer, who succeeded Monsignor Burke as head of the Board for Catholic Missions Among the Colored People, wrote in 1934: "Trepidation, fear prevailed. Why? Because of a spectre . . . and that spectre, the soulless, terrifying ghost of 'what our Catholic people might . . . do.' . . . It is said that our [white] students . . . will leave if Negroes are enrolled."

It is true that from the early 1930's onward the national Catholic Student Mission Crusade, led by the late Father John Gillard, S.S.J., passed strong resolutions in favor of interracial justice and put them into practice within the organization. Furthermore, some Catholic colleges (for example, Loyola in Chicago, Loyola in Los Angeles, Seton Hill and Villanova in Pennsylvania, Fordham University Law School, among others) were accepting Negroes in the early 1930's and have never ceased doing so. In 1938 Mother Grace Dammann, R.S.C.J., president of fashionable Manhattanville College (then on the edge of Harlem), shocked conservative Catholic opinion in a widely reprinted speech called *Principles Versus Prejudice:* "The Pope and the Bishops insist upon Catholic education on all levels for Catholic students," she said. "A Catholic colored girl who meets the requirements of a Catholic college and applies for a Catholic education has a *right* to it and in consequence the college has a *duty* to give it to her." In a secret ballot taken that year, 80 percent of her students voted to accept Manhattanville's first Negro applicant. But a far greater number of Catholic colleges and universities (including some of the most famous), made timid by their own definition of "prudence," have begun to admit Negroes only in the last 10 or 15 years.

The pressure against the discrimination barriers began to rise under the old "G.I. Bill" which paid the tuition and living expenses for World War II veterans who decided to resume college after the war. This brought increased numbers of Negro applicants to Catholic institutions. In 1954 the Supreme Court decision, declaring segregation *ipso facto* unconstitutional, further undermined the "prudence" argument which had become so convenient a rejection device. By way of generalization it can be said that those colleges which catered only to nonresident students dropped their barriers first. Catholic boarding institutions did so slowly, and only a few at a time.

A dearth of factual information prevents any conclusive judgments about the admission policies of Catholic hospitals. No nationwide investigations have been made; but here again, though overt discrimination is a thing of the past, documented instances of widespread racial bias do exist. A Negro refused admission to a Catholic school may never be sure he was turned away because of his color; a Negro unable to get into a Catholic hospital knows the reason why.

Ever since racial injustice became an issue in the North, individual Catholics—lay and clerical, black and white—have fought it, though in many cases their valor has cost them dearly. One of the earliest group protests was launched by Catholic Negroes themselves. During World War I, Dr. Thomas Wyatt Turner, then a botany professor in Howard University, organized a Committee Against the Extension of Race Prejudice in the Church. Small but militant, the Committee protested to Church authorities whenever an instance of racial discrimination by a Catholic institution came to its attention. In major cities of the North pastors, bishops, archbishops—even the papal delegate—were approached directly and insistently. But while its demands were justified, the Committee's approach left one factor—human nature—out of the equation. It was not ecclesiastical policy which assigned the Negro a pew in the choir loft or kept his children out of the parochial school; it was—at the level of the individual pastor or administrator—deep-rooted prejudice, or the human tendency to conform. But Dr. Turner and his Committee ascribed their failure to make lasting progress to their own lack of impressive numbers and to their loose organization. Since the Irish, they reasoned, apparently owed their influence in the Church to their talent for shaping mass organizations like the Ancient Order of Hibernians and the Knights of Columbus, members of Dr. Turner's Committee began, in 1925, to group the Holy Name, Altar, Rosary and other laymen's societies in Negro parishes from New York to New Orleans into a new movement called the Federated Colored Catholics of the United States. Under Turner's leadership the federation demanded immediate and direct reform within the Church.

The Federated Colored Catholics did not long remain alone in the fight for interracial justice. In 1933 a group of white priests involved in the Church's apostolate to the Negro met in Newark to form the Clergy Conference on Negro Welfare. Within a few years this group sired others—one in the Midwest, another in Mobile, a third in the dioceses of Richmond and Raleigh. The aim of the Conference was, as an early member put it, "to make our priests and nuns color conscious by every available form of publicity—pamphlet, press, radio and even, if possible, by singing."

The Conferences, which met three or four times a year for a decade, sent out a series of letters to priests and nuns in their respective regions; one of the most effective bore on its cover the slogan "Keep the Negro in His Place"—inside, it was explained that his "place" was within the Catholic Church. In New York and Philadelphia, debates, lectures and skits on the radio explained Catholic interracial doctrine. Letters were sent to colleges and schools conducted by nuns, encouraging them to enroll Negro students and offering to furnish speakers on race relations.

Meanwhile, in the New York editorial offices of the Jesuit weekly *America,* Father John LaFarge, a veteran of fifteen years in the Negro missions in Maryland, was meeting with a number of colored Catholic business and professional men who called themselves the Catholic Laymen's Union. Through his experience in these meetings and in the Clergy Conference, of which he was one of the founders, Father LaFarge began to formulate a new approach to "the race problem." It was based upon two central ideas: first, that repeated stressing of grievances brings, in the long run, diminishing returns: "If you have made little impression by telling your story once," he wrote some years later, "you may fail to make any impression when you relate it for the second time, and encounter more stubborn resistance from then on"; second, that in the fight for interracial justice whites and Negroes must work together, not separately: "If the children of light . . . do not join forces, the children of darkness will take over and exploit their apathy and division."

This approach was made explicit on Pentecost Sunday, 1934, when the Catholic Laymen's Union sponsored a mass meeting in New York City's Town Hall. Some 200 people had been expected, but more than 800 came; almost all of them voted for the formation of an interracial organization for the promotion of better race relations along the lines of Catholic doctrine. Toward the end of that year, with the financial backing of the Clergy Conference, the First Catholic Interracial Council was formed. George Hunton, a white Catholic lawyer from Brooklyn who had participated in the joint legal defense of the Scottsboro Boys[1] and had later worked with the Catholic Laymen's Union, gave up his practice to become the Council's executive secretary.

The Clergy Conference on Negro Welfare ceased to function around 1942, partly because of the war, partly because of the death of some of its founders. By that time, too, the strength and influence of the Federated Colored Catholics (which had changed its name to the National Catholic Interracial Federation) had dwindled considerably. But all three organizations—the Federation, the Catholic Laymen's Union and the Clergy Conference—had helped shape the ideas and the spirit which today make the Catholic interracial councils one of the Church's major instruments in the fight for interracial justice.

For many years the Friendship House movement was another major voice, though never numerically impressive. It began in 1939, when a Russian émigrée, the Baroness Catherine de Hueck, assumed a personal responsibility to help the people around her and, with some financial help from the Catholic Interracial Council of New York, rented a flat in Harlem. The essence of the Friendship House movement (which at its apogee in 1949 maintained houses in New York, Chicago, Washington, D.C., Shreveport and Portland) is that its members shared the lives of those they sought to serve. White and Negro staff members (who volunteered for at least a year) got a salary of $6 a month plus room and board. They lived in tenement houses above or near the store-front Friendship House itself, their meals were of the simplest kind, and they chose their wardrobe from among the castoffs donated for distribution to the poor. But from their meager stock of donated money, clothing, books and food they gave to all who came in need.

Moreover, members of the Friendship House movement

1. This was a trumped-up charge against five Southern Negroes accused of rape, which came into international prominence in the early 1930's.

championed Negro rights, not in an abstract way but concretely: they fought unjust evictions; helped get jobs for fathers out of work; ran summer day-camps which took slum children out of their depressing surroundings for a few hours a day; directed the sick to free clinics or hospitals—and fought to get them admitted if prejudice barred their way. They also conducted open forums. The permanent staff members of each house organized an Outer Circle, a cultural and educational group; each summer at the two Friendship House farms (one in Burnley, Virginia, the other in Montgomery, New York), short summer courses on the interracial apostolate were given; and every month from the Chicago house about 6,000 copies of the movement's newspaper, *The Catholic Interracialist,* were mailed to priests, religious and laymen all over the country. The "Credo" of Friendship House summed up the movement's aims; it concluded: "As long as a Negro in America is not treated as a brother in Christ and a child of Our Father in Heaven, not given due recognition of his dignity as a man . . . Friendship House has work to do."

For various reasons the number of Friendship Houses has declined in recent years, and today only the Chicago house remains, though the Friendship House newspaper, renamed *Community,* has retained its national circulation. The Chicago House has developed into an influential force in the state and through its Home Visitation Project it has also become effective on a national scale. This project, with the endorsement of President Kennedy, engaged an estimated 100,000 people in interracial home visits in 112 cities in 1964.

In the decade since the Supreme Court's decision of 1954 the Catholic interracial movement has made notable gains. In 1958, at their annual meeting in Washington, the Catholic bishops of the United States issued a strong statement entitled "Discrimination and the Christian Conscience." It said, in part:

> No one who bears the name of Christian can deny the universal love of God for all mankind . . . Our Christian faith is of its nature

universal. It knows not the distinctions of race, color or nationhood . . . Every man has an equal right to life, to justice before the law, to marry and rear a family under human conditions, and to an equitable opportunity to use the goods of this earth for his needs and those of his family. . . . we are bound to love our fellow man. The Christian love we bespeak is not a matter of emotional likes and dislikes. It is a firm purpose to do good to all men . . . The question then arises: Can enforced segregation be reconciled with the Christian view of our fellow man? In our judgment it cannot.

Recalling the bigotry and injustices to which Catholic immigrants had been subjected, the bishops continued:

The immigrant, fortunately, has achieved his rightful status in the American community. Economic opportunity was wide open and educational equality was not denied to him. Negro citizens seek these same opportunities . . . They wish acceptance based upon proved ability and achievement. No one who truly loves God's children will deny them this opportunity. To work for this principle amid passions and misunderstandings will not be easy. It will take courage. But quiet and persevering courage has always been the mark of a true follower of Christ.

Catholic laymen, too, have shown an increasing concern for civil rights. In 1959 the Catholic interracial councils, which had been dwindling in membership and influence for some years, were revitalized by being brought together for the first time in a nationwide organization, the National Catholic Conference for Interracial Justice, with headquarters in Chicago; a Southern field office was added in New Orleans in 1962. The number of local councils has rapidly increased: today there are close to 100 of them from coast to coast, and their programs are beginning to show the influence of the trained professionals being attracted to their leadership. For many years the local councils performed a valuable function in spreading "the Catholic viewpoint on race" within the Church and in the community at large. Today they are becoming conscious that "the race problem" will not yield to principle alone, however sound and however often reasserted; that it requires involvement—and above all, professional competence—in such fields as housing, education, equal employment opportunities and urban renewal.

At the initiative of the National Conference, the first national interreligious organization in the field of civil rights was formed. In January of 1963, the centennial of the Emancipation Proclamation, almost 700 voting delegates and 500 observers from 70 national religious bodies—Catholic, Protestant and Jewish—met in Chicago to dedicate themselves to a common effort "to work, to pray and to act courageously in the cause of human equality and dignity while there is still time, to eliminate racism permanently and decisively, to seize the historic opportunity the Lord has given us for healing an ancient rupture in the human family, to do this for the glory of God." The new organization, called the National Conference on Religion and Race, voted to set up interfaith civil rights units in ten cities: Chicago, Detroit, St. Louis, Seattle, San Francisco, New Orleans, Atlanta, Pittsburgh, San Antonio and Oakland. Many Conference members participated in the March on Washington and the Selma to Montgomery March, and joined in the lobbying that brought about the passage of the civil rights bill in the summer of 1964.

Despite these impressive advances, "the trail of the serpent," in Archbishop Ireland's words, "yet marks the ground." When in September of 1963 a Negro named Horance Baker sought to move his family into a new home in Folcroft, a heavily Catholic suburb of Philadelphia, his white neighbors stoned and vandalized the house. Two months later, in Chicago, a Negro Catholic named Joseph Bertrand, a former Notre Dame basketball star, was blackballed when he sought to join a Knights of Columbus council. A week later, meeting in Washington, D.C., the National Catholic Conference for Interracial Justice felt constrained to criticize some Catholic hospitals for discriminatory hiring practices. And a survey conducted by a priest-sociologist and published in the fall of 1964 revealed that although young Catholics educated in Catholic schools attend Mass and receive the sacraments more regularly than Catholic graduates of the public schools, their attitudes in racial matters are not significantly more Christian—a fact confirmed in Chicago during the summer of 1966.

Clearly, the thinking and actions of the Catholic people lag behind the Church's moral teaching on interracial justice, behind the official statements of the bishops, and behind the progressive positions taken by laymen in the Catholic interracial movement.

II.
THE SOUTH

THE basic context for an analysis of the impact of a social problem on an institution is its immediate cultural unit. Institutions, such as a Catholic diocese, exist simultaneously as functional units of a regional culture, a national culture and, of course, the more extensive Western civilization. Obviously, it would be going the long, hard way around to work the analysis from the larger unit downward. It is more sensible and helpful that the smallest cultural unit that can be defined be taken as our starting point.

A second reason for starting with this smaller unit is its differential function with respect to the larger cultures. A man who takes the marriage vow today can be assumed to be making a commitment to monogamy. He is, in other words, acting on a value or ideal learned by his ancestors and passed on to him with little or no reflection. This particular marriage form is peculiar to Western civilization. However, when the same gentleman, a Brazilian, let us say, accepts monogamy with a woman of a different race, he is exhibiting a behavioral form peculiar to a smaller cultural division. For the more detailed understanding of behavior, the smaller unit seems to perform this differential function.

But undoubtedly the most cogent reason for focusing on the smallest cultural unit is the role which it plays in shaping the mentality of its members. In the process of socialization the cultural group in its day-to-day patterns of speech and behavior socializes the young by the process of imitation. The imitated behavior and speech patterns, which are the unwitting vehicles of norms and values, become habitual and thus internalized. The end result for the group or society is the order that comes from shared norms, common ways of looking at life and common ways of behaving. If one is going to gain any insight into the people of a diocese and the way they look at the problems that relate to the white-Negro issue, then one must keep in the forefront of attention that cultural unit which differentiates these people from other Americans.

The unit of culture we refer to is, of course, "the South." In accepting it as a viable entity, however, we do so with the full realization that we are leaning heavily on a historical reality that is undergoing rapid change. To ignore it, on the other hand, and deny "the South" as an effective socializing medium is to fly in the face of some very obstinate realities. Despite the inroads of industrialization and unionization, for example, "the mind of the South" (to borrow the title of W. J. Cash's classic) still prevails. The Crown-Zellerbach Corporation in Bogalusa, Pan American World Airways in Atlanta, Royal Crown Cola in Birmingham and even the liberal-oriented Christian Family Movement in New Orleans all have had to adapt to "Southern ways." Economic and religious organizations or movements have not altered this environment simply by their entry. Whatever long-term influence they might exert, even their very survival depends on an initial adjustment to the customs and mores of the region. After that, the modulating influence of such organizations or movements is governed by a number of complexly interwoven variables. To discuss these is not in order here. Our point is simply that "the South" lives on as an influential cultural entity which continues to shape the mentality of individuals, influence the policies of organizations and institutions, and set the tone, the style of response to the revolutionary changes under way in the nation at large. Such changes, corrosive as they are of the patterns of attitudes and behavior through which they course, nonetheless are still patterned.

If the South is the cultural soil of such dioceses as Lafayette, Louisiana, New Orleans or Atlanta, it should also be noted that there are local variations of it. While a lingering affection for the Old Confederacy, a mythology and "the Southern way" constitutes its main theme, white attitudes toward the Negro and segregation patterns here and there do vary. In these respects southern Louisiana, for example, differs from Jackson or Birmingham. The explanation seems to lie in the different historical ancestry—one French and Spanish, the other Anglo-Saxon. It might be well to look at some of these Southern dioceses, noting particularly their distinguishing features and how these have influenced the reaction of the Church and her people to that problem complex we call civil rights.

With the exception of the diocese of San Antonio and those in southern Louisiana, the Church in the South has been, at least up to the 1950's, an alien or minority group institution. This relationship to the regional culture has been designed by history. The first Catholics to enter the area came, in the late 18th and in the 19th century, from Ireland, a nation persecuted for religious reasons and enslaved economically. The migration was therefore a flight for survival. This fact plus the relative paucity of their numbers required a process of accommodation. Economic dependence shut off other alternatives. Thus the history of the "Old South" depicts the newcomers as supplying the need for manual laborers. The few clergy who were able to follow them likewise had their task clearly defined. It was one of helping a despised minority to "keep the faith." In a more personal vein the task called for administering the sacraments, offering solace in suffering and bereavement, and warning the wayward. For close to 200 years the activity of the Church in this overwhelmingly Protestant and for the most part hostile region can best be described as a "holding action." By 1960 only some 4 per cent of 36 million Southerners were Catholic and most of these were in southern Louisiana.

Recalling what was said earlier about the pervasive, formative influence of culture on personality, and given the nature of the Catholic way of life, the end result in terms of attitudes, values and behavior toward Negroes was a foregone conclusion. Even from the point of view of theology, a more enlightened approach to race relations was hardly possible. The address of Bishop Gross of Savannah to the Third Plenary Council of Baltimore in 1884 typified the best possible attitude, namely, paternalism. Thus, by default, Southern culture shaped not merely Catholic personalities, but also, through them, the institutional response.

In all the dioceses of the South this response has been segregation and discrimination in church, school, hospital, seminary and charitable institutions. But if we can understand why this had to be so, from the force of history, we must now seek to discover where and how the Church is desegregating its institutions. We must endeavor also to determine if a leavening process is replacing that of accommodation, and if so, how this reversal is being accomplished.

As to where and how the Church in the South outside of Louisiana is desegregating its own institutions, it might be well to start with the first dioceses to do so. In 1953 Virginia-born Bishop Vincent Waters, whose diocese of Raleigh includes the entire state of North Carolina, wrote a pastoral letter to be read in all his parishes. It stated in part: "There is no segregation of races to be tolerated in any Catholic church in the diocese of Raleigh. The pastors are charged with the carrying out of this teaching and shall tolerate nothing to the contrary." The reasons he offered for this drastic change he took directly from the Gospel. "The Church does not propose tolerance, which is negative, but love, which is positive. If Christ said love your enemies, we certainly can love our friends. These are our friends and members of our own body . . ." The letter outlined briefly the obligation of Catholics to help the Negroes secure their just rights in all sectors of life from education to the vote.

The response to his appeal ran the gamut of expected response in a state where less than 1 per cent of the population is Catholic: from the threat of violence to reluctant obedience. He faced a mob, straining to do violence, at a pair of churches about 100 yards apart as he supervised their first integrated service. Undaunted, Bishop Waters proceeded to "down" the barriers in Catholic schools and hospitals.

In 1954 Bishop William Adrian of Nashville integrated the parochial schools of that city despite the existence of local ordinances to the contrary. In San Antonio, Bishop Robert Lucey had effected the desegregation of Catholic institutions with relative ease, the high ratio of Mexican Americans probably accounting for the difference. Not so easy was the task faced by Bishop Peter Ireton of Richmond, Virginia, where again violence threatened. In the diocese of Dallas-Fort Worth, Jesuit High School admitted two Negro students in 1955, thereby setting the pace for the other schools on both elementary and secondary levels.

The actual results of all these moves left much to be desired. They represented for the most part courageous decision; they also represented the application of the power peculiar to social organization. As such they had a questionable impact on the mind or heart of white Catholics. And they certainly could not have been expected to muster courage in the parents of Negro children who were for the most part reluctant to expose their children to the threats of violence, intimidation or insult likely to follow their admission to white schools. In fact, a survey made by *Jubilee* claimed that in February, 1959, "With the exception of North Carolina (a liberal oasis), there are only two integrated parochial schools out of a total of 568 grammar schools and 177 high schools in the hard-core racist states of the Deep South."

Whatever the reasons, a reaction apparently set in among Catholic bishops after 1955. For the next few years the desegregation process seems to have halted. Only the diocese of Charleston (and here only in Rock Hill, South Carolina) is reported to have admitted Negro students to Catholic schools. Churchmen, where they were at all inclined to be liberal, evidenced the decision to "wait it out." With the inauguration of President Kennedy and acceleration of the civil rights movement, pressure for desegregation began rising in the Church, stimulating courage where there was a will at all. In 1962 Catholic dioceses throughout the South resumed, one by one, the march to the inevitable. By the end of that year, the following dioceses had been added to the list with desegregated schools: Houston-Galveston (but only in the former city), New Orleans, Atlanta, Miami, St. Augustine, Savannah, Charleston, Little Rock, Amarillo, Austin, Corpus Christi, and El Paso. In January, 1963, added momentum came from the historic meeting of the three major faiths at the National Conference on Religion and Race held in Chicago. In Miami, Bishop Carroll sought vigorously to organize a Mayor's Human Rights Commission to head off social conflict building up in that city. He succeeded and Miami escaped violence. Only where the bishop himself was not convinced that integration was spiritually mandatory did there remain any resistance. The diocese of Natchez-Jackson in Mississippi was one such diocese, while in Mobile-Birmingham there ruled a paternalistic bishop whose theological outlook could, apparently forever, tolerate segregation.

LAFAYETTE: A RURAL DIOCESE

The Diocese of Lafayette covers roughly the southwestern half of the State of Louisiana. It coincides with an area of 14 parishes (counties) whose population is about 60 per cent Catholic. One of the most thoroughly Catholic areas in the nation, it also has the highest number of Negro Catholics of all the dioceses in the nation—approximately 75,000. This diocese, together with New Orleans, St. Mary's and Charles parishes and Maryland, is one of the few where Negroes themselves have a long tradition of Catholicism. Covering the 14 parishes extending from the southeastern border of Texas to the south-central part of Louisiana, this diocese more than any other warrants the title "the Catholic South." It is an ideal area to study the interaction of culture and Catholicism. Given the dominant Southern pattern of race relations, what is the effect of Catholicism on that pattern? Is it corrosive? Ameliorative? Supportive? Does the Church, or do Catholics, lead in social reform movements when found in such a dominant position? Before handling such questions directly, it might be well first to look at segregation as an intramural problem.

Recalling the history of the segregated Catholic Church—that it was a practical solution to the intolerable conditions under which Negroes worshipped in the "white" churches during the Reconstruction Era—the question as to whether or not the original hostility and alienation still prevails is basic. There is not much point in expecting the separate Negro church to disappear while the white state of mind makes such a segregated Church the only peaceful arrangement. While there can be no doubt that profound psychological changes are in process in the South, on the other hand its viable culture continues to form the traditional mentality. The habits of generations have worn such deep behavioral ruts that one can justifiably say that basically conditions have not changed. Furthermore, Lafayette is by no means a prosperous diocese. The people, who are for the most part farmers, are less well off than their counterparts in Texas or the Midwest. The Negro farmer is in particularly difficult straits and almost seems to be outside the central currents of American life itself. Many of them have never even heard of Martin Luther King. For people such as these it should come as no surprise that they would continue to worship, untroubled in their own mind, in "their own" church. In 1963, for example, one of their churches was destroyed by fire. The ordinary of the diocese, Bishop Maurice Schexnayder, took the occasion to integrate the congregation into a nearby white parish. Neither whites nor Negroes minded, believing it was only a temporary arrangement. When it became known that it was not, the Negroes sent a delegation to ask the bishop to rebuild their old church. So earnest was the plea that he felt that he had no alternative but to accede to their request. It is also against this background, therefore, that desegregation within the Church must be examined.

Officially, all Catholic churches of the diocese are open both to Negroes and to whites. But as indicated above, Negro Catholics have their own separate parish churches and chapels, staffed primarily by members of three missionary communities: the Society of St. Joseph (Josephites), the Society of the

Divine Word, and the Congregation of the Holy Ghost.[1] Sprinkled over the area are a few churches and chapels where both races attend service, but in each case the church retains its identity as "colored" or "white," and those of the other race enter more as a matter of privilege than of right. The chapel of Our Lady of Good Hope in the see city of Lafayette is an illustration: as an outpost or "mission" of the Negro parish of St. Paul's the chapel is regarded as "colored," but since it is located near a white neighborhood, some white Catholics attend Sunday and weekday Masses there. (Interestingly enough, they seat themselves apart from the Negro congregation, and approach the Communion rail last. This segregation-in-reverse occurs only *ad hoc:* when the whites come to this chapel for Mass because of its convenience. For all other services and parish activities, they go to their own "white" churches.) For all practical purposes, then, there are in this diocese two sets of churches.

Yet on the diocesan level degrees and varieties of "integration" may be observed. Meetings of parochial school teachers have for the past 15 years been mixed affairs, with no distinction in seating arrangements or even in the serving of meals. Negro Catholics recall in glowing terms the formal dinner and reception for Bishop Schexnayder on the occasion of the tenth anniversary of his elevation to the see: the same receptionists greeted white and Negro guests without slight or offense to either. Seating was by individual preference, and although most of the Negroes tended to gravitate toward tables occupied by other Negroes, there was mixing at many other tables. Diocesan meetings of the Confraternity of Christian Doctrine (a clerical-directed but lay-staffed group which among other activities teaches religion to children in public schools) are likewise integrated. Diocesan sodalities and youth organizations, as well as competitions in music and oratory, once totally segregated, are now conducted on a biracial basis. Marriage preparation courses

1. A few diocesan priests have been assigned to posts in Negro parishes since June, 1962. As the increase in vocations allows, the diocese will gradually assume responsibility for all parishes.

on the deanery level (a deanery is a subsidiary unit of the diocese grouping several parishes in the same area) are attended by engaged couples of both races, and at deanery parades held on the feast of Christ the King the parish contingents line up in alphabetical order; Negro parishes are not expected, as they have been in other places, to "march behind the elephants." The religious ceremonies at such affairs are conducted by priests of both races.

Thus there is evident at the deanery and diocesan levels a considerable degree of desegregation or integration. How soon this will carry over to other areas of Catholic activity remains to be seen.

Elementary Education

Considering the number of parochial schools available to Negro Catholics in proportion to their numbers and in comparison with the number available to white Catholics, Negroes have more than equal access to a Catholic education. In fact, more Negro parishes have their own schools than do white parishes. The comparative quality of the two sets of schools is another matter; many of the priests working among the Negroes say they "know" there is no comparison; in their opinion the Negro parochial school is quite inferior. Judging by physical appearances alone, this would seem to be true. Further substantiation comes from a look at the quality of teacher training for Negroes. This is perhaps an exception, but a pastor in one parish gave a standardized test of sixth-grade level to his two teachers—both of whom handled all eight grades—and both failed. But there are exceptions in the other direction, too: such Negro schools as Sacred Heart Elementary in Lake Charles and Our Lady of Lourdes in Abbeville were claimed as equal to or better than the local public schools. All seven elementary schools conducted by the Sisters of the Blessed Sacrament (Sacred Heart is one of them) are reported to be acceptable or at least "equal," probably because these sisters are trained in Northern schools.

Whatever the merits of these conflicting opinions, it would be a mistake to generalize on this question solely in terms of race. Poverty is no mere spectre in southwestern Louisiana; it is a reality. And "rurality" is another vital consideration. One-room schoolhouses still dot the countryside, and it would appear irrelevant to compare the one or two-room parochial school in a poverty-stricken farming area with the nearest (and understandably better) white Catholic school in town. The location of the Negro Catholic, his consequent lack of aspiration and low economic status—all these things, along with his race, have much to do with the quality of his school.

In September, 1965, the parochial schools of four civil parishes were "integrated." What this meant in practice was that some 12 to 15 Negro families, sensitive to the quality difference between the schools, transferred their children to the white school. Although there were ruffled feelings among many of the "host" parents and a few threatening phone calls to the Negro parents, the transfers were accomplished peacefully. The bishop had announced his intentions as early as 1963 and word got around the diocese that it was not a question of "whether" but simply "when." It was also believed that it would not amount to much of a change in the old order—and it has not. In January 1967, the U.S. Office of Education ruled that the diocesan schools were not complying with the provisions of the Civil Rights Act of 1964. What this meant was simply that there were too many Catholic schools exclusively white and exclusively Negro—(a fact also true of the public schools). This situation prevails despite the fact that in ten or twelve cities of the diocese Negroes may enroll in "white" Catholic schools.

The Negro parochial school is part of the parish, part of the small world that belongs to the poor Negro farmer. To move beyond it, particularly into white territory, requires not merely some extraordinary courage, but also a sophistication about the value of education. This, in itself, is uncommon. Desegregation, then, is not the significant event in Lafayette that it is in cities or places where affluence and the pace of social change are more marked. Yet the devastating effects of racial isolation demand action. The necessary leadership seems to be lacking.

Secondary Education

Secondary education presents a similar picture. From the viewpoint of adequacy, the five Catholic high schools for the colored appear to match the 24 for whites. The question of relative quality seems a little clearer and, for the Negro, sadder: he does not, according to informed sources, get the same quality of education.

Sacred Heart High School in Lake Charles was, until 1965, the only accredited colored Catholic high school. Holy Rosary Institute, a vocational school in Lafayette, has a good reputation among the colored people, but it is overcrowded. Thus in Lafayette, as in other parts of this region, most Negro Catholic students go to the public schools. Economics, the level of aspiration and demographic factors, as well as race, play the determining roles in the number and quality of Catholic high schools. There are no diocesan high schools except one in Lake Charles and the minor seminary. This whole situation demonstrates the economic weakness not only of the Negro individually but of his parish as well. The money for schools must ultimately come from him. His condition being what it is, the odds against building any high school at all are high; and of building a good one, even higher.

Unschooled themselves, Negro parents seem almost unaware of the value of education for their children. Their principal concern is over their crops and over jobs for their children. Since he lacks wide or free access to the range of employment opportunities available to white people, the Negro progresses so slowly economically as to appear to be standing still. This has been his perennial plight, and unhappily he seems to have adjusted to it: both his level of aspiration and his level of expectation are low. Thus there seems to be among the Negroes of the diocese little demand for more or improved Catholic high schools. For better or worse, the public schools seem to meet their requirements.

From the diocese's point of view, the problem seems to be manpower. Even were the parishes to build more or better-equipped high schools for Negroes, the decisive factor would, in the opinion of diocesan authorities, be supplying competent faculties. The drop in religious vocations and the Sister Formation Program have sharply reduced the number of nuns available to staff the schools. The latter program—begun in 1954 and now spreading to more and more religious communities of women across the nation—has ironically slowed the rate of availability of sisters in favor of a longer period of training for them.

In brief, then, secondary Catholic education for Negroes may not be equal to that for whites, but it is not yet the urgent problem it would be in a more urbanized or more prosperous area. Nor is it as urgent as the problem of economic security, nor as deep as that of restoring the Negro's self-respect. And yet, paradoxically, these underlying problems cannot be solved without better secondary education—of a type which will not merely prepare the colored youngster for his economic role but raise his level of hope and awaken him to his own rights and essential dignity.

Seminary Education

It has already been pointed out that priests of the Holy Ghost, Divine Word and Josephite communities administer most of the Negro parishes. As for the diocesan clergy: the Lafayette diocese itself has only a minor seminary; its graduates pursue their advanced priestly studies at the archdiocesan major seminary of New Orleans, or other university centers. But at Immaculata Minor Seminary in Lafayette there are no restrictions based on race. Negro students with the proper qualifications are admitted as they apply. No "quota" exists. But the number of Negroes who apply and are admitted is small: in 1961 there were five in training—the maximum Negro enrollment in any one year since the seminary opened in 1948.

As the diocese with the largest number of Negro Catholics in the country, Lafayette does, as might be expected, rank first in the United States in the number of Negro priests ordained—most of whom have been and are in the Society of the Divine Word. But the number is not at all large, or proportionate to the over-all Negro Catholic population. During the whole span of American history up to 1953, only 68 Negro priests were ordained, 17 of whom were natives of Louisiana. As of 1967 the total number will not be much over 150. Compared to the total number of Catholic priests in the country—55,581 this year—this is almost infinitesimal. Yet in terms of the total number of Negro priests the achievement of the Lafayette diocese is significant. Here, spiritual and moral principles have triumphed over the cultural: as a matter of justice and ecclesiastical need, the doors of the minor seminary from the first have given entry to all regardless of race.

But once Negro priests are ordained for the ranks of the diocesan clergy, there is a problem as to where the bishop can assign them. It seems to be taken for granted that the "place" for a Negro priest is a Negro parish. Unfortunately, these are manned by the various religious orders. The social atmosphere is still not clear enough to predict how Catholics in white parishes will react to the assignment of a Negro curate. A few years ago a Holy Ghost Father, A. A. McKnight, received a temporary assignment to Our Lady of Good Hope chapel. Upon his first appearance to celebrate Mass, a number of whites in the congregation—though they were there only on the sufferance, so to speak, of the Negro parishioners—walked out. Yet that was the end of the affair: no further trouble ensued, even when Father McKnight heard confessions. With this and similar experiences in mind, and considering Bishop Schexnayder's benign and objective attitude toward Negroes, it is entirely likely that if circumstances warrant, a Negro diocesan priest would be assigned to a white parish. It is just as likely that there will be trouble, or at least protest. And it is equally probable that the protest will be of no avail.

The Care of the Sick

Until 1964 all Catholic hospitals of the diocese which had accommodations for Negroes segregated them. In Lafayette proper, Our Lady of Lourdes, a private institution run by the Franciscan Sisters of Calais, had about 25 of 110 beds set apart for Negro patients. Negro doctors were permitted to visit and treat their patients; there were no Negro interns or residents. Only one Negro nurse was employed (for the Negro patients, of course) but more would have been hired if they were available. Charity Hospital in Lafayette, although operated by the Daughters of Charity of St. Vincent de Paul, is a state hospital. It is, as its name implies, open only to "charity cases," white or Negro. Of 381 beds, about 185 were set aside for Negroes. Negro doctors or interns, according to the hospital administrators, were barred by state law. Negro nurses, on the other hand, first accepted after World War II, were needed (for the segregated wards) but have been in short supply. In Lake Charles, St. Patrick's is the Catholic hospital. Sisters of Charity of the Incarnate Word are in charge. Before 1964, out of a bed capacity of 120, there was an allotment of 30 for Negro patients—in a separate ward. There was one Negro Catholic physician on the staff, an associate, and one other "courtesy staff physician." Their services were restricted to the Negro ward. There have been three Negro nurses employed at various times. Again, the number needed for the segregated ward would have been hired, apparently, if they were available.

In Opelousa General Hospital, administered by the Marianite Sisters of the Holy Cross, there were about six beds out of 50 available to Negroes. It is worth noting that in the drive for funds to build the hospital, the Negro community agreed to contribute only if the hospital were "integrated." To these people the term meant simply admissibility; the fact that the ward was segregated from other sections of the hospital apparently was irrelevant. The one Negro doctor in the community, incidentally, was allowed to treat his own patients there. While there were no Negro nurses on the staff, there have been Negro nurses' aides. In New Iberia, the Iberia General Hospital can be described as having had policies similar to Opelousa General. Although neither is a Catholic hospital, they are the only ones.

The Hill-Burton Act, which brought subsidization for the building or expansion of all the above hospitals, was probably a decisive factor in making available the relatively high percentage of beds for Negroes. (The Act requires, as a condition of Federal aid, that the hospital be available to all citizens.) At Our Lady of Lourdes in Lafayette, for example, the opening of a new wing in 1958—subsidized under this law—meant more beds for Negro patients; an old wing was turned over to them. But to the credit of the Lafayette diocese, it must be noted that some beds were always available to Negroes. This was not the case in some Catholic hospitals in dioceses farther north.

The important question of the comparative quality of the accommodations within each hospital was beyond our resources to investigate. We feel quite sure, however, that in almost any hospital in the South they are not comparable. "The best and the first for whites" is a realistic rule of thumb for judging or comparing facilities and institutions. The release of the old wing for Negro use at Our Lady of Lourdes upon completion of the new one illustrates the point, and this rule is probably just as much a function of majority-minority relations as of race relations. It should also be noted in passing that in the South the number of equal or in some cases even superior Negro schools and hospitals is growing, as the region makes a belated effort to live up to the legal requirements of Medicare.

It is difficult to gather statistics for hospitals covering the period since the passage of the Medicare Act and the 1964 Civil Rights Act. Some indication of the continuance of discriminatory practices can be obtained from the NAACP Legal Defense and Education Fund files as of the fall of 1965; the following hospitals were charged by the above with failure to meet the requirements of Title VI of the 1964 law: St. Francis Xavier in Charleston; St. Joseph in Augusta; Mercy in Charlotte; Our Lady of the Lake in Baton Rouge; St. Mary's and Good Samaritan in West Palm Beach; St. Vincent's in Birmingham; Providence in Mobile; St. Patrick's in Lake Charles (Lafayette diocese); St. Luke's in Jacksonville; and St. Joseph's in Tampa. Nothing can be concluded about those hospitals not listed but according to lawyers in the NAACP, religious-affiliated hospitals are generally easier to bring into compliance with the law than are the non-religious-affiliated. Similarly, a *National Catholic Reporter* survey published in August, 1966, noted that out of 100 Catholic hospitals in 11 Southern states, less than 24 failed to qualify for Medicare on grounds of racial segregation or discrimination. By December, the number dropped to one: St. Francis, a 373-bed general hospital in Monroe, La.

Religion and Culture

The large numbers of Negro Catholics in the Lafayette diocese, and the fact that the area as a whole is so largely Catholic, immediately suggest the question we raised earlier: Given the dominant Southern pattern of race relations, what is the effect of Catholicism on that pattern? Does the Church, or do Catholics, lead in social reform movements? We have already noted that segregation within the Church is a rather flexible arrangement. The rules are there, but they are not so inflexible as in, say, Jackson or St. Augustine. But what of the area beyond the Church?

Among historians, politicians and other knowledgeable people, there is a commonly held conviction that French-Catholic Louisiana—the 25 Southern parishes—differs from the rest of the South in the quality of its race relations. The belief has some firm ground under it. It coincides, too, with a body of scholarly opinion, of which Frank Tannenbaum and Gilberto Freyre are the best known spokesmen, that slavery as it existed in Latin America was more humane than the chattel slavery of Anglo-Saxon United States. Yet the historical development of these differences is not traceable to either culture or religion. The point was unwittingly made by one Southern bishop who attributed the excellent progress in desegregation made in the archdiocese of San Antonio to its favorable Latin atmosphere and the slower progress in his own to the long-term migrations from southern Louisiana!

The belief that Lafayette is different because of its Catholic influence is also held by the Jewish scholar Benjamin Kaplan, chairman of the Department of Sociology in the University of Southwestern Louisiana, who has remarked: "The best place for a Jew or a Negro who lives in the South is in a Catholic community." Yet he also noted that while there have been no race riots or disturbances in the Lafayette area in the last 20 years, the problem has not yet come to a head.

Again, one hears it said over and over that whatever sentiment there is for desegregation in the state is to be found in the southern parishes. In the Democratic gubernatorial primary of 1960, the decisive election for the office in this one-party enclave, the moderate, liberal and Catholic elements were for the most part behind the mayor of New Orleans, the late DeLesseps Morrison, a Catholic. If one could equate ambiguity with pro-integration sentiments, then Morrison was as close to an integrationist as a Louisiana politician dared to go. Then, too, the Negro vote (inconsequential as it was) fell into his column.

There was no doubt, on the other hand, that Jimmie Davis, Morrison's guitar-strumming Protestant opponent, stood four-square for segregation. Victory for Davis showed that the eighteen parishes with populations 50 per cent or more Catholic cast about 60 per cent of their votes for Morrison. Yet that may not indicate much about the reasons for the Catholic backing Morrison received. Some pro-Morrison Catholic voters undoubtedly identified him as the one under whom desegregation was most likely to come. But how many, no one knows. The commanding factor remains—as Davis's ultimate victory shows—that segregation sentiment throughout the whole state (French-Catholic parishes included) triumphed.

Still, if no convincing case can be made, on the basis of election returns at least, that Catholic Louisiana stands behind desegregation, there is strong evidence that its patterns of segregation are less rigid. Perhaps the strongest piece of evidence is the voter registration statistics. According to the "Negro Registration in Louisiana," an article which appeared in 1957 in the *American Political Science Review,* the percentage of Negroes registered for voting in the French-Catholic parishes of southern Louisiana is twice as great as in the northern Anglo-Saxon parishes. "Permissive attitudes toward Negro registration in French-Catholic parishes," the article declares, "seem expressive of the basic value that the Negro is spiritually equal in a Catholic society." Further substantiation of this belief is to be found in Margaret Price's study, *The Negro and the Ballot in the South,* published in 1959 by the Southern Regional Council. The author found that the white man's attitude toward the Negro's participation in the political process is quite different in the Catholic parishes from what it is in the Protestant parishes. Crowds at political meetings in the southern part of the state are integrated; those in the northern area tend to be segregated. In 1966 this same organization made a study of voter registration in the South. Its data indicate that the 25 "Catholic" counties of Louisiana have registered 53 per cent of the eligible Negro voters as compared to 35 per cent in the rest of the state. White Citizens Councils have strong backing in the North but less support in the South—despite the activity of Catholic segregationists like Emile Wagner and Leander Perez.

Further evidence is to be found in the city of Lafayette. The Lafayette Public Library, for instance, was integrated before 1960. The Municipal Golf Course and lunch counters in the 5-and-10's were desegregated without incident. There seems to be little evidence of vigorous White Citizens Council or Klan activities. This holds pretty much for the southwestern part of the state. But perhaps the most impressive single example of successful desegregation in the whole South is the University of Southwest Louisiana, a state institution located in Lafayette.

By court order, the University admitted Negro students to its Lafayette campus in 1954. Negroes enrolled, appeared for classes and have been continuing to do so ever since without significant incidents or difficulties. Negroes now in attendance number more than 350 out of a total enrollment of about 5,000. They are free to use all University facilities including the dormitories.

More than a proportionate share of these 350 colored students can be seen freely using the facilities of the Newman Center, focus of Catholic student activities. No obstacles are put in the way of their full participation in all the Center's facilities. In 1961, for example, the president of the Center's Commuters' Club was a Negro boy. There is concurrent use by both races of the lounges and game rooms. There is not, on the other hand, any forced or deliberately planned mixing or socializing of the two races. Genuine racial integration, it is expected, will come in slow but natural course. This is the policy of the Center's moderator, Monsignor Alexander Sigur. The progress made so far on the campus at large, and in the Newman Club, are naturally attributed to the Catholic atmosphere of Lafayette.

The case can easily be overstated. What may pass at first sight for "integration" at the university or its Catholic center is perhaps more accurately to be described—thus far, at least—as co-existence. Social intercourse is not at all evident; by four in the afternoon the Negro students have departed, leaving the night life of the campus—social, cultural and intellectual—to the whites. This is not a matter of Newman Center policy; virtually all of the Negro students are commuters and most of them have jobs after school hours. Thus although the legal and traditional barriers have dropped with an ease that contrasts sharply with the experience of "Ole Miss," the psychological barriers remain.

Any attempt to analyze the Catholic factor in race relations here or elsewhere would be incomplete without a sounding of Negro opinion. Do Catholic Negroes feel they are better off in Catholic Louisiana, and especially in Lafayette, than they would be in other parts of the South? Do they believe that Church influence and leadership makes and has made the big difference in Lafayette?

Negroes here show much the same range of opinions and resentments as those in other parts of the South. They voiced their most urgent complaints against economic and educational discrimination. The lay principal of a Negro elementary school, for example, was quite worried about the lack of opportunity for the middle third of his graduating class. The upper third, he said, could go on to Holy Rosary Institute or Holy Ghost High School. He continued: "The lower third don't want any more schooling anyway. But these kids in between who want to learn a trade—they have no place to go. The Opelousa Vocational High is strictly white. So what do I tell their parents? That their kids are finished with schooling?"

A Negro priest spoke in the same vein. His people were "economically depressed," he said. He did not go so far as to imply that the region is in the grip of a full-fledged depression, but he did speak quite convincingly of the growing inadequacy of the farm to support both parents and their grown children. The future of young Negroes approaching marriageable age is bleak; local opportunities for better jobs are almost non-existent. Even the new industries coming into the South do not greatly widen Negro horizons; colored workers are still "last hired, first fired," and even the unions discriminate against them. The chances to learn a trade and enter the ranks of skilled workers are minimal due to the segregated policies of the public technical schools; the curricula and facilities of Catholic Negro vocational schools are inferior.

The plight of these Negro farm families cannot be blamed exclusively on the pattern of Southern race relations. It is to a considerable extent a reflection of a national problem: the decline of the small farm—and consequently of the small rural community—under the stress of competition with the larger and more scientific business-farm. Often, and certainly in the diocese of Lafayette, the small Negro farmer works marginal land. These two factors, combined with a general drop in farm prices, squeeze him in a vise. If he does manage to hold on to his farm until his children are raised, it is certain that they have no future on the land. As the small farm disappears, so too does the small town dependent on it as it attempts to compete with its larger, more diversified neighboring city.

Whatever the larger, non-racial dimensions of the Negro farmer's plight, its racial aspect in the diocese of Lafayette is still real and no doubt just as painful. What follows is a migration, particularly of the young, the ambitious and the talented, to the North or to a more promising Southern city like Lake Charles, or even across the Texas line to Galveston or Houston. Very often, Negro spokesmen label this migration as the flight of an elite which will ultimately deplete the community's resources in brainpower and manpower.[1]

However favorably the record of Catholic Louisiana may compare with that of other areas, Negro leaders here as in other parts of the deep South refer bitterly to the psychologically debilitating effects of segregation, the loss of self-respect particularly. Both Negroes and whites to whom we spoke in this diocese marked this loss as a major problem. The long-term denial of respect and equal standing in the community—a natural consequence of slavery and, later, of the reign of Jim Crow—has eroded the self-respect of Negroes as individuals and as a race. The elders did not seem to be aware of this until comparatively recently—until, as one Negro father put it, "my boy saw these African leaders on TV shaking hands with Khrushchev, Kennedy and all those other big shots." The restoration of racial pride and self-esteem—psychological assets which the cry for "black power" has focused on—is now only just beginning. The only question that remains is: How long will it be before the effects of self-respect are felt by the community at large?

Inquiries as to what Martin Luther King means to Lafayette Negroes, for example, elicit from many the reply that they see

1. Human-relations leaders here and elsewhere in the nation might reëxamine their approach with an eye to the implications of this larger dimension. As Harry Golden, editor of the *Carolina Israelite,* has pointed out, white segregationists often rejoice in this migration of the Southern Negro—without stopping to realize that those who stay behind are the aged, the ill, the indigent and the ignorant—so that in terms of relief funds and public-assistance programs, segregation is not only unjust but terribly expensive.

just these qualities in him—the image of a new, self-respecting Negro. There is much evidence to indicate that in Lafayette King is a symbolic leader even among Catholic Negroes, at least those of the upper and middle classes. Among the more remote rural people, however, the awareness of King, of the rise of black African leaders, and of the other indications of Negro progress cropping up in the world news, varies directly with the number of TV antennas—and these, among the poor black farmers, are not at all common.

The principal locus for the Negro's new attitude toward himself seems to be among the young, even school children. A Negro father told us: "My boy isn't going to take what I took. He asks me when we went over to the Carvel stand here last Sunday, 'Daddy, how come we have to go round back to get our ice cream?' And he just don't like my answer."

It is among these younger Negroes, too, that instances of discrimination within the Church—and they still occur occasionally—rankle most deeply. Undoubtedly, some Southern bishops today quietly and without press releases, take remedial action when such instances occur. Bishop Schexnayder, for example, demanded and received a prompt apology and statement of repentance from three white Catholics who attacked an outspoken liberal priest, pastor of a Negro church. The bishop pressed the attack on bigotry by a strongly worded letter to all the parishes of the diocese noting the strong penalties which can be incurred by Catholics who oppose the teachings of the Church on race relations. The letter, read at all Masses on Sunday, August 2, 1964, specified that the penalties are applicable to anyone who interferes with Negro Catholics in the practice of their religion, or who join organizations whose aim conflicts with the teaching of the Church on racial justice. This teaching, in the form of a syllabus, has been made obligatory in all Catholic schools since the fall of 1963. The following year the bishop directed each deanery to establish a Human Relations Council. There can be no doubt, then, of the stiffening posture the official Church is assuming here and elsewhere in the South. This new attitude, however, important as it is, does not change white attitudes.

But for the increasing numbers of Negro Catholics the conflict between belief and practice on the part of their white coreligionists is a scandal more and more difficult to accept. This scandal has, since the Civil War era, driven unknown numbers from the Church. But in general, although the Catholic variety of racism is sometimes more humane, the Negro finds that fact irrelevant; he has no real knowledge of worse varieties, hence the reality he suffers is as strongly resented as though he were in Mississippi. It is significant that white Catholics point out the difference often with a touch of satisfaction.

Yet there are noticeable differences between Catholic Louisiana on the other hand and the rest of the state (and the rest of the South) on the other. Organized efforts at improving the lot of the Negro do take root in this diocese. But they rarely fructify. The Crusade for Justice, an organization started in 1960 by Father Wilfred DesRosiers, S.S.J., aimed to unite the Negroes of the Opelousa area toward achieving a larger measure of self-respect, economic advantage, and a means of defense against brutal police treatment. It aimed also to teach the Negro farmers the principle of the cooperative and the other advantages of working together on problems of mutual concern. But there is in this Catholic region a great deal of opposition to "stirring up trouble," and Father DesRosiers has been threatened with physical harm. Still, the work was continued. Bishop Schexnayder gave the Crusade his episcopal approval and it succeeded in mustering some white lawyers as allies. Except for the threat to Father DesRosiers, there was not the kind of devastating counteraction one might have expected.

Membership in the Crusade stood at 1200 in July, 1961, yet the organization lacked the technical know-how, the resources in money and manpower to help the Negro farmer stem the tide of economic forces running so strongly against him. On the other hand, the Crusade had a chance to minimize some effects of racial discrimination in employment and education. Eventually, it might also have expanded the Negro's use of the franchise and helped him combat a common Southern phenomenon: police brutality. But so devoid is the area of Negro leadership that the organization succumbed within a year after the transfer of its founder, Father DesRosiers.

Similar efforts at helping the Negro help himself have been made by the Jesuits at Grand Coteau and Bellview. Father John Millet attended Southwestern Louisiana Institute (now the University of Southwest Louisiana) on his own time for years taking a degree in agriculture, so that he might help his parishioners. Father Cornelius Thensted also concentrated his pastoral efforts on helping the Negro farmers improve their methods of farming and marketing. Father Albert McKnight, now assistant pastor of Our Lady of Lourdes in Abbeville, spent the summer of 1960 studying cooperatives at the world-famous St. Francis Xavier University in Antigonish, Nova Scotia, and the summer of 1961 taking business courses at Duquesne University in Pittsburgh. With the background he has organized a Producers Cooperative that operates successfully in six parishes (counties). The Coop purchases pecans, a tree-grown product likely to be found on most farms and green properties in the area. With these and other ingredients, it makes and sells a Louisiana Fruit Cake that has found a wide market throughout the South. Father McKnight has weaned the organization from dependence on himself and is now in the process of starting another in the Lake Charles area. Bishop Schexnayder, meanwhile, sends one of his priests each year to Nova Scotia to study the Cooperative Movement with an eye toward its further development in the diocese.

Such efforts as these have their roots deep in Christianity. More than any other diocese in the Deep South Lafayette has shown some response to the demands of the times. It has been able to do so most likely because it is "at home" in this locale. Bishops and priests here, in contrast to those in Jackson or Atlanta, speak and act with the air of people living in their own house.

On the other hand, the number of priests and the investment of time, money and effort by the diocese do not add up to any impressive attack on the problems. The plight of the one-third of the graduating class in the Opelousa Elementary School, which sorely needed vocational training but was denied it by a largely Catholic community, illustrates the point. The efforts made by Fathers DesRosiers and McKnight and the Jesuits should not obscure the pattern of discrimination and inferior segregated schools and hospitals that actually did prevail and to a much lesser extent still does today, though desegregation is now official policy. For an answer to the ambivalence of the Catholic position to this deep-rooted problem of racial injustice it might be well to look at it through the eyes of the bishop.

For one thing, it is only one of several major problems facing a bishop—in the South or anywhere else. The shortage of vocations to the priesthood and to the teaching sisterhoods and brotherhoods which staff his parishes and parochial school system—here as in the suburban areas of the North—is an important concern. And there are, of course, the urgent and immediate tasks to which all administrative officers fall heir. Too often, the race problem to a bishop's mind is, by virtue of his spiritual calling, acknowledged and defined only insofar as it has direct moral or spiritual implications. And from place to place these implications vary. The late archbishop of Chicago, Cardinal Albert Meyer, for example, envisioned the race problem as simply one aspect, albeit a very important one, of the over-all Catholic objective of informing the whole social order in the Chicago area with the spirit of Christ. In that archdiocese emphasis has been placed on the formation of apostolic-minded lay Catholics to be leaders and pressure groups for the reformation of the whole temporal order. Such an approach requires of a bishop a different theology, energetic, positive action and vigorous leadership. It contrasts sharply with the older—and in America the more traditional—theological outlook: "The salvation of souls is the supreme law."

Quite clearly the ordinary of Lafayette belongs to this older tradition. "It really doesn't matter whether or not a Negro can ride next to a white man on the bus," said Bishop Schexnayder, "if he's not in the state of grace." Not man's temporal but his spiritual condition is the ultimate concern of a bishop who operates from this theological position. Charity and social justice, while they are prime concepts, cannot command the dynamism of what might be called "centrifugal theology." In this traditional view sin and eternal damnation are risks too grave to be subordinated to "social problems." Hence what the Church can do for the Negro beyond furnishing him the opportunity to hear Mass and receive the sacraments is limited by what the material framework of sacramental administration costs in time, money, personnel and planning. It is true that by order of the bishop, sermons have been preached in every parish of the diocese embodying the Christian viewpoint on race relations. In general, however, the building of churches, missions, schools and seminaries and the recruitment and training of priests and teachers seem to command such a high priority that everything else is relegated to secondary importance.

It must be realized, of course, that a bishop in Louisiana—at least until recently—was not entirely a free agent: state laws enforcing segregation bound his hands. Bishop Schexnayder's minor seminary, for example, lost its free-lunch program because it accepted both white and Negro students. In addition to legal restrictions, there is always the danger of activating the Klan or the White Citizens Councils. And within the Church, the likelihood of alienating white Catholics is omnipresent. (Alienation of Negro Catholics seems never to have been a problem—from the white-Catholic viewpoint.) There is no overestimating the dangers in any Southern diocese that threaten any Christian response to social justice.

This, then, in brief, is the interrelationship between the Church and the cultural environment of southwestern Louisiana. Although not to the satisfaction of Negroes, it has mitigated slavery and its sequel, the segregated society. The latter, on the other hand, has established the framework of law and custom, that shape the Catholic vision and enervate its will. The seeds of conflict grow within the diocese itself as self-respect takes root among young Negroes. On the horizon play the storms of change from other sections of the state and nation. Visions of a better life seduce the Negro imagination via the TV set while invitations to organize come daily by mail and phone. The rate of change has always been slow in the rural diocese of Lafayette. But a priest in Bogalusa said the same thing in the fall of 1964.[1] The challenge the diocese faces is painful and perplexing. Yet the theological orientation of the bishop, the traditional Southern mentality of the Catholic people which overrides their religion, the high priority which internal or organizational problems have in the chancery and the depressed economic condition of the Negro people—all these factors seem to indicate that the role of the Church in the reform of customs and social institutions will be minimal. The basic relationship between the Church and its cultural setting remains precisely what it was before the Civil War. It can ameliorate slavery and segregation, it temporizes with them and even cooperates in their maintenance. Then as change becomes inevitable, again its best effort seems to be acceptance and cooperation with the new order. This remarkable ability to adapt to environment has been made possible, unwittingly of course, by an introverted theology narrowly focused on personal salvation via the sacramental system.

NEW ORLEANS: AN URBAN DIOCESE

We have explored so far the interaction between Church and culture in a congenial rural setting. We now explore that relationship and ask the same basic questions for a city that is markedly Catholic. New Orleans, with its present population more than 40 per cent Catholic, is the largest such city in the Deep South. In the total number of Negro Catholics, 55,000, it ranks fifth of all dioceses in the country as of 1967. For these reasons this archdiocese, combined with the diocese of Lafayette, offers a unique area in which to explore the interaction of Church and culture.

The Catholic Church in New Orleans, perhaps more than in any other diocese, is intricately woven into every sector of the

1. In the spring and summer of 1965 demonstrations, strikes and violence shattered Bogalusa's peaceful ways and seriously threatened its economy.

life of the city. Catholics may be found at all levels of the economic and political power structure: among large landowners, sugar planters and processors, oil men, coffee traders, shippers, factory owners, lawyers, politicians and judges. The informal as well as the formal networks of power and influence are manned from these groups, over half of whose members, it is estimated, are Catholic. From this leadership class, recipients of ecclesiastical honors are chosen; and from it the Church seeks advice and consultation for its operations in the material or secular order. The lines of demarcation between the spiritual and material realms are not always clear, however, and it happens frequently that influence or pressure from the secular order is exerted on Church authorities in matters moral or spiritual. For the last decade of his life Archbishop Rummel, for example, had been under heavy pressure from the state legislature not to desegregate the Catholic schools. This perhaps is the price the Church must pay when it is too tightly woven into the framework of the social order.

Historically, New Orleans is a Catholic city. Much of the history of greater New Orleans, from early 19th century anticlericalism to the Mardi Gras of today, can be written in terms of French Catholicism. Negro Catholicism, too, like that in Lafayette, has a long history in this city. The first segregated Catholic Church in the Deep South was opened here in 1895. But we need not trace these threads of history into the distant past. For the essence of the relationship between Church and culture can be observed by following the course of a moral problem that has profound implications for both the Church and the culture.

The desegregation of Catholic institutions is such a problem, for in studying it one gets an unusual view of the closely woven network of ties, personal and official, between the political, economic and religious (Catholic) institutions of a city. This network of relationships connects to others in the state and national capitals. Contemporary issues, too, are involved: educational fringe benefits, tidelands oil and, as might be expected, public school desegregation. The time span is relatively short, for New

Orleans was still a thoroughly segregated city when the Negro veteran returned from World War II.

Even within the Church, the returning veteran found the lines of racial separation to be as rigid as ever. Here and there Negro Catholics could attend Mass in a "white" Church—provided they "kept their place." But for the most part, they could not even enter any but "their own" churches. Separate churches, a segregated covenant, so to speak, devised as a *modus vivendi* for two alienated peoples, had devolved into a state of humiliating ostracism.

As far as the number of parochial schools was concerned, the Negroes had a proportionate share. The quality depended on the wealth and educational sophistication of the parishioners. But parents who desired better schooling for their children and who lived within the territorial bounds of a white parish with a good school suffered most. Canonically, any person living within the geographical boundary of a parish "belongs" to that parish. If he is a non-English speaking national, he may opt for the nearest national parish. In the case of the American Negro, however, "local custom" has simply nullified canon law. It was simply out of the question for a Negro child to attend a white school no matter how high his ambitions or aspirations. Catholic high school education, although limited in capacity in all American dioceses, was simply beyond the reach of some 90 per cent of the Negro families of this archdiocese. Hospital care, perhaps more than anything else, presented the most frustrating and embittering deprivation along the whole spectrum of injustice. As late as 1963 the two Catholic hospitals, ironically called Hotel Dieu and Mercy, were simply not available to Negroes. To compound the irony, they were non-discriminatory with respect to religion. A white Protestant could enter for an appendectomy or a check-up; a Negro Catholic wishing to die in a Catholic atmosphere could not. This, in brief, is the starting point of the desegregation process in the archdiocese of New Orleans. Whether the date is 1945 or 1955 makes not much difference; the return of the Negro soldier from World War II is the watershed.

He had endured the hardships of a war for the preservation of democracy. At home and abroad he had had some experience, although limited, in unsegregated situations. Such experiences stirred the first rumblings of discontent. Indeed no Southern city, New Orleans not excepted, was to remain unshaken. The wall of racial separation, destined as they were to stand for years to come, had been cracked in the foundations of Negro acceptance. Not many Negroes themselves seemed to have been aware of this. Among the first in New Orleans to realize what had happened was a group of Negro community leaders, mostly Catholics, who undertook to sell the idea of practicing medicine in the city to the Negro doctors recently discharged from the service. The doctors made their reasons for refusing perfectly plain. Said one: "I can stay in the service, go to New York or Chicago and be a free man. Why should I sacrifice a future for this!"

The inventory of social and economic injustices was a long one and it was applied against all sectors of the Negro community. For the first time, perhaps, Negroes saw—really saw—the second-rate eating facilities in the 5-and-10's and department stores, the inferior Negro waiting rooms in transportation terminals, the countless attractive restaurants, hotels and bowling alleys barred to them, the severely limited hospital facilities, the inferior schools and the exclusively menial job opportunities that were theirs. A. P. Tureau, the local NAACP chairman, observed: "I think these fellows who went in the service saw more of New Orleans abroad than I ever saw living in it." Fighting for democracy apparently sharpened their eyes to its absence at home. Experiences of some Negro servicemen in the more permissive atmosphere of Northern cities, retold no doubt with exaggeration and wishful thinking, induced many to leave New Orleans. Scores of doctors, dentists and other professionals left the area for points North. And countless technicians, mechanics and other skilled laborers also stored New Orleans into their past. The white community meanwhile lived on in its own world, oblivious to the ground being dug from under its foundations.

The Negro who remained was not the same either. The contrast between fighting a war for "the four freedoms" and living in a city where his freedom was restricted was brought into even sharper focus by several factors. These were sprung from a war-changed economy. The new demand for factory labor drew increasing numbers of rural Negroes into the city and moved countless others from one city to another; or from one urban section to another. Increased war wages brought many to the movies for the first time. It introduced others to the white man's picture magazines. Car sales among Negroes rose rapidly in the late war years and thereafter, thus increasing their mobility and their vision. War-time savings brought TV sets—and another window into the glittering white world. All these developments contributed to the Negro's awareness of the contrast between his rights and his meager opportunities.

Within the Church Negroes began complaining not so much against segregation as against its implications. Even today there is not much evidence that they wanted their own close-knit parishes abolished, but starting in the late 1940's they began to reject the idea that, where the congregation was mixed, they "belonged" in the rear or in the choir loft. They resented, too, the notion that their "place" was at the end of the Communion or confessional line. Other humiliations seemed to be more frequent. Even the basic right of any Catholic to attend Mass was denied to more and more Negroes by white ushers. And it was not unknown for colored Catholics to be forcibly expelled if they happened to enter a "white" church unnoticed. Matters seemed to be worse than before the war.

What had happened to increase the frequency of such incidents in the post-war years was, of course, an increase in the number of Negroes now living in the cities where these incidents invariably occurred. War-begotten employment opportunities having drawn many from the country, pressures on urban Negro neighborhoods increased, and many found housing in areas heretofore white. (Due to a historical pattern—the fact that slave quarters were adjacent to the owner's house—housing segregation in New Orleans does not follow the typical ghetto pattern common to the north.) War-time population shifts therefore brought many more residential and in-church contacts between white and Negro than the South had ever experienced before. The frequency of these contacts and the resulting humiliations brought forcibly to the colored man's mind the real implications of segregation. Further dissatisfaction was generated by the increased pressure on hospital facilities brought on by the rise in population after the war. Later the same pressures were felt by the Negro parochial schools, for whether a Negro family lived in a "white" parish or not, only the segregated school was available to it. As the 1950's advanced it became apparent that the Negro Catholic high schools, too, could no longer carry the load they had in the pre-war era. But now the attitude of accommodation that once had sustained segregated institutions was rapidly dissolving.

Catholic Negro leaders of the Knights of St. Peter Claver (the Negro counterpart of the Knights of Columbus) and the NAACP brought their case to the highest court available, the archbishop himself. The decade following the war saw these delegations seeking redress of grievances on a broad front, from the simple right to enter any Catholic church to staff privileges in Catholic hospitals.

From the very beginning of his administration of the diocese in 1935, Archbishop Rummel had excellent rapport with the Negro laity. An opinion commonly held among them was that "He never did like the way Negroes were treated in the South." Reports of these conferences and subsequent events indicate that the archbishop took Negro remonstrances seriously. At the diocesan synod of 1949 he brought the substance of the complaints to the attention of his pastors and curates, and in the pastoral letter which he subsequently sent out, Archbishop Rummel directed that signs reading "For Colored" be removed from the churches. Pastors were directed to instruct their ushers in particular, that Negroes were to have access to any Catholic church in the diocese. The letter expressed the archbishop's wish that "priests avoid anything which would discourage or impede Negro participation in the life of the Church."

The offending signs were promptly removed. But it proved to

be nothing more than an act of external compliance. If there was any change for the better it was too slight to be evident. The principal consolation as far as the Negro was concerned was the positive knowledge that in the archbishop he had a friend and ally. The belief spread, too, that "he was taking action." The removal of the signs was but one indication. Another was the integration in the early 1950's of the deanery and diocesan unions of the Holy Name Society, Sodality, and the National Councils of Catholic Men and Women. In 1951, when a delegation of Josephite and Divine Word Fathers informed Archbishop Rummel that their Negro parishioners refused to participate in a Holy Name rally being held in the segregated City Park Stadium, he promptly cancelled the whole affair. As critical reports and complaints continued to reach him, he wrote another unambiguous pastoral letter, which he ordered read in all churches on March 15, 1953. The letter directed that "there be no further discrimination or segregation in the pews, at the Communion rail, at the confessional and in parish meetings. . . . Our colored Catholics . . . should not be harassed when they attend services in any parish church or mission, or when they apply for membership in parish organizations."

The lack of any substantial improvement in race relations following this and the earlier directive undoubtedly made it evident to the archbishop that letters or directives would not solve the problem. Meanwhile, the Catholic Committee of the South, a group of progressive priests and laymen organized and subsidized by many Southern bishops, was studying this problem in greater depth than any one bishop could. A local division of the Committee was set up in New Orleans with episcopal encouragement. Educational programs particularly for the parish clergy were proposed, as well as programs (planned by integrated committees) on a wide range of community problems. In only a few cases were they actually launched. The advisability of joint action, or at least a common statement of Catholic principles, by all the Southern Catholic bishops was also discussed by the New Orleans group and by the parent body in Rock Hill, South Carolina. It is evident, in other words, that there was in the early 1950's, in New Orleans particularly, considerable thought and discussion of the problem of interracial justice.

But the efforts of Archbishop Rummel and the CCS were not to fructify—at least not in the 1950's. For one thing, the resistance and inertia of the diocesan clergy were far more formidable obstacles than had been estimated. Priests born and raised in Louisiana and conducting their ministry in parishes populated overwhelmingly by segregationists could not be expected to shed what was actually part of their own personality. This would be particularly true in the rural parishes, where a priest's constituency might comprise a network of kin and friendships dating from before the Civil War. Even where a priest might himself be somewhat more enlightened on the race question than his parishioners, it would take more than the common allotment of courage to risk the inevitable hostility, ridicule or ostracism that would follow the expression of untraditional views. Some priests and pastors, too, are blood relatives of White Citizens Councils leaders. What this all means, in other words, is that racial attitudes here and in the South in general are ingrained in personality. Despite the fact that segregation was termed a moral problem by Archbishop Rummel early in 1956, it was not, to state the obvious, amenable to moral solutions.

French Catholic Louisiana, it has been observed, reflects a typically Latin hedonism. Unlike the stereotyped Puritan who views life as a matter of toil, struggle against sin and rigid adherence to the moral code, the allegedly typical Latin views life as something to be enjoyed. Attitudes toward moral behavior, religion and the other serious concerns of society (politics, perhaps, excepted) tend to be more permissive or relaxed. Viewed as opposite or polar attractions rather than as descriptions of actual attitudes, these cultural contrasts explain much. Harsh as they are, the discriminatory barriers in New Orleans, for instance, are not as rigid or extensive as in Jackson, Birmingham or other parts of the Deep South. But if this Latin tendency ameliorates interracial problems, it also tends to enervate Christianity itself. In the hard world of business and politics, for example, Catholicism is not taken too seriously. The ritual and tradition of French Catholicism may inform the folklore, name the streets, initiate the Mardi Gras, mark public ceremony and govern superficial behavior in countless ways, but the doctrine and moral teachings of that same religion are not commonly regarded as at all relevant to economics, politics or social problems. Priests of the archdiocese have often remarked how easily antagonized their parishioners become by social-action sermons. A layman from Plaquemines Parish, the bailiwick of the notorious Leander Perez, remarked that "a priest's popularity and effectiveness correlate positively with his ability to fish, handle a shot-gun competently, enjoy good meals, and otherwise manifest the tastes of his communicants." This hedonistic aspect of the problem he summed up by quipping that "South Louisiana Catholics do not concern themselves with ideologies and abstractions, but rather, with really fundamental matters such as slot machines, horse races, good food and drink, hunting, fishing and beautiful women."[1] This one element of the region's culture goes a long way in explaining the widespread resistance to the archbishop's efforts. Matters were to get worse before they would get better.

It seems that the Church was ill-equipped to handle moral problems with such deep cultural roots. The Church itself was partly responsible for the problem. It had, for generations, held up eternal salvation as the reward for enduring the misery of slavery. Unwittingly, it put theological props under the evil. Its principal message to the white man could be reduced to the simple formula which even today is still commonly regarded as comprising the essence of Christianity: "Avoid sin, frequent the sacraments and perform the duties of one's state in life." Probably because of the variety of "states in life" there was no clear set of norms, certainly none with any implications of social reform. And for the slave, paternalism was the outer limit of advocacy. Buttressed by an emphasis on sin and the threat of

1. Alfred Hero, in an unpublished manuscript, "The South and American Foreign Policy."

personal damnation, this orientation toward religion supported Southern institutions before and after slavery, and down to the recent post-war period. Moreover, it produced a mentality which, on the one hand, could serve God on Sunday, honor His name in public ceremony and even use public funds for subsidies to Catholic education; and on the other hand accept all forms of social injustice such as slavery, *laissez-faire* economics, plutocracy, destitution, barbarous treatment of the insane and the criminal. By its own history of accommodation to Southern culture via minimal spirituality the Church in New Orleans was not ready for the fast pace of either social or theological change. Both the widespread public demand for interracial justice and the concomitant development in recent years of the doctrine of the mystical body caught Catholics in a state of mind which could barely comprehend either. It was, then, with a geat deal of historical and even theological cogency that a Leander Perez could ask: "How come we could have slaves, separate schools and churches for these Negroes for ages and ages and now all of a sudden it's a sin? Seems to me like some Communist got some kinda spell over that man [Rummel]."

It seems, then, that while the problem of interracial justice had its roots in the cultural, economic and theological orders, the abilities of the Church to do anything about it rested on the number of its friends in politics. Clearly, it was an unequal struggle. When its political allies, as we shall see later, could not muster the votes to defeat punitive legislation against the Church for its pending desegregation, the Church ceased its efforts. For approximately seven years, 1956–1963, it remained in a stalemate with its political opposition in the legislature, many of whom were, ironically enough, "good-living Catholics."

In a sense the stalemate was of its own making. Not only New Orleans but all American dioceses with their bureaucratic structures have by that very fact defined themselves as organizations. As such the Church carries within it the same tendencies, the same strengths and weaknesses of all organizations. One such tendency is called "goal displacement," or the non-deliberative substitution of means for ends, procedures and rules for objectives. "The phenomenon is perhaps the most frequently noted pathological aspect of large-scale organization."[1]

Thus in the Catholic experience, the Mass and the sacraments, originally defined as means to sanctification, became ends in themselves. The practice came close to superstition in the sense that the good Catholic (the saved one) could be identified by the frequency of his church-going and the observable intensity of his prayer (goods works). Brotherhood and community were lost sight of. In the memory of the contemporary Catholics of New Orleans, the means were always the goals. The effort on the part of Archbishop Rummel to desegregate Catholic institutions simply did not make sense.

Human institutions also face the crucial problem that in order to solve problems or execute policy, people on the lower echelons have to be organized and instructed. This raises the temptation to contribute to the decision-making, its "necessary" modifications and the ways and means. Again Archbishop Rummel's policies and directives were frequently "modified" and so executed as to defeat his intentions. Catholics in the state legislature knew, too, that he had exceeded the "policy" of "the organization" as they had known it for generations. As part of the rank and file they therefore felt no qualms of conscience in controverting the new rules. The attempt to desegregate the parochial schools thus devolved into a conflict between a political organization and a religious one. Though the archbishop defined the problem as a "moral and spiritual" one, it was implicitly defined internally as a disciplinary one and externally as a power conflict. We shall now examine how these definitions developed.

The Desegregation Sequence

Shortly after the historic Supreme Court decision of 1954, the archdiocesan school board issued a news release stating that the decision, while not legally applicable to the parochial schools,

1. David Sills, *The Volunteers: Means and Ends in a National Organization,* The Free Press, Glencoe, 1957, p. 62.

was morally so. The archbishop in a press conference about the same time confirmed what the board had said. While there had been no decision as to the time at which the desegregation would take place, the archbishop inadvertently left the impression that it would take place in 1955, for when a reporter asked, "Will the schools be desegregated this year, Your Excellency?" he answered, "No, not this year." Early in 1955 his chancellor, Monsignor Charles Plauche, left the same impression in replying to questions from the press by saying that steps would be taken soon. But the 1955–1956 school year opened under the old segregated system.

Meanwhile, members of the state legislature let the archbishop know that in order to counter any such move on his part, bills were being formulated which would remove the subsidies the state was giving to the Catholic schools, namely, free textbooks, the school-lunch program and bus service for parochial school children. It was the news of these threats that caused the chancery to delay. The loss of these advantages, it was believed, would strike hardest at the Negro Catholics, who for the most part needed them more than the whites. "There was nothing we could do until that threat was removed," said Monsignor Plauche as he described the plight some years later. "No one believed that the state could not or would not take such measures to stop us." To the question as to the legality of such discriminatory state action, he replied, "Of course it wouldn't be legal. But it would take years to stop them in court, and even then you might lose. No telling how they might tie up the whole subsidy with the Church-state issue."

In February of 1956 Archbishop Rummel, in an effort to arouse favorable opinion and weaken the segregationist forces, issued his most famous pastoral letter, in which he condemned segregation as "morally wrong and sinful because it is a denial of the unity and solidarity of the human race." The state legislature countered this move by assigning the prepared bills to the appropriate legislative committees for action. It was the archbishop's move next. With the advent of spring registration, word came from the diocesan superintendent's office that desegregation would not be effected until September, 1957, and that it would be organized gradually, one grade at a time. The threatening bills in the legislative committees were moved down on the calendar and the confrontation was put off for another year. The deadlock continued until 1962.

Liberal Catholics all over the South were chagrined. Most people did not realize the terms of the Catholic dilemma. Even in New Orleans itself the viewpoint was commonly held that the opposition of priests and laymen in the parishes was responsible for the delay. Whether deliberately or not is hard to determine, but Archbishop Rummel gave support to this view by telling a group of white and Negro laymen who had come to urge him to desegregate the schools: "It's your move, gentlemen; you know the state of mind of the people as well as I do. You create the atmosphere necessary for the success of such a move and I'll make it." Frustration and demoralization settled over the liberal camp. There was some relief as the focus of attention shifted to the public school fiasco in the fall of 1960.

Around that time Monsignor Henry Bezou, the Superintendent of Schools for the archdiocese, was preparing to give the order for desegregation concurrent with or immediately following that of the public schools. Shortly after his intentions became known he received two phone calls which forced him to retreat. One was from a member of the state legislature who stated that a bill was ready for introduction on the calendar which would deprive integrated religious institutions of their tax-exempt status if the monsignor went ahead with his plans. The second call, received the same day, came from Mayor DeLesseps Morrison, who merely wanted it known that he had his hands full with the public school crisis and could not guarantee police protection at the Catholic schools as well. Archbishop Rummel was in a hospital some 40 miles from the city and he was not expected to recover. Apparently, his subordinates felt that in view of the seriousness of the threat from Baton Rouge and the risks involved in the lack of police protection, they could not issue the order. They cancelled their plans, and the public saw an image of the Church standing by silently while mob rule prevailed around the Frazier and McDonough schools and the Catholic schools continued securely in their segregated status.

But even in the summer of 1961, disillusionment, anger, bitterness and cynicism were rampant among the "integregationists." The archbishop's age and near-total blindness mollified whatever personal antagonism existed toward him. But except at the chancery, the opinion was almost unanimous that the grand opportunity had been lost. The time to act was in 1954, right after the Supreme Court decision. A move then, so the argument ran, would have caught the opposition unorganized and faced with an irreversible *fait accompli.*

March of 1961 saw the establishment in New Orleans of a Southern Field Service of the National Catholic Conference for Interracial Justice. A few months later Archbishop John Cody of Kansas City was appointed coadjutor of the diocese with the right of succession to Archbishop Rummel. The object of the Southern Field Service was to crystallize the forces for desegregation and prepare, insofar as possible, the "atmosphere" needed for a successful desegregation program in all sectors of the diocesan structure. The appointment of Archbishop Cody was aimed at the gradual retirement from active service of the aging Rummel.

By the summer of 1961, Archbishop Rummel, however, had appointed a Board of Directors for the Catholic Council on Human Relations, key members of which were also in the Southern Field Service. Although a variety of views were represented by the personnel chosen, the significant representation on the Board was from the city's political power structure. Several of the members then met with the archbishop in an attempt to persuade him to desegregate the schools at the next registration, the spring of 1962. Present at the meeting was Monsignor Bezou, the Superintendent of Schools.

Chastened no doubt by the experience of the previous year, the monsignor was reluctant to back the recommendation. Nonetheless, it was learned later that the meeting had marked a turning point in the archbishop's thinking. Meanwhile, individuals from the Human Relations Council had been writing letters and phoning various chancery officials as well as the archbishop urging him to make the move. Considerable support seemed to mount behind him. The Council leaders now realized that Monsignor Bezou's conversion was crucial, too. He would have to have some assurance that the state legislature would not enact the legal measures that had been threatened. This assurance was given to the Monsignor from an authoritative source. The punitive legislation, it was explained, could not be enacted for several reasons. First, among the various pressure groups in the city there was sufficient evidence that even though they did not like desegregation they wanted their public schools kept open. There was, in other words, a limit to the price the people of this Catholic area were willing to pay for segregated schools. This was news to many in the legislature. Secondly, the state budget was faced with a deficit of $73 million, and the executive branch was trying to negotiate a favorable settlement with the Federal government on two issues which might help reduce it. The National Aeronautics and Space Administration was developing a plant in New Orleans for building Saturn rockets. This alone, it was estimated, would add $90 to personal income in the state. Governor Davis was hoping, too, for some $50 million in tidelands oil funds, totaling an estimated $400 million which was being held in escrow pending settlement as to where Louisiana's tidelands boundaries lay. Knowing how the Kennedy administration felt about integration and civil rights, the state government, according to authoritative sources, would not be likely to flout its wishes. The chances were as favorable as ever for the Church. Judging from subsequent events, Monsignor Bezou was convinced that at long last the time was ripe.

In November, 1961, at a meeting with leaders of the Council and the monsignor, Archbishop Rummel stated his decision to desegregate the schools at the next registration period, in April, 1962. The Director of Southern Field Services, Henry Cabirac, who was also a member of the Board of the Catholic Human Relations Council, put into operation the procedures which had become more or less standardized by the experiences of many other cities and institutions. This was the knowledge which had long since been available to any and all dioceses, not only through Cabirac but through Matthew Ahman, the Executive Director of the National Catholic Conference for Interracial Justice and the Southern Regional Council. It involved the coordination of the Mayor, the Chief of Police, the appropriate Federal offices, the Superintendent of Schools, pastors and school principals. Carefully worded press releases were also part of the procedures as well as the responses to the expected questions in press conferences.

Although it was not planned this way, the Federal District Court had ordered, at about this same time, the desegregation of the public schools to be resumed. What the effect of this order meant was that those Catholic families who might have considered transferring their children from integrated Catholic schools to segregated public, had this vent cut off. And, of course, the archbishop's order had the same effect for the reverse of this case.

The decision firmly made, and all supporting liaisons with governmental agencies and the press established, the archbishop summoned the clergy to a meeting on the afternoon of March 27, 1962. Here he made known the decision. Quite unexpectedly, he was interrupted by applause that lasted several minutes. He was halted three or four times more by applause before concluding his remarks. Long-time observers of the diocesan scene say, however, that the applause stemmed from several factors besides approval of integration: admiration for his tenacity in the problem, polite respect for a man of his age and relief that the inevitable had finally come.

Late the same day the press carried the story. Then began the last fight of the Catholic segregationist forces. The hard core of this resistence, estimated by several local observers to be not more than 20 per cent of the Catholic population, apparently gathered greater strength from the watery allegiance of many Catholics whose sentiments and ties were to the old order but who were not so bold as to oppose authority openly. The resistors dominated the news, however, picketing the archbishop's residence and the seminary, boycotting Sunday Mass, raising funds for a private segregated school system. On March 31 Archbishop Rummel sent a letter of admonition to 11 leaders of this resistance movement, citing their efforts to incite disobedience to his authority. Unless they desisted, he warned, they would incur excommunication. There being no indication of an end to the activties of three of the 11 the Chancellor, Monsignor Plauche, sent a letter of excommunication to Leander Perez, Mrs. J. B. Gaillot, Jr., and Jackson Ricau on April 17, 1962.

While this move undoubtedly checked the growth of the faction, it nonetheless raised the spectre of schism. The three excommunicants and their more intimate followers started a drive to collect funds for a "Church for excommunicated Catholics and segregationists." The potential for a successful schism lay not so much in their numbers as in the fact that there were a number of priests among their supporters. These priests were widely known, for they had frequently attended segregationist rallies and private meetings. The clergymen involved soon received stern warnings from the archbishop himself, one in fact being transferred to an assignment outside the diocese. As these priests separated themselves from the resistance movement, the threat of schism soon passed.

But opposition continued for at least two years. "Parents for Catholic Schools" was organized. This group used a variety of techniques to discourage parents from support of the Church. One was the "dial-a-message" gimmick. On dialing a well-advertised phone number, the caller heard a message to the effect that Archbishop Cody was taking over parish funds to finance his "race-mixing" plot. He was, as a matter of fact, but for the purpose of centralizing funds, investments and fiscal procedures.

It is worth noting also that there arose among the laity, within days after the initial announcement of desegregation, a movement of positive support. A group of men and women numbering about 30 and not representing any particular organization or parish notified the press of their support of the archbishop, adding that they were circulating a petition for signatures; this, they asserted, would indicate that most Catholics of the archdiocese were in favor of the desegregation decision. They also indicated that they were forming a bureau so that speakers would be available to take the side of integration. The same night that this statement was released to the papers, Monsignor Plauche phoned the group leaders and indicated that the archbishop wanted to speak to them. Late that same evening they went in a body to the archbishop's residence. Expressing his gratitude to them for their courage, the old prelate took them by surprise by asking them to discontinue their efforts immediately. "There is a serious danger," he said, "that the Catholic populace might be divided into two camps . . . antagonism might be intensified among the people." Despite their arguments to the contrary, the archbishop maintained his position, ultimately making his request an order. Very much dejected, they complied.

The dispersion of this supporting movement destroyed whatever chance there was of determining how many Catholics were actually behind the Archbishop. It has been estimated that there were probably 20 per cent of the Catholic people of the archdiocese at either pole at the time of the desegregation announcement. Most of the people were in the middle where racist opinions were probably traditional but were neutralized by loyalty to the Church.

The first test of the basic acceptance of Church discipline came in mid-April, with the collection for the Bishops' Relief Fund. The results were heartening to diocesan officials, for although the amount was down several hundred dollars from the previous year's total of $56,719, it was high enough to indicate that the loyalty and discipline of the people were for the most part intact. In several parishes where the residential pattern of mixed housing indicated that the schools would be desegregated, the collection exceeded that of the previous year.

About the same time, the diocesan Superintendent of Schools, Monsignor Bezou, announced that registration for the fall term would be held April 13 and 14. This, of course, would be an even more direct test, if not the only one prior to the opening of school itself. Here again the results were far better than anticipated. Except for the schools in Perez's Plaquemines Parish, where there were minor disturbances and what could be interpreted as a boycott, registrations went off smoothly and close to 200 Negro children were registered in 23 previously all white parochial schools.

The summer passed without incidents of long-term significance. The schools opened on August 30 with only some minor, mostly verbal, clashes. By October it was evident that the majority of white New Orleans Catholics had accepted this decision reluctantly, but attendance at Mass, reception of the sacraments, collections and attendance at school were encouraging. The peak enrollment in 1961 was 65,000. In the first week of school in August, 1962, the figure was 60,000 and in 1963 it rose to 63,000. There were, of course, instances where the clergy reneged. But this was more or less to be expected. The over-all results seem to have been far better than had been expected. There were actual enrollments of from two to 20 Negro children in some 23 previously white parochial schools in the school year 1962–1963. The number has slowly risen, but not to the point where racial isolation can be described as ended.

Only one school has been forced to close. In the heart of Plaquemines Parish where Perez has been in political control for nearly 40 years, lies Buras, an unincorporated community of 5,000 people. The parochial school, which had an enrollment of 359 white children in 1961, opened in August of 1962 with five Negro and 38 white students in attendance the first day. In the face of threats to both the Negro and white families of these students, Father Christopher Schneider, O.F.M., the pastor, closed the school. Approximately 100 pickets gathered around the school the first day. Placards read: "We want our school back." After the closing the number dwindled steadily, there being a dozen or so women each day maintaining the vigil down to the summer of 1963. Explaining their position, one of these women said: "The archbishop said he would not integrate our school until the public school had 'Niggers.' There aren't any in there now [she pointed to the public high and elementary schools down the street] and there won't be. Maybe the public schools in New Orleans are integrated. So let the Catholic schools up there have 'Niggers.' But not us." About that time the school was demolished by a bomb. Father Schneider had it rebuilt, but it has failed to pass inspection by the parish (civil) authorities. Thus the political power of one Catholic layman, still excommunicated, remains as a symbol of the vanquished forces of racism in the diocese.

On the high school level, fruitful results of the desegregation order have come more slowly. Cultural factors play a more decisive role here. Financial and academic abilities particularly govern the slowly increasing number of Negro admissions. Even though the high schools are mostly private or parochial, as distinct from diocesan, Archbishop Cody had made it clear to the religious orders operating them that he wanted no racial barriers. The four diocesan institutions enroll a significant number of Negro students and thus prove the sincerity of diocesan policy. There is no evidence of either discrimination or a quota system. However, the total number of Negroes in Catholic high schools is insignificant and this undoubtedly is related to economics. The median income for Negro families in the New Orleans metropolitan area is $2,900 while the figure for the white population is $4,800. Clearly, the influence of the Church in the social order is rigidly defined by factors beyond its control —at least as it is presently structured.

Meanwhile the fact that there are a significant number of Catholic schools, on both levels, which are still exclusively Negro, prompted the U.S. Office of Education to order a speed-up of the desegregation process. Failure to do so would bring a cut-off in Federal funds for auxiliary aid. With a Catholic enrollment of some 79,000 pupils—over one-third of the total for the city—the Federal Government apparently feels that if the problems of desegregation in New Orleans is to be resolved it cannot be done by ignoring these schools. The public schools are no less a problem. They are, however, on a timetable set by the courts. The price of slavery and its cruel aftermath seems to be rising daily for both the city and the Church.

MISSISSIPPI: THE LAND OF "NEVER"

In Mississippi, the diocese of Natchez-Jackson was, down to the summer of 1963, totally impervious to even any discussion of desegregation (of Catholic institutions). Bishop Richard Gerow, the ordinary, conveyed the impression to many who sought to prepare the diocese for the inevitable that he was a frightened man. Since 1954 various groups and individuals, including the Catholic Committee of the South, had tried to mount programs, conferences or simply publish statements that might implement or clarify the teaching of the Church on interracial justice. But the bishop rarely saw fit to join such endeavors. Pastor of a flock of some 67,000 Catholics in a total population of 2.1 million, he apparently was convinced that, if a change in race relations were possible at all in Mississippi, it would have to come from outside the Church. For its own safety, the Church could not even give the appearance of participating in such change. Since 1963, however, a marked change has taken place in the bishop.

In June of that year the State Chairman of the NAACP, Medgar Evers, of Jackson, was assassinated. Although not a Catholic, Evers was known to be a religious man. His reputation was spotless and those who knew him well recognized the heroic and spiritual stature of a man who lived daily with the threat of death. The Evers' two children were students in Christ the King parochial school and the family was well-known among the clergy, including Bishop Gerow. Visibly moved by the tragedy, the bishop attended the wake—an unprecedented move in a state where NAACP leaders had been randomly murdered before. Afterwards, he issued a statement to the press in which he laid the blame for the murder on the white community at large. In the context of Mississippi mores, the statement was a forthright and courageous one. In fact, according to the New York *Times,* it was the only one ever made by any white man of prominence in the state. Coming from a man of some 80 years, whose understanding of the psychological, economic and theological dimensions of the problem was restricted, the statement seemed to mark a turning point.

It is difficult, of course, to assert that the Evers tragedy was the event that caused a change of heart in the Catholic leadership. What is evident, however, is the change of course both the bishop and the tiny diocese have taken since then. Contrary to the description of him as a "frightened man" given earlier, one integration leader, in the summer of 1964, remarked: "I was much impressed with Bishop Gerow when I talked with him in Jackson. He seemed to be acting with great courage in a fearfully difficult situation."

This was the summer when the Council of Federated Organizations (COFO) was operating its voter registration project. Tension gripped the whole state. Three civil rights workers disappeared and later were found murdered. The diocesan paper, the *Mississippi Register,* in measured and moderate tone took a firm and favorable position on the project. Bishop Gerow also publicly supported it. Meanwhile, several Negro Protestant churches which had served as headquarters for the voter registration and other uplift programs had been bombed or burned to the ground. A committee of white clergymen organized themselves to raise the $300,000 needed to rebuild these churches with Bishop Gerow as one of their leaders.

In August he began preparations for the desegregation of the parochial schools, calling on the Southern Field Service of the National Catholic Conference for Interracial Justice to help plan the move. Later he joined with other religious leaders of the city and approached the Chamber of Commerce, urging it to advocate public compliance with the Civil Rights Acts. This it did.

Meanwhile, with the passage of the Economic Opportunity Act, the Auxiliary Bishop, Joseph Brunini, together with two priests, Fathers Bernard Law and Lawrence Watts, began working with some business leaders and politicians to develop a proposal for a state-wide attack on the problem of poverty. The attendant political implications threatened the project, but by some astute handling and talking, Governor Johnson was persuaded to cooperate. By late spring, 1965, the project was approved by the Office of Economic Opportunity. Star, Incorporated (Specialized Training and Rehabilitation), Mississippi's first large-scale attack on poverty, was launched with Bishop Brunini as Chairman and Father Lawrence Watts as its Executive Director. The Board of Directors, white and Negro, includes clergymen of other faiths and leaders from the business community. The project operates from the physical plant of mostly Catholic parishes throughout the state. Literacy, vocational training and home-making programs constitute the core of the effort. Financed by a grant of 7 million dollars over a two-year period, Star, together with the beleaguered Child Development Group of Mississippi (CDGM), is expected to provide the knowledge, experience, manpower and blueprints for a more permanent program to lift the large proportion of the state's population from the level of poverty and ignorance in which they have existed since the Civil War.

Mississippi, at the same time, continues as the police state it has always been. Its Advisory Committee to the United States Civil Rights Commission reported in 1963 that there exists a full-scale regime of legally sanctioned police terror, violence and oppression. In fact, the committee's fact-finding efforts were actively opposed by agents and instrumentalities of the state government. In the summer of 1965 George Metcalf, the Natchez NAACP chairman, turned the ignition key in his car and touched off a dynamite charge that totally demolished his car, but by some quirk of fate left him alive. Charles Evers, the brother of the late Medgar Evers, gave a desperate warning after Metcalf's narrow escape: "The Negroes have taken all they can take. We've armed ourselves and we are going to fight back." They have active support from churches and clergymen within and outside Mississippi. In a protest march on the state capitol in June, 1965, some 75 demonstrators were arrested. Among their number were six white ministers. Catholics, however, were conspicuous by their absence. They are not at all evident in this aspect of the struggle, although several of the diocesan priests are with it in spirit. Some few Catholic laymen have likewise opposed the excessive violence and intimidation at the cost of their political careers. Joel Blass of Wiggins, John Kennedy of Holly Springs and Karl Wisenberg of Pascagoula all failed in reëlection to the state legislature, having identified themselves as "liberals" for publicly decrying the violence that marked the state's recent history.

The nature of the problem within the Church as it struggles to overcome the impact of a racist culture is illustrated by an interview we had with a pastor in Hinds County. He does believe integration should and will come throughout the state, yet in his long years of association with his white parishoners, as he says, "I've come to know and love these people. You can't expect me to turn on them or to hurt them. Asking me to advocate or work for integration is like telling me to abandon my flock." A monsignor, shortly before Bishop Gerow ordered the desegregation of the schools, asserted: "Now you know segregation is not sinful. If it is, how come we've had it in the Church for so long?" When the desegregation order came through he gave a sigh of relief: "Thank God we have no school in our parish." In a sort of apology for the bishop, the monsignor explained to his congregation "that with all the nonsense that passes for reason today, and all the pressures on him, His Excellency had to do this. I think we all understand what's going on." In another case a white pastor of a Negro parish approached his counterpart in a white parish with the proposition that white and Negro Catholics should get to know one another. "Perhaps we could plan some sort of an affair that would simply offer the opportunity to break down the barriers." The "white" pastor showed not the slightest interest.

As for the desegregation of the schools again, there is a wide gap between policy and practice. A handful of Negro Catholics in the Gulf counties, which partake somewhat of the more lenient Latin culture of southern Louisiana, have entered Catholic schools. In Jackson some 30 Negro pupils now attend "white" schools. There are another 10 schools in the diocese now desegregated. The total number of Negroes involved is small, of course, but even the most optimistic liberal would never have anticipated even this degree of desegregation two years ago. Clearly, Catholicism in Mississippi is a cultural religion. But with the assistance of the poverty program, the civil rights movement, its two bishops and a handful of farsighted priests and laymen, the Church is clearly reorienting itself away from its cruel heritage.

III.
THE BORDER STATES

THE archdioceses of St. Louis, Baltimore and Washington, D.C., are remarkably similar in the history of their internal interracial problems. The break-away from the over-all pattern of segregated parishes, discriminatory practices in school and hospital and non-involvement in the community-wide struggle for Negro rights came with the appointment of the present ordinaries. Cardinal (then Archbishop) Ritter put the archdiocese of St. Louis in the forefront of all national institutions with the desegregation of the parochial school system in 1947. Archbishop O'Boyle put the capital archdiocese on a more gradual timetable starting in September of 1948. By 1952 all Catholic elementary and secondary schools were "open" and actually enrolling qualified Negro students as they applied. Within weeks of his assumption of office in January, 1948, he cancelled the questionable canonical barrier that pastors and ushers had been relying on to prevent Negroes from entering white churches.

In Baltimore discrimination in schools and hospitals was still prevalent when Lawrence Shehan was appointed ordinary in 1961. Although the Josephite Fathers, the Catholic Interracial Council and its militant moderators, Fathers Richard Swift, S.S.J., and Joseph Connolly, had been waging a long struggle for Negro rights in these two areas, their progress was painfully slow until the appointment of Archbishop Shehan.

Notwithstanding the fact that in pastoral letters and administrative directives Cardinal Shehan has made it perfectly clear where he stands with respect to the race problem, his influence on the thinking of his flock has been hard to detect. In the spring of 1964 Senator Daniel Brewster vied with Governor George Wallace of Alabama in a presidential primary. Because of the governor's racist views the chancery, in a very unusual move, endorsed the senator. But a CBS Vote Profile Analysis revealed that in six representative Catholic precincts only 39 per cent of the voters had followed the chancery lead, while 56 per cent voted for Wallace.[1] The cardinal appeared the following year at an open meeting of the City Council to urge the passage of a fair-housing ordinance. Heckled throughout his talk, he persisted in completing his remarks and continued privately to work for the passage of the law. The City Council, heavily Catholic, has rejected fair housing three times in the last few years. James Griffin, chairman of Baltimore's CORE chapter, in April, 1966, cited housing as the city's number one problem. The city was set up as a "target city" for 1966 by CORE for this reason. Yet despite the chancery efforts, and those of the CIC, the rank and file of Catholics and other residents of the city yield very reluctantly to a leadership which is trying desperately to head off impending violence.

In St. Louis and Washington too, there were small interracial groups which had already begun the labor of social change. Working without the active support of the preceding bishop, their measurable accomplishments were meagre. Scandalous injustice and harassment in parish, school and hospital were rampant in the border dioceses in the decade following World War II. However, the war gave the Negro population a new mobility as it enticed it from the rural South to border cities, and gave it an inflated income with which to seek a better life. Compared to the slow pace before the war, the high rate of white-Negro contact during and after it accentuated the mutual irritation simply by multiplying it. Although working for more tangible results, the people in the Catholic interracial councils of these three sees, plus the Josephite Fathers in Baltimore and Washington, were undoubtedly achieving more than they realized.

1. New York *Times,* May 20, 1964, p. 1.

They did, on the other hand, realize how hampered they were without episcopal support.

After the new episcopal appointments the course of events in the border dioceses seemed to follow an identical pattern. Integration of the schools was tried first; the hospitals proved far more difficult. Effective assistance was rendered in the public fight for interracial justice by diocesan support for appropriate legislation at the city, state and national levels, and by joining with other churches or civil rights groups. By examining in detail the development of desegregation policy and community-wide involvement in the civil rights movement in the archdiocese of Washington, we will see a typical case. In the latter sections of this chapter we will recount the main features of the St. Louis story.

WASHINGTON, D.C.: CRISIS IN THE CAPITAL

Washington's peculiar position as the federal capital turns upon it a bright and inescapable spotlight. Until relatively recent years one of the most obvious blemishes revealed was the abysmal state of Washington's race relations. As late as 1947 the President's Committee on Civil Rights, in a blistering report entitled *To Secure These Rights,* summed up that treatment: "If he [a Negro] stops in Washington . . . with very few exceptions he is refused service at downtown restaurants, he may not attend a downtown movie or play, and he has to go into the poorer section of the city to find a night's lodging. The Negro who decides to settle in the District must often find a job in an overcrowded, substandard area. He must often take a job below the level of his ability. He must send his children to the inferior public schools set aside for Negroes and entrust his family's health to Medical agencies which give inferior service. In addition, he must endure the countless daily humiliations that the system of segregation imposes upon the one-third of Washington that is Negro." Public and private recreational facilities were strictly segregated. Negro professional men could not join the District of Columbia Medical Society or Bar Association. Fire and police departments, too, were segregated; for a Negro, a job nearly always meant a menial job, except in the agencies of the Federal government.

To the Negro the Catholic Church in Washington showed the same face as did the District itself. To begin with, Washington was until 1947 a part of the archdiocese of Baltimore, which had always had a Southern tradition. Negro Catholics prior to 1914 were expected to attend either St. Augustine's Church on 15th Street, N.W., then regarded as the "mother church" of the city's colored Catholics or St. Cyprian's, at 13th and C Streets. Between that time and 1949, six other parishes for the colored were established. All these parishes were operated by the Josephite Fathers, except St. Augustine's, which was staffed by diocesan priests. White and Negro parish lines overlapped so that Catholic Negroes often found it more convenient to attend Mass at the nearest Church.

Those who did attend white parishes were expected to sit in a specially designated section to the side or rear. Even when the white section was but sparsely occupied and the Negro section crowded, Negroes were made to stand at the rear of the church rather than occupy empty pews in the white section. When Communion time came, the whites approached the altar railing first, the Negroes last. In one instance, when a Negro was reported dying in the alley behind a white church, the pastor sent for a priest from the Negro parish half a mile away rather than go himself. It was an isolated act, but the fact that it could happen at all was evidence that the virus of prejudice was strong and pervasive.

The same pattern prevailed in the parochial school system. Both the elementary and the secondary schools were strictly segregated; until after the Second World War, a Catholic Negro girl who wished to attend a Catholic high school had to go to Baltimore to do so, and for Negro Catholic boys there was only Cardinal Gibbons Institute, a vocational school located at Ridge, Maryland. Conditions were brighter on the college level. Dunbarton College (for women) frequently admitted upper-class

Negro girls; Trinity College, also for women, followed Dunbarton's lead. Catholic University, a national institution established by the American bishops as a group and supported by the contributions of Catholics all over the country, had accepted some few Negroes before 1920, but accepted none until 1936, when it began a slow return to the original policy of non-discrimination. Patients and inmates in the District's Catholic hospitals and charitable institutions, as in those under municipal auspices, were separated according to color.

Such was the general picture some 15 years ago. In that brief decade and a half, Washington has undergone a striking social revolution with virtually all the public and private facilities once closed to Negroes now open to them. Employment, however, remains a major stumbling block. Though they comprise some 55 per cent of the District's population, Negroes still face serious obstacles when they look for a job, even though the building trades once tightly closed are now open. So too are many types of white-collar work: banks, savings and loan companies, and brokerage houses. Here the problem of unemployability is showing its head. Several of these institutions had deliberately sought Negro applicants, only to discover that very few could qualify. Meanwhile, the most serious problem seems to be housing. Coupled to the growing rate of Negro unemployment and unemployability is the massive problem of poverty. Underneath all these problems is demographic change. Population shifts have made the city proper 55 per cent Negro and the surrounding suburbs almost totally white.

The civic revolution has had its counterpart within the Catholic Church; nor has the Church been, as in some other places, a foot-dragging follower; in important respects it has been a leader, helping to make the civic revolution possible.

The change within the Church began in 1947, when the District of Columbia, along with five counties in neighboring Maryland—Montgomery, Prince Georges, St. Mary's, Charles and Calvert—was made a separate archdiocese. As its first archbishop Rome appointed Patrick O'Boyle, a Scranton-born Irish-American who had spent much of his priestly life in

New York as executive director of Mount Loretto, a huge child-care institution of the archdiocese. He also had directed Catholic war-relief for the American hierarchy overseas.

Consecrated and formally installed in January, 1948, Archbishop O'Boyle seems to have decided almost at once that desegregation of the Church and its institutions should receive priority. In those parish churches where segregation at Sunday Mass was most blatant and most strictly enforced, he called in the offending pastors and firmly insisted that it be stopped. For some time, lay groups from the Catholic Interracial Council formed in 1944 had been organizing sit-in demonstrations in these churches, white and colored members showing up together for Mass on Sunday unannounced and sitting in a body in the center aisles. The Council's protests—and those of others—to the new archbishop did not go unheeded. For more than 10 years now, there is no Catholic church in the archdiocese where a Negro need sit in a segregated section or take second place at Communion time. Moreover, a firm policy has been adopted which stipulates that whenever the residential pattern of a parish changes from white to Negro, diocesan priests will stay and continue to administer it.

Concurrently, Archbishop O'Boyle decided to do something about the schools. Relying on the experience and advice of his Director of Education, Father John Spence (now his auxiliary bishop), he called a meeting of the newly appointed officials of the archdiocese in the summer of 1948. It was determined that the beginnings would be made in the Federal District and the two northern Maryland counties, Montgomery and Prince Georges. The counties of southern Maryland posed a different problem which will be considered later.

The change was to be made without delay, but quietly. "We could have had headlines all over the country if we had made a public statement of our intention," the archbishop has said, "but I don't think the operation would have worked as successfully as it did. Pockets of resistance would have had time to form and develop." Accordingly, no public announcement was made. Instead, a series of private meetings were held for pastors of parishes with parochial schools, for the administrative officers of religious communities of men and women teaching in the diocese, and finally for school principals. Both types of schools —those operated by the parishes or by the diocese and therefore directly under diocesan supervision, and those operated privately by the religious orders—were asked, and they agreed, to accept the new policy. "We couldn't afford to have any holdouts," the archbishop said.

Integration was, at the outset, extremely modest. That first year—the academic year 1948–1949—one Negro boy was enrolled in a parochial high school. The following year it was decided to admit three Negro applicants in the freshman year of each Catholic high school, two in each of the first three grades of the elementary schools. In 1952 all limitations were dropped, and by 1954, when the Supreme Court handed down its integration decision, the Catholic schools of the District of Columbia had been integrated on all levels. Washington thus joined a small company of other Southern and border dioceses, St. Louis, San Antonio and Raleigh, in anticipating the Court's action. In general, the change was quiet. "At least," says the archbishop, "we had no one leaving the Church, so far as I know." Today, 7,500 Negroes attend Washington's 88 Catholic elementary and 35 secondary schools. Community leaders believe that the leadership of the Catholic Church in integrating its schools was in some measure responsible for the generally peaceful integration of the District's public schools right after the Supreme Court's decision.

The churches and schools in the southern part of the diocese presented the archbishop with a special situation that thus far has not permitted the same rapid progress toward integration as in the District of Columbia and the northern Maryland counties. This heavily Catholic area, consisting in the main of St. Mary's and Charles counties (there is only one parish and a mission in Calvert County), contains some 25 parishes with 12 elementary and six high schools, accommodating altogether some 5,564 students.

This is what the old historians called the cradle of American

Catholicism; St. Ignatius Church in Port Tobacco was founded in 1641. But so far as racial democracy is concerned, the area is one of the most backward. Until the Civil War the colored people there were slaves; even Archbishop John Carroll and the Jesuits, who have always ministered to the region's Catholics, held slaves at one time. After the war Negroes became house or tenant farmers for the dominant white Catholic families. The Catholics among them sat in special sections at Sunday Mass, and their children did not attend Catholic schools with the sons and daughters of their parents' employers.

Archbishop O'Boyle was not able to make a beginning toward school desegregation until 1956. He decided to begin with a series of instructions on the race question. He directed that between September, 1955, and May, 1956, seven sermons on the subject be delivered weekly in the 25 parishes of St. Mary's, Calvert and Charles counties. Each week following the sermons, he and one of his aides visited the parishes in turn to discuss the progress with the pastors. At its conclusion he suggested to the pastors that they simply begin that fall to accept Negro children in the parochial schools—without fanfare, as had been done in the northern part of the archdiocese. The clergy demurred, asking instead that an official archdiocesan announcement be made. Accordingly, on Pentecost Sunday in 1956 the following statement was read from every Catholic pulpit in southern Maryland:

The Archdiocese of Washington, conscious of its sacred obligation to provide parochial school education, wherever possible, for all its children, began to accept colored pupils in many of its schools in 1948–1949. There are now 91 Catholic Schools and Colleges of the Archdiocese in the District of Columbia, Montgomery and Prince Georges Counties enrolling Catholic colored students. Beginning next September all elementary parochial schools of St. Mary's, Charles and Calvert Counties will begin to admit colored children to the first two grades.

As usual the pastors and principals will select the applicants according to standard educational procedures.

We are confident that all Catholics, who wish all possible blessings to their neighbors, will cooperate in this action as true believers in the teachings of Christ, the Redeemer and Savior of all mankind.

White parents did not take kindly to the new plan, and in PTA meetings they frankly expressed their opposition. The archbishop was visited by official delegations and told, in effect, that he was going too far too fast. Why didn't he wait, they wanted to know, until the public schools of the region had made a beginning?

Faced with this kind of opposition, archdiocesan authorities have proceeded more slowly than they would have liked. Still, progress is being made. In two large consolidated schools, one in St. Mary's, the other in Charles, there are Negro students scattered through all the grades, and in the latter county several other schools have seen the beginnings of integration.

So far as seating arrangements in the churches are concerned, no easy generalization is possible. The official policy is that Negro Catholics are free to sit wherever they wish, but in some parishes, whether influenced by timidity, tradition or pressure on the part of pastors and/or fellow parishioners, Negroes still sit apart from their white co-religionists. A good deal depends, of course, on the attitude of the pastor: where he lets it be known unequivocally that segregation is a thing of the past, it tends gradually to disappear; where he gives tacit approval to its continuance, it goes on.

"The situation [in these two counties] is not as good by any means as I'd like to see it," the archbishop has said, "but it's on the way." It seems likely that the progress will continue at the same rate; current enrollment figures indicate that over 150 colored children are in attendance at formerly all white Catholic schools.

There are only three Catholic hospitals in the archdiocese: Providence, conducted by the Daughters of Charity of St. Vincent de Paul, and Georgetown, under Jesuit administration but staffed by the Sisters of St. Joseph (Baden, Pa.). Each has about 400 beds, with Georgetown in the process of adding about 100 more. Holy Cross Hospital in Silver Spring with 260 beds is the newest, opening in September, 1963, under the administration of the Sisters of the Holy Cross.

Until 1964 the older two hospitals, while they never excluded Negroes as patients, did segregate them and did exclude colored doctors from their staffs. In its out-patient department, Providence had separate facilities for whites and Negroes. Colored patients were housed on sun-porches—one for men, one for women—instead of in the regular rooms and wards. However, when the hospital moved to its present location about seven or eight years ago and constructed a new plant, the policy began to change. Through the efforts of Archbishop O'Boyle and the Urban League in 1957 the medical staff was opened to Negro doctors, and four or five were admitted. Their number, nonetheless, has remained small. An Urban League report of May, 1964, listed two on the Active Staff and 16 on the Courtesy Staff. Incidents such as the one which follows illustrate the problem faced in fully integrating the hospitals.

One day in 1963 a Negro doctor in Washington got a call from a white member of the resident staff at Providence regarding a 70-year-old Negro woman who had fallen and apparently broken a hip. She had been given emergency treatment at Providence, and the white resident, in calling his Negro friend, inadvertently spelled out the hospital's policy. The Negro woman would have to be moved, he said, as no single room or bed in a room occupied by other Negroes was available. The patient was kept in the emergency area for 36 hours, then finally given a bed. Operated upon, she subsequently died. Again, there was no evidence that lack of a regular bed in a regular room was a contributing cause of death, but it remains true that this was a situation which should never have occurred. A complaint was made to the archbishop, who wrote to the nun in charge of the hospital. No action was taken, so a Negro doctor familiar with the situation went to see her in person. The nun said that her primary interest was in the welfare of her patients, and that if some of them did not want to share a room with Negroes, she was not going to force them to do so. She had had requests from Negroes themselves, she said, not to put them in rooms with whites. As far as she was concerned, the existing policy would remain in effect. And so, apparently, it had.

On the other hand, Providence Hospital employed Negro nurses even before Archbishop O'Boyle came, and its nursing school freely admits Negro candidates. There seems to be no discrimination in its general employment policies; Negroes as well as whites are to be found among nurses aides, secretaries and laboratory technicians.

Traditionally, Georgetown University Hospital also segregated its Negro patients. They were cared for in a separate ward, and there were no accommodations at all for Negro maternity cases. But Georgetown, too, built a new plant—in 1950—and thereafter its policy, like that of Providence, began to change. It opened its doors to Negro patients who could pay, and took in a limited number of Negro charity cases as well (though fewer than comparable public hospitals). At first there were no Negro doctors on the staff, but five were admitted shortly after the new buildings were opened.

That number has remained constant, but in justice it must be said that there may be a reason for the limitation which Providence cannot advance. Georgetown is a university hospital, with a relatively closed staff. Also, it is a teaching hospital affiliated with a medical school which uses the hospital to provide clinical experience for students in their junior and senior years and, subsequently, opportunities for internship and residency. Any such hospital would naturally give preference to its own medical school graduates when making staff appointments, and there have been very few Negro graduates of the Georgetown Medical School. The hospital has, however, taken occasional Negro residents and interns.

As to patients in the hospital the pattern seems similar to the one in force at Providence. Occasionally, Negroes and whites share the same rooms. Like Providence, too, Georgetown has hired Negro nurses who are treated as well as their white colleagues and seem to enjoy working there. Negroes occupy other responsible posts—in laboratory work, for example—and the hospital's nursing school admits qualified Negro girls. Holy Cross Hospital, starting anew with no tradition or vested interests and a clear mandate from the archdiocese, operates with a clear policy and record. Since 1965 there have been at least five Negro doctors on the active staff; white and Negro patients share semi-private accommodations as well as wards. Hospital administrators have also voiced the hope that affiliation with the Howard University Medical School may be in the offing.

A Plan for the Year 2000

The greater Washington area is one of the fastest growing metropolitan complexes in the country. It has been expanding rapidly, in fact, since the 1930's; by the year 2000 its population, presently estimated as 2.4 million, is expected to double.

To plan for this growth there are two major agencies, the National Capital Planning Commission and its subsidiary, the National Capital Regional Planning Council, created by an act of Congress in 1952; and the Maryland National Capital Parks and Planning Commission (together with several local planning groups in Maryland's incorporated cities over which the state Commission does not have jurisdiction). They have a threefold aim: (1) to arrest the deterioration of the so-called "metro-center," the heart of the city; (2) to supervise the planning of future suburbs in "suburban development corridors" radiating from it; and (3) to help preserve the open character of the countryside between these corridors.

For some time a priest acted as the Church's informal liaison officer with these agencies. In the fall of 1963, like the archdioceses of Chicago and New York, the archdiocese of Washington set up its own Office of Urban Renewal. The operating head of the urban renewal office was a young layman, Floyd Agostinelli, who was a staff worker in Friendship House in Chicago and at the Peter Claver Center, its Washington affiliate. Agostinelli also had professional training in the field of city planning and a master's degree in urban sociology from Catholic University. He worked under the archdiocesan director of charities, a priest, but he had a good deal of autonomy and seems to have had cordial access to and strong support from the archbishop.

The scope and importance of Agostinelli's tasks are indicated by a startling statistic: of 38 parishes in the District of Columbia, 26—just under 70 per cent—are affected in one way or another by municipal plans now in operation or on the drawing board. Most of these are in areas already or about to become heavily Negro; like their non-Catholic brethren, white Catholics in Washington have fled the urban limits for the suburbs, leaving the city with all its problems behind. Some of these 26 parishes are located in "urban renewal areas," neighborhoods in such an advanced stage of decay that they are being completely torn down and rebuilt. Others are in "conservation areas," where determined efforts are afoot to preserve existing buildings and facilities. Still other churches and schools stand in or near the paths of freeways and other roads planned or actually under construction to speed the flow of traffic into, out of, through or around the District.

Agostinelli's task was twofold: to interpret the plans of the planners to the archbishop and his pastors, and to inform the planning commissions of the present and future needs of the Catholic Church.

As a beginning, the Office of Urban Renewal sponsored in March of 1964 a workshop to which the pastors of the 19 parishes most seriously affected by city planning were invited. It is a measure of their realization of the gravity of the situation that all but one of the 19 came—and the lone absentee was confined to a sickbed. With the aid of slides Agostinelli explained the over-all "Plan for the Year 2000," and told each pastor how his parish would be affected. Each priest also received information on housing conditions in his parish, statistics on relative incomes of Negro and white wage-earners, data on the kinds of jobs open to members of each race, and plans for public housing. More of these workshops were scheduled in the District of Columbia, and in suburban areas as well.

One of the special problems that the office tried to ameliorate was the plight of homeowners in conservation areas, many of whom are Negroes. In such areas planning officials are charged with the responsibility for inspecting dwellings to see that they are clean, decent and safe. If they are not, the housing law provides that homeowners can obtain loans to make necessary repairs and improvements. The banks, however, will not risk such loans, so Agostinelli's office encouraged the formation of parish credit unions for the purpose. At least one has already been formed.

On the parish level, there is only one (so far as we know) that has established working relationships with community groups in a planned effort to maintain its interracial character and upgrade its housing and public facilities. The Church of Sts. Paul and Augustine is, in other words, pioneering a new parish-community relationship.

But the paradox is that an office with such an essential role to play in the future development of the archdiocese and in solutions to problems of race and poverty was operated with a staff of one full-time professional, a secretary and a few part-time helpers (from time to time). Early in 1965 Mr. Agostinelli resigned and there has been no apparent effort to continue the operation. With the exception of Detroit and possibly Chicago, there seems to be in episcopal circles an astonishing indifference to or incomprehension of urban man's emerging ability to control the development of his environment. This is not to suggest that the Church can perform this task; it is to suggest, however, that as planning does materialize, the diocese must learn the language of planning, the issues and proposals so that it might exercise its moral judgments in a sophisticated and relevant way. A diocese whose central city is over 55 per cent Negro and whose suburbs are overwhelmingly white is one with a bewildering future. It would seem mandatory to have, not a one-man Urban Renewal Office, but a full staff of social scientists. This failure to develop scientific competence will guarantee the continued irrelevance of the Church in a world of change.

The Lay Frontier

In Washington, as in other cities, the vanguard of Catholic lay activity in the field of interracial justice is the Catholic Interracial Council, affiliated with the National Catholic Conference for Interracial Justice. The moving spirit of the Washington Council since its founding in 1944 has been Dr. John O'Connor, a professor of history in Georgetown University who was elected first president of the National Conference when it was founded in 1960. Much of its dynamism now stems from its current president, Joseph Nuesse, professor of sociology in Catholic University.

The membership of the Washington Council, a figure which has fluctuated sharply over the years, is now at about 125. It did a good deal of pioneering in its first four years, before the archdiocese was established, and afterwards as well. But the record of Archbishop O'Boyle and the 1954 decision of the Supreme Court has tended to give lay Catholics a feeling that the major victories in civil rights have already been won. Lately, however, there is a new and youthful leaven working within the Council which had led to some interesting developments. In 1964, for example, members of the Council joined a picket line to help force integration of Montgomery County's principal amusement park, Glen Echo. They also picketed National Football League games of the Washington Redskins in an effort to induce the owners to hire Negro players. They joined in a doorbell-ringing campaign in the suburbs, soliciting signatures from white homeowners willing to pledge themselves to welcome newcomers regardless of race. The Council also sponsors a regular weekly paid radio program over a local station.

In an effort to muster support for the various civic efforts to bring about fair employment practices, to secure an equitable share of the housing market and to promote non-discriminatory practices in the area of public welfare and education, Archbishop O'Boyle called a clergy conference in April and May, 1963, with attendance by all priests of the diocese compulsory. The archbishop presided over the opening conference to indicate the high priority which he gave this general problem. The workshop technique was used in order to maximize participation and freedom of discussion.

A similar program was repeated in the fall for the various religious orders of priests, sisters and brothers working in the archdiocese and for lay leaders. Meanwhile in May, there was established an Archbishop's Committee on Human Relations to implement within the entire organizational structure of the archdiocese the principle of equal opportunity in such fields as education, welfare and employment. The Commission was also instructed to coordinate its efforts with those made by the other church bodies of the metropolitan region. It was made up of some 31 members, white and Negro, half laymen and half clergy. Archbishop O'Boyle retained the presidency, giving executive responsibility to his auxiliary, Bishop John Spence. Much of the Commission's work is aimed at education of the clergy at the deanery and parish levels and the provision of competent consultation at the parish level when crises appear.

Perhaps the major accomplishment of the Commission was the drawing up of a fair employment practices policy. The concluding paragraph of the publicly announced policy stated:

> We shall continue to select our contractors and suppliers on a competitive basis but we shall also be guided by their employment practices and will, wherever possible, favor that contractor or supplier who demonstrates an affirmative employment program of equality of opportunity.

Implementing such a policy has proved difficult. The pressure it exerts on contractors is often counteracted by the de facto absence of Negroes in many of the unions. Contractors cannot police the unions. But as we noted before, the building trades unions are, as a result of pressures from many sectors, opening up their apprenticeship programs. As unemployability grows into the stature of a major social problem, the Commission apparently will have to seek Federal "poverty money" to inaugurate retraining programs for the purpose of providing a supply of skilled labor from the ranks of the Negroes. Otherwise, its pressure on companies and unions to lure non-white labor will fail. It goes without saying, of course, that this is not the exclusive responsibility of the Commission, but of the community at large. The point remains, however, that policies and demands of the Commission have to be drawn up in terms of actual conditions in the labor market.

In addition to this Commission, Archbishop O'Boyle joined with religious leaders of the other major faiths to form an Interreligious Committee on Race Relations. Through working subcommittees, the ICR is actively engaged in seeking to widen the employment and housing opportunities for Washington Negroes. It acted as a lobby for the passage of the Civil Rights Act of 1964, helped organize the March on Washington (August, 1963) and solve its logistics problems, and through such programs as the "Good Neighbor Pledge" it works for the peaceful integration of Negro families into all-white neighborhoods.

Lest a mere description of these activities and programs lead to false optimism, it must be reported that criticism is still leveled at the archdiocese. It comes most frequently from the front ranks of those involved in the civil rights struggle and in the day-to-day life of parishes in the inner city. Here one hears the charge that "the archdiocese has no effective over-all social action program." Or as one priest put it: "Time is running out. Revolution comes when the goals are in sight. And these people in the slums see them. The leisurely pace of diocesan efforts and the inability of pastors to understand what's going on around them, seem to me to be the makings of a dangerous situation."

Given the deep psychological and economic roots of poverty and prejudice, running deep for centuries, it does not seem logical to expect that much progress can be made in the few years that religious and other institutions have given to the working of solutions. In the eyes of civic and religious leaders everything possible is being done, that is, everything possible within the framework of priorities, commitments, personnel and financial policies of the established institutions. The question implicit in the complaints is whether there is time to solve the problems within these present institutional limitations. More specifically, what the Catholic critics seem to be calling for is a drastic reform of the existing ecclesiastical structure.

ST. LOUIS: FROM LEADERSHIP TO ESTABLISHMENT

In St. Louis the situation is pretty much the same. The recent history of the Church's involvement in civil rights in St. Louis dates back to 1943 with the formation of the St. Louis Conference on Negro Welfare. Fathers Patrick Molloy, Donald Corrigan, C.Ss.R., and Charles Reinalt, S.V.D., were the founders. A similar group for sisters, the Sisters Conference on Negro Welfare, was formed the following year, and also a Catholic Interracial Council, which included both clerical and lay members.

Abortive attempts by members of this group to obtain enrollment of a Negro girl in Webster College ultimately led St. Louis University to open its doors to Negro students in September, 1945. This move brought many others in its wake. Within two years both Fontbonne College and Webster College opened their doors to Negro students. In the fall of that same year Father John Smith, pastor of Visitation Parish, had moved three classes of Negro children into previously all-white Visitation Parochial School in segregated classrooms, but with joint use of the lunch room and playground. From December, 1945, until June, 1946, 12 Negro children moved into Visitation's formerly all-white classes and by the fall of 1946, St. Bernadette's Negro school and Visitation formally merged and integrated. Other previously all-white schools accepted a handful of Negro children that same fall.

In October, 1946, Archbishop Joseph Ritter assumed leadership of the St. Louis See. In the spring of 1947, he instructed pastors in the archdiocese to "accept all children into parish schools without regard to race." From the beginning of integration at Visitation, only very minor opposition was felt. When a group of Catholics organized to oppose the new policy by civil court action, the archbishop warned them, in a pastoral letter read from all the pulpits of the diocese on September 21, 1947, that they ran the risk of excommunication. Shortly thereafter, the group withdrew their action at court and disbanded.

It was in 1947 that Washington University in St. Louis first enrolled Negroes, and in 1950 the University of Missouri followed suit. The 1950's saw the Supreme Court ruling on desegregation of public schools. The actual history of desegregation in St. Louis schools parallels what has been said above with regard to other border dioceses. The issue is still a very prominent one today, for there are not a few schools Catholic and public on both the elementary and secondary levels where integration is minimal or non-existent. While there have been some efforts made to achieve a better balance, these have met with varying degrees of success. The largest obstacle in this area, of course, is the all-too-evident fact of neighborhood segregation. There are at least 13 parishes (and schools) which are still or have become totally Negro. Under pressure of discrimination and poverty, the Negroes in St. Louis are packed into a ghetto in the center of the city, a ghetto that was narrowed and elongated into a corridor running through the entire north-central section of the city by public land clearance and urban "development" programs in the 1950's.

In the field of employment the picture is even less bright. Employers have clung tenaciously to discriminatory policies in hiring. Unions, the only effective weapon workers have traditionally had, have maintained exclusionary practices in job apprenticeship and membership. In the face of this pincer-like force from employers and unions (somewhat curtailed in the last two or three years), the employment plight of the St. Louis Negro has been a despairing one.

Not until the 1963 National Conference on Religion and Race awakened the consciences of religious people of all faiths, did the Church in St. Louis declare itself committed to any specific course of action for civil rights. In May of that year Catholics joined with Protestants and Jews in calling the St. Louis Conference on Religion and Race (CRR). Planning for this conference was due in no small measure to Paul Hanlon, Executive Director of the CRR, and it was to him that the various religious groups entrusted the leadership of the new organization that grew out of the conference. Also called the St. Louis Conference on Religion and Race, it was undoubtedly the most notable achievement of the May, 1963, meeting. Its function was that of a coordinating and planning group with official status among all major religious groups in St. Louis. It assisted these religious bodies in working out both racial policy and its practical implementation.

The St. Louis Conference on Religion and Race found real scope for its work in the succeeding months of 1963. In August, it gave full support to the proposed March on Washington, and the sizable delegation from St. Louis at the march gave evidence of its success. In this same month Cardinal Ritter took another step toward involvement of the Church in the race situation by establishing the Archbishop's Commission on Human Rights. This is a group of priests and laymen headed by Auxiliary Bishop George Gottwald, whose purpose is "to advise and recommend procedures which will bring about a rule of justice and charity in the community; to initiate a program that will enable all to understand the principles involved in the current civil rights issue; and, thirdly, to formulate programs of action that will overcome the obstacles that now impede the use of God-given rights." This commission, and the St. Louis Conference on Religion and Race, in trying to collaborate, have suffered some setbacks from the considerable disagreement as to the nature, the composition, the purposes and the practical procedures of both groups. However, the very fact that these problems (particularly disagreements over causes of the basic racial issues) could be brought to the level of free discussion by religious persons of both races, is itself an advance.

Since 1963 much work has been done by both the St. Louis Conference on Religion and Race and the Archbishop's Commission. In the early fall, Catholic laymen, priests and nuns gathered at St. John's Church in the downtown area and proceeded in prayer and by candlelight to the courthouse to hear a

Catholic lawyer speak on civil rights. On November 25, an estimated 30,000 persons of all faiths marched down Market Street to the steps of the old courthouse where the notorious Dred Scott Decision had been rendered, and heard a Negro Protestant minister, a Jewish rabbi and a Catholic priest appeal for an end to residential segregation.

On the last day of January, 1964, the St. Louis Board of Aldermen passed a fair housing bill. The final passing of this bill was due, in no small measure, to the efforts of religious leaders of both organizations who spent weeks in mobilizing support for this bill.

Renowned and informal speakers came to St. Louis during 1963 and 1964 to address themselves to the problem of racial injustice, several at the invitation of the religious organizations. Dr. Martin Luther King, Jr., spoke on different occasions to capacity audiences and John H. Griffin told groups, at times numbering in thousands, of his experiences as a "temporary Negro." In early May, 1964, St. Louis played host to the second National Conference on Religion and Race.

During this same period of time, the problem of discrimination in employment was highlighted by CORE demonstrations at the Jefferson Bank. Continuing from August, 1963, to the end of the year and into the new year, the demonstrations spread to downtown department stores and the Gateway Memorial Arch then under construction. Catholics, usually the same few, had more than a token representation among the demonstrators. An indication of St. Louis involvement by religious organizations in civil rights was the active participation in the Montgomery-Selma March of March, 1965. The large delegations of persons who went to both Selma and Montgomery were either sponsored or brought together through the joint efforts of the St. Louis Conference on Religion and Race and the Archbishop's Commission on Human Rights.

At the parish level there have been some impressive but spotty efforts. Pastors and curates in several parishes involved in racial changeover have met to discuss and plan activities on mutual problems; Catholic interracial councils have been formed and have worked on freedom of residence projects and community planning. But perhaps the most impressive parish project uncovered in the research undertaken for this book is the Bicentennial Civic Improvement Corporation, the successor to the St. Bridget of Erin Housing Fund. The latter was established by Fathers John Shocklee and Joseph Kohler.

The experience of working daily in the deteriorating neighborhood in which St. Bridget's parish was located, convinced these priests that poverty was a spiritual problem—a poverty of personality as much as an absence of wealth. The primary difficulty they encountered was the pervasive atmosphere of despair and resignation among the inhabitants. Those who did achieve success financially moved out to better homes. Most of the time they were forced to move since they exceeded the allowable income rule of the public housing project. Thus, stripped of natural leadership, the neighborhood could not help itself.

What the Corporation does to get at the root of this problem is to buy the uninhabitable homes in the area. It arranges for their renovation and remodeling. The cost of this operation is used in lieu of a 20 per cent down payment on the house by the purchasing family. When over the course of years the latter repays the 20 per cent, a mortgage is then arranged, and the 20 per cent goes into a revolving fund to do a similar service on another house. Meanwhile, viable families are offered the opportunity to buy. Families with pathologies of alcohol, addiction or perversion are screened out. The husband is invited to participate in a Voluntary Improvement Program where he learns to read, compute and master a household budget. The wife enrolls in a Basic Household Educational Course. Both are encouraged to join the parish credit union. The new home with a manageable financial foundation can thus become an abode of dignity and promise for a family that has been allowed to rise to its own inherent potential. Between 1963 and 1967, 55 families have been placed in these new homes. Sixty-five are on the waiting-training list at this writing. The Corporation meanwhile has been near the point of financial exhaustion—further evidence of the inability of existing political, economic and religious institutions of the American city to assist grass roots efforts such as this.

While the picture of the work done in the Archdiocese of St. Louis appears to be rather impressive, one must in fairness and objectivity admit that the actual situation today still gives basis for real concern. One cannot fail to see that on both the archdiocesan and parochial levels, despite good intent, the achievements have not kept apace of developing problems. Due to population shifts, for example, desegregation has turned into resegregation. The promising and vigorous St. Louis Conference on Religion and Race collapsed in 1966. Problems internal to the supporting churches and the difficulties of financing the programs led to its dissolution. Also, from what we can determine, there seems to be considerable difficulty on the part of interested laymen in working on or with the Human Rights Commission. The mode of communications peculiar to institutions or complex organizations prevails in the Commission and even more so in the chancery; while it may facilitate communications within, it tends to alienate those trying to maximize the leadership potential of the cardinal. Dozens of highly competent people have given up working with what they call "the establishment."

The excellent four-phase program designed by the Commission to involve the parish in the solution of race and poverty programs does not, on the other hand, constitute the pressure necessary to move the reluctant. Much, if not most of the compliance, while sincere, seems to the outside observer perfunctory and ineffective. One reason is that many of the clergy to whom the initiative is given for solving local problems are, themselves, part of the problem. As noted earlier, the Bicentennial Civic Improvement Corporation represents a unique parish reform and achievement. It is significant, however, in its uniqueness: it involves two, perhaps three, parishes at the most. Dying a slow death from financial starvation, it was saved in February, 1967, by a grant from the U.S. Office of Economic Opportunity. It might have been possible to get some assistance from the diocese. Yet, it would not be fair to expect anything but an emergency loan or grant, for the diocese has a wider range of responsibilities. It has, among others, internal responsibilities to its own members (for example, a parochial school system) which limits severely what Cardinal Ritter and many of his clergy and laity would like to contribute to the cause. As in all other large dioceses, the freedom of action in St. Louis is defined by a bureaucratic form of organization whose orientation is still basically internal stability, and whose major problem of the moment is communications up and down the echelons.

IV.
NORTH AND EAST

FROM the Civil War onward, the North has been the source of most, it not all, of the liberal or reform movements in American Catholicism. Here are to be found its numerical strength, its economic and political power, and its larger universities. Programs for rural life, labor schools, Catholic social-action movements and liturgical reform have originated in the cities of the east and midwest. The 19th-century flood-tide of immigration in washing up on the East Coast brought the resources necessary for these movements.

The leadership of the Catholic interracial movement itself came and continues to come from the North. Here the late Father John LaFarge, S.J., and George Hunton—the movement's pioneers and long-time guides—laid the groundwork for the eight-year-old National Catholic Conference for Interracial Justice now headquartered in Chicago. Our purpose in this chapter is to examine the work and influence of this movement, but more importantly to look beyond it to the whole area of contact between Catholic institutions and Negro Catholics, and the relationships of both to the series of national problems we today call "civil rights." The focus is on the diocese and its institutions. We have selected those dioceses which make our sample representative statistically and geographically.

Insofar as the heaviest proportion of Negroes and Negro Catholics particularly is to be found in New York, Philadelphia and Chicago, we shall deal with these cities in depth. To do this, historical perspectives are necessary and these we have sought to establish. But the key to the future seems to lie with the suburbs, for it is here that the next major development shall occur, when Negroes in large numbers attempt to join in the demographic movement called "urban sprawl." There being vastly more suburbs than cities, and an equally unmanageable variety, the wisest course would seem to be the selection of a diocese that combines the greatest variety of suburbs. One such diocese is Rockville Centre, comprising the counties of Nassau and Suffolk, just east of New York City on Long Island. It is also the largest such diocese and ranks fifth among the dioceses of the United States.

The great migration of Negroes from farm to city, from South to North, has profoundly affected race relations in Northern cities and communities. It implied a challenge to Catholic institutions, of course; it also faced individual Catholics with a whole spectrum of personal choices involving prejudice and fears and responsibility. In big cities in particular the challenges have been unique. Residential life is dense, civic life diverse, social affairs complex. In some ways, the social and religious problems of Catholics in the North are compounded. Their parishes are rather static: limited geographical areas rooted in a system of canonical and bureaucratic directives that do not permit a high degree of flexibility. Despite the breadth of social mission implied by Catholic history, the Church is not easily adaptable to the new dimensions and swift pace of metropolitan change including racial problems.

In large cities of the North the influx of Negroes is evident. In the 22-county Greater New York City area there live 1,700,000 non-whites; by 1975 that total is expected to reach 2,400,000. In 1960 Negroes numbered 823,000 in Chicago and just over 500,000 in Philadelphia. About 80,000 reside in Milwaukee. Most of this influx into big cities has occurred in the last 20 years. From 1940 to 1960 the Negro populations of New York and Philadelphia doubled, those of Chicago and Detroit tripled, and that of Los Angeles rose fivefold. As many urban sociologists have discovered, the large cities of America are becoming Negro cities. Today only one major American city—Washington—has a Negro majority. But by 1980, if present population trends continue, Negroes will be the majority in Detroit, Cleveland, Baltimore, Chicago and St. Louis. These trends, if unchanged, will give America a civilization in which seven of her ten largest cities (all except New York, Los Angeles, and Houston) will have Negro majorities while the whites will live in racial isolation out in the suburbs.

The population explosion of Negroes in the North should have brought home to Catholic leadership a realization of the huge dimensions of the racial problem. However, anything short of a sudden or tremendous calamity tends to be overlooked. Or perhaps it is simply a matter of administrating dioceses without a flow of data from reliable and competent sources at the parish level. At any rate, the formulation of a long-term, well-informed and coherent approach to social problems is still a thing of the future for all but a handful of dioceses.

The Commission for Catholic Missions Among the Colored People and the Indians is the only agency (secular or religious) that claims to keep statistics on the stated categories. The data is compiled at the diocesan level from figures supplied by pastors. It is at this source that trouble begins, for it is commonly known that statistics and the techniques for gathering them is the subject about which a pastor cares least and knows even less. The forwarding of reports on social statistics to the diocese is often given to the youngest curate with instructions to "do the best you can" or "add about 10 per cent to last years report." It is, then, with this caveat that we give the following information.

These figures are culled only from those parishes officially known to be or to have been "colored." They do not include the people who constitute small minorities in white parishes. Nonetheless, they afford minimal membership estimates, relative standing of the various dioceses and clues as to the direction of population movements.

As far as Northern dioceses are concerned, it is evident that Brooklyn and Detroit more than doubled their Negro member-

NEGRO CATHOLICS REPORTED*

Diocese	*1956*	*1966*
Lafayette	75,000	77,988
Washington, D.C.	48,258	65,832
New York	46,425	62,678
Galveston-Houston	24,671	62,000
New Orleans	71,000	55,000
Chicago	41,000	45,000
Philadelphia	23,037	41,637
Los Angeles	22,542	40,000
Detroit	8,500	30,000
Brooklyn	10,000	28,500

* In *Our Negro and Indian Missions,* Annual Report of the Commission for the Catholic Missions Among the Colored People and the Indians, 1966.

ship in a decade. The proportionate gains of New York, Chicago and Philadelphia, although much smaller, still leave them as the Northern strongholds of Negro Catholicism, a position these cities have held since the turn of the century.

As we mentioned earlier, the geographical stability of the Catholic parish has by that fact itself made it a part of practically every community into which the Negro moved. With the passing of time it actually became "his" parish. Even though he may have been excluded from attendance at a more distant parish, there could never be any doubt that, as long as he wanted to remain so, he was a Catholic. Then too, it is worth noting, there never was an African Catholic Church. What this suggests is that segregation and discrimination were not the ultimates. If rights and privileges were denied to Negroes in the Church, membership—and more important in the psychic realm, identification—was not. This is probably the explanation for the relative stability of Negro Catholic statistics. Leakage no doubt has always been a problem, although no one ever got excited about it; but mass defection, schism or secession has never even been a threat. The ability of Negro Catholics to identify with Catholicism undoubtedly has something to do with it.

One index of Negroes' attitudes might be their press. Recalling the history of Irish-Negro relations, one might expect that Catholicism would be a favorite target of Negro journalists. Yet one finds among them a rather unbiased approach. Even in the 1920's when lynching reached its height, North and South, the *Afro-American* chain, the Chicago *Defender,* the *Amsterdam News,* the Cleveland *Gazette* and others handled news from the Catholic sector in a variable manner. Praise and criticism were meted out as the occasion seemed to demand. It is of more than passing interest to note the near universal condemnation of the Church for its supporting role (blessing soldiers and war matériel) in the Italian invasion of Ethiopia. Other than this, Catholicism has emerged nearly unscathed from the Negro press.

From the point of view of social stratification there is some evidence indicating that the strongest attraction of the Church is for the middle-class Negro.[1] Interviews with converts in Philadelphia, New York and Chicago reveal that the most attractive features of the Church are: the celibacy of the clergy, the discipline in the Catholic schools, the absence of money scandals, and the reticence and restraint of Catholic ritual. A survey of converts in a dozen parishes in the Germantown and West Philadelphia areas show them to be families of teachers, other professions and white-collar workers. Undoubtedly, the universality of the Church confers on it a prestige or "respectability" that makes it acceptable to middle or upper classes, but also, on the other hand, socially distant from the lower ranks. This feature undoubtedly became salient as the Church emerged into national prominence with the entry of John F. Kennedy in 1959.

Such considerations do not suggest, on the other hand, that skepticism, criticism or even hostility toward the Church is lacking.

In September of 1960, a Chicago Negro priest, Father Rollins Lambert, addressing a Clergy Conference on "The Negro and the Catholic Church," made a class analysis of Negroes and attitudes toward the Church. He stated that the lower-class

1. This is also the view of Franklin Frazier, for example, in his *The Negro Family in the United States* and *Black Bourgeoise.*

Negro regarded the Church as the Church of Charity, the middle-class Negro was satisfied with the local parish, and the upper-class Negro was critical and skeptical of the Church. Today, it seems, Negroes regardless of class are developing a "show me" attitude toward Catholicism. There is no one reason for this tendency. It is tied in with a general and total intolerance of any kind of racial discrimination and segregation. "The time has come," said a Negro professor from Los Angeles, "for the Church to 'deliver' on its teaching about racial justice. Negroes are sitting back and waiting, and watching." Many things are going on in dioceses throughout the country, and they are being observed and evaluated. The fruit of these activities—and the judgment Negroes make about them—may not be known for a decade.

In September, 1928, W. E. B. DuBois wrote these lines about the presidential election campaign between Al Smith, the first Catholic candidate for the presidency, and Herbert Hoover: "Even the nomination of Alfred E. Smith does not relieve our situation . . . Smith is an excellent administrator and his attitude on liquor is at least honest, [but] he has consistently vetoed every bill and movement which Negroes advocated." The reference was to anti-discrimination legislation passed up to Smith as Governor of New York. DuBois continued: "The Catholic Church, to which Smith belongs, knows no color line in all the world, except in the United States; but here it is 'Jim Crow' from top to bottom, in church attendance, in education, in philanthropy, in missionary endeavor . . . first vote for him and then commit suicide."[1]

From Boston to Baltimore and from the Atlantic to the Ohio, DuBois' view of the Church summed up, not only a *de facto* situation in the Northeast, but the mood and attitude of Negroes —at least those who were aware of the Church.

A clue to the mentality of the "liberal" clergy (and by inference to the more conservative elements) is to be had in the remarks of a white priest (a chaplain to an eastern branch of the Federation of Colored Catholics) to the annual convention

1. *The Crisis,* 1929, official journal of the NAACP.

in 1929. Speaking to a motion on the floor calling for the training of more Negro priests, he said: "Under present social conditions, Negro priests could not mingle with whites socially in the South, they would have to undergo unpleasant experiences, Negro congregations would be unwilling to obey them . . . the whole subject of Negro priests had better be dismissed for the present." The priest added, however, that he would favor separate seminaries for Negroes, as a sort of preparation for the day when a Negro clergy might be possible.

In the four decades that have since passed, the situation in the North has almost been completely reversed. Some parishes, in fact, are enrolling non-Catholic Negro children in their sparsely enrolled parochial schools as an enticement for their parents to come to Catholic "informational" classes. In March, 1965, Bishop Bernard Kelly, auxiliary of Providence, marched with the episcopal bishop of Rhode Island at the head of a civil rights march on the Statehouse. Priests and nuns from several dozen Northern dioceses not only participated in the famous Selma-Montgomery March but repeated this or a similar form of protest in their home dioceses. It is difficult to estimate how great the number of these incidents is, but there is no doubt that the number is large enough to be significant. The problem here is: What do these events signify? Has the Church closed its chapter on race prejudice? Has the Negro Catholic been completely assimilated into the parish structure, its schools and colleges? How effective is the prejudice that still lingers among white Catholics? Does it keep the Negro "in his place" in Church organizations? Does it establish *sub rosa* quota systems? How does a Catholic neighborhood react when a Negro family moves in? These questions, plus the larger one of how much progress has been made and how it has come about, constitute the remainder of this chapter. We shall now review the archdioceses of New York, Philadelphia and Chicago. Our focus then shifts to the more affluent sector of Northern Catholicism, suburbia, where the social problems are less complex and the resources relatively greater.

NEW YORK: THE PREËMINENT CITY

Of all American cities, New York is the most extraordinary. Its sheer size makes it the despair both of city planners and of social critics, the while it remains a powerful magnet for the nation's talent, resources and decisive wealth. Thus because of its population density and concentration of special opportunities, what is thought, printed and done about religious affairs and race relations in the nation's premier metropolis—that now spreads from mid-New Jersey up into Connecticut—has national resonance. In particular, the response of the Catholic Church to the racial changes that have occurred in this metropolis have far-reaching import in the struggle of American Catholics to overcome generations of estrangement between Negro and white citizens.

The Catholic Church in the New York area is populous, gifted, diverse and wealthy; moreover, it is becoming increasingly involved in the region's urban problems. Like so many other institutions and organizations, the Church is hard pressed to cope with the expansion and change in a metropolis that resembles nothing so much as a volcano, so powerful and swift are the social changes and eruptions within it.

Perhaps the outstanding characteristc of the Catholic Church in New York is its resources. It has drawn tremendous variety and vitality from the vast population, but, in its basic social outlook the archdiocese, like most great Eastern Catholic centers, has not been notable for ingenuity or inventiveness. The trials and growth-crises of the Catholic Church on the Northeastern seaboard have never permitted the fresh outlook and flexibility possible in other areas of the country. From New England to Washington, D.C., Catholic bishops have constantly been required to live within an established social order at once assured of itself, dynamic and rapid in its movements. They have also been required to provide for repeated waves of Catholic immigrants—to contend with repeated cycles of arrivals, adjustment and assimilation. It is not surprising, therefore, that circumspection has characterized the policies and views of New York Catholics and their leaders.

Yet if these repeated influxes of new members have created great problems, they have also been the source of great strength and richness. The archdiocese today, functioning under a cardinal, a coadjutor and 10 auxiliary bishops, has over 2,400 priests serving more than 1,650,000 Catholics. It has 23 seminaries and scholasticates, 400 parishes, 15 colleges and universities, and 438 high schools. There are 20 Catholic hospitals and 21 orphanages and "homes." There are a great number of chapels, libraries and centers for apostolic and charitable activity. The size of many of these institutions is remarkable. Most of the leading Catholic magazines and publishing firms are located in New York or have New York offices and ties.

New York's cosmopolitan character endows this huge network with spirit and creativeness, however reserved may be the outlook of the archdiocese's leaders. If one takes into account the adjacent dioceses of Brooklyn (Brooklyn and Queens), Rockville Centre (Nassau and Suffolk counties on Long Island) and Newark, then the area's Catholic resources are nothing less than awesome.

The first Negroes to arrive in New York came to the Bowery in 1620. During the colonial period and the early 18th century a small grouping of non-whites concentrated on Manhattan's West Side in what came to be known as "Little Bohemia." One of the ornaments of early Catholic life in New York was Pierre Toussaint (d. 1852), an immigrant slave who performed charitable works in Old St. Peter's parish for over 50 years. The cosmopolitan French connections of colonial Catholicism in the city permitted a degree of tolerance that would not remain possible as time went on.

The massive immigration of the Irish during and after the great famine deeply affected race relations. The Irish, beset with every kind of social disability short of slavery, were a constant irritant in intergroup relations. Rubbed raw by discrimination, and themselves considered almost as a separate race by native-born Americans, they were ill-disposed toward other ethnic groups with which they shared the frightful conditions of slum life and industrial disorder.

During the long and bitter national controversy over slavery, the Church itself took no clear position, but the powerful Irish Catholic press in New York generally was antagonistic toward abolition or emancipation, and toward the idea of equal rights for Negroes. The strain of job competition with Negroes was constant, and in the world of the immigrant a job was the difference between life and death. There was a steady rash of racial conflicts in the slum areas, and on occasion a major conflagration occurred. One such tragedy took place in 1863, when a series of riots, beginning as a protest against the inequalities of the draft laws, turned into a city-wide reign of terror that pitted white mobs—largely Irish—against Negroes. Dozens of Negroes were killed or injured and a Negro orphanage was burned. The Irish, the dominant ethnic group in New York's immigrant Catholic Church in the 19th century, can only be described as virulently anti-Negro, even if this disposition did not always take such violent form. This condition lasted with only very small modifications up to 1920. It definitely retarded the missionary work of the Church among colored people; Father John Gillard, S.S.J., the pioneer historian-sociologist of the Church-Negro relationship, conjectured that a great many Negro Catholics coming to New York were lost to the Church as a result.

After World War I, however, the Catholics in New York began to achieve status and release from the social disabilities that had long been their lot. The physical stature of the Church grew as it built more and more schools and institutions; churchmen could now turn their attention toward missionary problems outside the immigrant groups. Several mission centers were established specifically for charitable and spiritual work with Negroes. Most of the youngsters at St. Benedict's Home, an industrial school at suburban Rye, were Negroes. Then in 1912 the Sisters of the Blessed Sacrament came to New York. They opened a school and convent in St. Mark's parish in Harlem, thus providing practically the first opportunity for a Negro Catholic child in New York to enter a Catholic school.

Between 1917 and 1929 the Negro population of Harlem grew from 150,000 to 400,000, the greatest Negro concentration in the nation. The reaction of the white families to the encroachment of the expanding Negro population was one of racial panic and disgruntled withdrawal. No religious scruples deterred white Catholics, most of them Irish, from separating themselves from the incoming Negro. But if their congregations fled, the Catholic parishes—and the clergy—remained.

As we have already noted, canonically the Catholic parish is an institution of locale. It is the Church in "this" place, with boundary lines juridically drawn. In contrast, most of the Protestant churches are congregational. If the congregation moves, the church follows. Or it closes its doors. The flight, therefore, of the Protestant churches and the continuation of the Catholic had its impact on the attitude of incoming Negroes.

In 1928 there were 13,800 Negro Catholics in New York. Up until 1929 only the Harlem parishes of St. Mark's and St. Charles Borromeo parishes would accept Negro children in their parish schools. In 1929 St. Thomas the Apostle parish opened its school to Negroes. This was symptomatic of a new era in the relations of the Catholic Church to Negroes in the city. During the 1930's the first moves of a conscious and substantial apostolate toward Negroes were made.

In 1931 Cardinal Patrick Hayes appointed Monsignor Thomas O'Keefe to St. Charles Borromeo parish. Monsignor O'Keefe had had some contact with Negroes at St. Benedict's parish on West 53rd Street; at St. Charles his priestly duties were carried out among an almost totally Negro population. This was the first time the archbishop showed any inclination to adopt the apostolate to Negroes as its own, and to supplement with the efforts of diocesan priests the work of such missionaries as the Holy Ghost Fathers, who were in charge of Harlem's St. Mark's on West 132nd Street.

In 1933 Father William McCann succeeded Monsignor

O'Keefe at St. Charles. In 12 years, in a remarkable display of missionary zeal, this pastor baptized some 6,000 converts. Father McCann's devotion to his Negro parishioners, his willingness to battle for their relief and aid during the terrible unemployment and despair of the Depression, became a legend in Harlem. Other parishes, like St. Aloysius, St. Thomas the Apostle and Resurrection, caught some of his spirit. Eventually, St. Joseph's, Our Lady of Lourdes and All Saints came within the orbit of Negro residence, as did St. Paul's in East Harlem and St. Anthony's and St. Augustine's in the Bronx. By 1940 there were 19,000 Negro Catholics reported to the episcopal board in charge of Negro mission work, and Gillard records 15 priests in missionary work to the city's Negroes in 1941.

In 1939, upon accession of Francis Spellman to the archbishopric of New York, the commitment to the old official policy of ethnic parishes for Negroes was abandoned. Archbishop Spellman's first episcopal act was to arrange to go personally to St. Charles and St. Aloysius to confirm Negro children. He decided to contribute to the building of a new school in St. Aloysius, and at its dedication, he pointedly remarked: "This is a Catholic school—not a Negro school—which any Catholic child who is qualified is entitled to enter." Negro nuns, Handmaids of the Pure Heart of Mary, were placed in charge.

Within a few years, Catholic Negro youngsters began to apply for and be accepted in Cathedral High School for Girls and later in Cardinal Hayes High School. The enrollments were at the rate of two or three at first, either by design or because of the paucity of aspirants. In 1938 Manhattanville College of the Sacred Heart now located in Purchase became the first of the area's Catholic colleges to enroll a Negro girl; indeed, it was one of the first in the nation to do so. Still, it was not until the 1950's that the archdiocese's major seminary—St. Joseph's at Dunwoodie—along with the Sacred Heart Sisters, the Sisters of St. Ursula and the Dominican Sisters at Sparkhill, enrolled their first Negroes.

The 1930's was a period of keen interest in Catholic social-action teaching on the part of an elite group of Catholics. The Depression, Communist activity, the teachings of Monsignor

John Ryan and Father Charles Coughlin, and Pope Pius XI's social encyclical *Quadragesimo Anno* in 1931—these things helped bring about a rebirth in the Catholic social-action movement dormant since 1919. Among this elite, strong Catholic voices began to speak out for interracial justice. In 1933 a group meeting at Manhattanville College drew up the "Manhattanville Resolutions" on interracial justice, and the following year a meeting at Town Hall resulted in the formation of the nation's first Catholic Interracial Council, under the leadership of Father John LaFarge, S.J. The Catholic Worker movement of Peter Maurin and Dorothy Day also spoke strongly in behalf of better race relations. In Harlem the Baroness Catherine de Hueck, with the financial aid of the Catholic Interracial Council, organized Friendship House, which was to establish centers in several U.S. cities in the years that followed; it became a highly controversial effort, for the Baroness was nothing if not forceful in her criticism of Catholic clergy and laity in Harlem. She criticized pastors for their stereotyped approaches to the Negro, and scathingly assailed laymen for their weakness and prejudice. Her stay in Harlem left a legacy among some clergy of strong feelings against any lay-oriented activity that might interfere with pastoral and parochial authority.

Still, it might be said that by the end of the 1930's the archdiocese had a fairly clear policy of non-discrimination, and had accumulated considerable pastoral experience in the Negro apostolate. This does not, of course, imply that segregation and discrimination had been exorcised throughout the whole archdiocese. From this larger viewpoint not much had changed; but from the view of the *avant-garde,* both Negro and Catholic, an *entente cordiale* had been reached. After decades of "one of the harshest intergroup hatreds in American history,"[1] the Church in New York had made a start in addressing itself to a Negro community largely Protestant or with no church affiliation.

Through the 1930's and 1940's the rapport between Catholic spokesmen and Negro leadership grew steadily stronger, largely

1. The reference, strictly speaking, is to the Irish. See Gilbert Osofsky, *Harlem, the Making of a Ghetto,* New York, 1966.

because of the new respect and communication established by the Catholic Interracial Council and other strong supporters of the true Catholic doctrine on interracial justice. Negroes were not unaware of the fact that the first interracial camp in the New York area was one operated by the Catholic Youth Organization. In 1946 Catholic voices strongly urged the adoption of an FEPC law on the state level. Despite the fact that the proportion of Negro Catholics was only a tiny percentage of the total colored population, Negro leaders were increasingly respectful of and attentive to the evident good intentions which the powerful Catholic establishment displayed toward them. As the formula of Protestant-Catholic-Jew became the accepted civic coordinate of religious activity, Catholics were constantly sought out for inclusion in campaigns, forums and activities aimed at interracial justice. Among Negroes themselves there was an active component of Catholics skilled and educated though small in numbers. West Indians, some of them, they were conscious of their responsibility to broaden Catholic interest in interracial matters.

All of these factors represented a good start, but the fact remained that however praiseworthy its official outlook was, the Catholic Church in New York was very far from having a broadly based approach to the Negro population. During and after World War II there occurred transformations of social life and race relations that were to outstrip the modest movement that had begun to work within the Catholic community.

By 1960 the 22-county area of Greater New York had grown to just over 16 million people, 7.8 million of them in the five boroughs of New York City. In 1930 only 5 per cent of the region's population was non-white or Puerto Rican; today it is over 15 per cent. In 1950 the non-white population of Manhattan was 390,000. While the Manhattan non-whites have leveled off at about 400,000, there is a total of 1,700,000 non-whites in the 22-county region. As noted earlier it is estimated that by 1975 the total will be 2,400,000.

Within the city the great increase of non-whites has taken place in four areas primarily: Harlem in Manhattan, Bedford-

Stuyvesant in Brooklyn, South Jamaica-St. Albans in Queens, and Morrisania in the Bronx. Non-whites in the Bedford-Stuyvesant area have tripled since 1940. The South Jamaica area in Queens has grown at a like rate; double the size of Harlem, it is the newest Negro ghetto and the one with the greatest growth potential.

The great population explosion among New York's Negroes should have brought home to Catholics in New York a realization of the onrush of a huge racial problem. However, vision starts with a mentality oriented toward seeing the old in a new light. Lacking this, the formulation of a consistent and coherent view of social issues did not come easy.

So far as the Church is concerned, what has occurred has been the movement of Negroes in significant numbers from Harlem—a localized base touching some dozen parishes—to a broad distribution affecting more than 60 parishes. In Manhattan there are six parishes that are more than 90 per cent non-white (St. Aloysius, St. Charles Borromeo, St. Joseph, St. Mark, St. Thomas the Apostle and Resurrection). There are five more in areas where non-whites make up 50 to 90 per cent of the population (All Saints, St. Catherine, Transfiguration, Our Lady of Lourdes and St. Paul). Nine others are in areas 20 to 50 per cent non-white (Annunciation, Ascension, St. Cecilia, St. Francis de Sales, Holy Rosary, St. James, St. Lucy, St. Rose of Lima and St. Teresa). Through the 1950's, the movement of Negroes and Puerto Ricans of color on the West Side of Manhattan distributed a one-in-ten ratio of Negroes through Notre Dame, Holy Name, St. Gregory and Holy Trinity parishes.

The Bronx has Negroes in St. Philip and St. James, St. Augustine and St. Anthony in heavy numbers and to a lesser extent in St. Francis of Assisi, Our Lady of Mercy, Sacred Heart and St. Pius parishes. Staten Island has a few Negroes, but the new Verrazano-Narrows Bridge from Brooklyn will soon change this. Beyond the city proper, in the Westchester County area of the New York archdiocese, towns such as New Rochelle, Mount Vernon and Newburgh received heavy Negro influxes.

The response to racial change on the part of these parishes—

and the schools, recreational facilities and social organizations that are part of them—has on the whole been *ad hoc*. A long-established tradition of reserve toward civic affairs has led the parishes to take a "wait and see" attitude. Except in a few cases, they have not devised special measures to allay the flight of whites or to meet the special needs of incoming non-whites. Only in Harlem, where experience taught the clergy the difficulty of working with an unfamiliar population, has there been a somewhat cogent and sustained effort to meet the problems peculiar to the life of Negro families. The approach has been one of pastoral initiative in small ways—an inter-parochial group of curates meeting on a voluntary basis with experts in intergroup relations, for example—rather than one of careful redefinition of parish policy and techniques. Here it must be pointed out that the recognition by individual priests of the problem's real dimensions—and their impulse to do something about it—is severely hampered by an archdiocesan tradition which discourages individual initiative and action.

In Brooklyn the Catholic welfare facilities have tried to devise special services for Negro clients, but here too the parishes —whether because of episcopal indecision or preoccupation, or the natural difficulty of changing the outlook and programs of a huge parochial network—have met racial change with a rather random posture.

Father Joseph Scheuer of Fordham University made a study of parishes in the Bronx not too long ago, and concluded: "Under conditions of swift social change, or situations where a parish is anything but homogeneous in its social character, this can lead to multiple frustrations and loss of prestige leadership. Typical cases are not hard to find." [1] Father Scheuer, a sociologist, noted that the parishes affected by racial change were faced with unprecedented conditions of community life, but that they had little or no constructive awareness of the problems involved and were making few if any inventive attempts to capitalize upon change.

There are, however, signs that diocesan officials are becoming

1. See "Changing Parishes," in *Catholic Interracial Review*, October, 1964.

increasingly concerned about finding new formulas for dealing with racial change and the social responsibilities of their parishes. They meet to discuss the situation with civic leaders and seek the advice of experts in the field.

Since the 1940's, there had been a quiet but nonetheless clear policy of refusing to tolerate discrimination and racial distinctions in Catholic facilities. Individual pastors or heads of institutions may have erred by their personal attitudes or recalcitrance, and the official policy did not impress itself upon the mass of the laity. But it was clear. The non-discriminatory admission policy of the schools, for example, was obvious to all by the early 1950's. Catholic Charities have for many years been administered without regard to race. Catholic residences, like the Leo House on 23rd Street, were open to Negroes as well as whites.

Hospitals represented a difficult problem. Large ones like St. Vincent's in Manhattan had Negroes as nurses, radiologists and service employees during the war years. Patients had long been admitted without regard to race, though private and semi-private rooms rarely had Negro patients until the 1950's. Medical staff positions for physicians did not reflect the general racial change in the city until the 1950's. Even then, the competition for staff positions and the intricate methods involved in medical staff placement caused difficulty. Nevertheless, though there were few Negro physicians, and fewer Catholic Negro physicians, Catholic hospitals did place Negroes on their staffs. As late as 1962 there were charges in the Negro press alleging placement difficulty because of race at Cabrini Hospital in Harlem. Upon inquiry, the Catholic Interracial Council found the charges groundless, but noted that this hospital was not very sensitive to race-relations concerns. Negro doctors themselves said that Cabrini, long close to the East Harlem community, was not attractive to them because of its limited facilities. With the closing of this case, Catholic institutions of the archdiocese entered a new era totally free of the taint of racial discrimination.

For many years there have been various spokesmen in the Catholic community who have maintained a ready relationship and communication with the articulate portions of the Negro community. Two groups of Catholics have shared in this process, rather independently of one another. The first is that cadre of priests and lay persons attached to the interracial movement or to heavily Negro parishes. Men like the late Monsignor Cornelius Drew, who was for some years pastor of St. Charles Borromeo Church in Harlem, Monsignor Gregory Mooney of the Kennedy Center in Harlem, and Father Kevin Kelly, a curate of St. Charles, have had steady contact with the NAACP, the Urban League, the Negro press and many prominent figures in the Negro population. Another is Father Henry Browne, a seminary professor who has been deeply involved in the development of the Stryker Bay Community and its conflicts with the religious and political establishments. Such Catholic lay and clerical leaders sought out Negro leaders to listen to them, speak to them and discuss the issues of interracial justice. On their part, conscious of the great scope and significance of the Church in New York, formal Negro leadership groups like the NAACP and the Urban League lent attentive ears to the views of these Catholics. In some cases, there was a divergence of viewpoint as to which issues should receive priority, but on the whole the Catholic pastors from Negro parishes and Catholics in interracial work saw the larger problems such as fair employment, housing needs and "poverty projects" in the same terms as their Negro counterparts. The major differences of viewpoint between Catholic clergy from the segregated areas and the Negro civil rights leaders derived from their different social positions. The clergy were very deeply enmeshed, as they served their parishioners, in the cruel social problems of ghetto life. Priests like Fathers Browne and Kelly frequently found themselves, involuntarily and unwittingly, playing the role of prophet, struggling to gain some effective voice in a "poverty project" for the unknowns—the politically impotent tenants of slums or changing neighborhoods. The opposition might be a Negro politician, a coordinator from City Hall or Washington, or even a civil rights organization. Thus, as a result particularly of the Federal poverty program, such priests are now in the forefront of the political revolution which seeks the dissemination of power among the poor.

A second group of Catholics with wide contacts among Negroes was that composed of Catholics in politics. The Irish Catholic political hegemony was a fixture in New York life for over 70 years. In the last two decades Italian Catholics have challenged that hegemony. The typical politician's "feel" for popular opinion and group affiliations, though intermittently compromised by bureaucratic blindness and conflicting loyalties, still is capable of recognizing important social themes. The urban political practice of deferring to the interests of any powerful ethnic group by according its members' status and patronage begins long before such a group actually achieves dominance. Thus the white Catholic politician espousing the general rhetoric of civic brotherhood also was attuned to many of the clashing loyalties and ambitions within the Negro population.

In New York this recognition began even before the reign of Mayor Fiorello LaGuardia, but it developed into a true utilitarian relationship during the 1950's when Hulan Jack, a Catholic, became the city's first Negro Borough President. Other Negroes have succeeded him in high political posts. However cynical or partisan the process might seem, the fact remains that politics and city business provided a wide sphere for contact between Catholic and Negro. The politicians, in turn, relayed their knowledge of and feel for race relations to key figures in the Church. This was an irregular and informal function, but a very real and largely constructive one.

These two kinds of social contact across racial lines were most intensive in Manhattan, then occurred later in Brooklyn and Queens as the Bedford-Stuyvesant area and the South Jamaica district became heavily Negro. There is less evidence of this same kind of contact in the Bronx, perhaps because of the absence of any clerical figure who characterized it on the religious level, and because of the continued strength and antique solidarity of the Democratic party machine under bosses Ed Flynn and later Charles Buckley.

One of the peculiarities of the Catholic relation to Negro leadership is the fact that it rests upon such a relatively small fraction of the Negro population. There are today only a little more than 90,000 Negro Catholics in the New York area.[1] Negro leaders have been drawn from the Protestant ministry, from the professions and from civil service. In Harlem one priest told us that Catholics had continually to assert their presence and insert themselves into the leadership echelons. The Catholic clergy are almost always white, and therefore cannot properly be called "Negro leaders." This condition has caused one priest to observe that the Negro Catholic is not too concerned about integrating himself into the heavily Protestant leadership-network of the Negro community itself.

Traditionally, the Church's strongest ties of cooperation in the civil rights field have been those with the NAACP and the Urban League. For many years George Hunton, the retired Executive Secretary of the New York Catholic Interracial Council, was an NAACP board member. Guichard Parris, a former president of the Interracial Council, was on the staff of the Urban League. As public concern about race relations grew during the post-war years, new city and state agencies were created, and the Catholic Interracial Council supported their formation and requests for budget and portfolio. Catholics like the late Julian Reiss, Judge Edward Conway and Monsignor Drew served on the State Commission Against Discrimination, later the Commission for Human Rights. Theophilus Lewis, a Negro writer and longtime CIC member, Mary Riley and Archibald Glover—all of them Catholics—served with the city Commission on Intergroup Relations, now the Commission on Human Rights. This association and support, however, represented only a fractional representation of the Catholic community. White Catholics in general continued to be suspicious or actually hostile toward the NAACP

1. The 1963 report of the Board of Negro and Indian Missions lists Negro Catholic populations in New York, Brooklyn and Newark totalling almost 90,000 (59,367 for New York, 22,500 for Brooklyn and 8,000 for Newark). This is almost certainly an underestimate according to experienced judges.

and what they believed it stands for, and they are unacquainted with the Urban League. Their notions of the methods and aims of these organizations are wildly distorted. In March of 1963, after reading an article on the Catholic Interracial Council in *The Catholic News,* the archdiocesan newspaper, one woman wrote to the editor: ". . . I shall not join the NAACP as suggested. I live on the border of Harlem and those Negroes boldly wear their NAACP buttons and push white people and try to instigate trouble." Yet the NAACP, of which Boston's Cardinal Richard Cushing became a life member in 1961, has been roundly criticized by many Negroes for what they consider its overly moderate policies.

There are two other types of agencies in the civil rights field in New York, one group of them religiously affiliated, the others militant organizations without formal sectarian connections. With the former—the race relations office of the Council of Churches, the American Jewish Committee, the American Jewish Congress, the Anti-Defamation League of B'nai B'rith—the Catholic Interracial Council and some of the editors of New York-based Catholic magazines have maintained steady and cordial liaison. Church officials and Catholics generally, however, have kept their distance from these organizations. Until the Vatican Council gave rise to an interreligious dialogue and spurred Catholic interest in the ecumenical movement, there was little disposition among Catholics even to recognize that these groups existed.

Catholic relationships with the non-sectarian civil rights groups—like the Committee for Civil Rights in Manhattan, the National Committee Against Discrimination in Housing, and CORE—have been more distant, despite the fact that the inspiration and techniques advocated by CORE have, until recently, been of a more religious nature than those of, say, the NAACP.[1] But, undoubtedly because of over-accommodation to

1. A vice-president of CORE, Rudy Lombard, is a Catholic whose philosophy of non-violent resistance he learned from a Josephite priest in New Orleans. James Farmer, the former president, formed his al-

the American middle class values and attitudes, the New York Catholic, priest and layman both, shies away from such techniques. So too do most other Christians. Hence as the struggle for political power among the poor mounts in intensity, Christians of all denominations, or at least those closest to that struggle, will have to reexamine their position. So too will the chancery.

Education

The contribution of Catholic schools to the educational advancement of Negroes in New York was delayed for some years, but in the last two decades it has steadily become more important. The number of scholarships and grants to Negro students has been quite limited at the high school and college level, but then, it has always been inadequate for the Catholic community as a whole. It is primarily at the elementary and high school level that Catholic schools are serving Negro families. This service is in larger proportions than the numbers or financial capacity of the Negro Catholic population would warrant. In heavily Negro neighborhoods there are usually many children of non-Catholic parents in Catholic schools—as high as 25 per cent of the student body in some cases. In New York, as elsewhere, non-Catholic Negro parents are often impressed by the Catholic school's discipline and by its allegedly higher standards of sexual morality.

The academic training which Negro children get in Catholic schools is generally on a par with that given in public schools. It is true that the latter have the edge in plant, language and science laboratories, and perhaps in the advantage that comes from offering higher salaries to teachers, but this is at least partially offset by the selective pupil enrollment of the parochial school. To illustrate: the impoverished Negro is not, typically, a Catholic. Neither is the crippled-marriage family. The church

---

legiance to non-violence at the Fellowship of Reconciliation, a school of Christian leadership in Nyack, N.Y.

of these people, in any racial category for that matter, is commonly the evangelical, pentecostal sect, housed in a store-front or renovated theatre. The children of these families are rarely found in parochial schools. Problem-laden through no fault of their own, such pupils create a more difficult educational atmosphere in the public schools. They also force on them a range of non-academic problems which they are not equipped to handle. The atmosphere in the Catholic school, preserved by social screening processes, is comparatively clearer and more conducive to learning. Furthermore, parochial school parents seem to have a vague awareness that the continuation of their children in these schools is conditioned on not only good behavior but also good academic performance. They therefore tend to pressure their offspring to live up to the norms. Abundant evidence for this view of the two school systems is to be had from interviews with the parents, Catholic and non-Catholic, whose children are transfers from public to parochial schools.

Another consideration is the fact that the Catholic school system has not been beset by the same furor about sub-standard facilities, bussing or *de facto* segregation as the public school. There has been some experimentation with bussing but this has been in response to under-enrollment in one school as contrasted with overcrowding in another. Some 150 Negro and Puerto Rican pupils travel from St. Athanasius parish in the Bronx to St. Catherine's School in an upper-middle-class area near Manhattan's Cornell Medical School, where there has been a marked exodus of the white Catholic population. Thus, the escape from involvement in the controversial "neighborhood school vs. bussing" issue has added comparative stability to the parochial schools.

The commitment of the religious orders staffing these schools likewise tends to offset the advantages of the public schools. These orders, and their individual members, are in Harlem by choice. They have in their own background and training a unique awareness of the race problem and a commitment to constructive solutions. In most of their schools, for example, the American history and social studies curricula have been revised so as to portray more honestly and realistically the contributions of the Negro himself to the abolition movement, the Union forces in the Civil War, the reconstruction of the South and to the various liberating movements of the 20th century. Study units on African culture and civilizations are also used. The hoped-for result is renewed pride of race and self.

It might be noted in passing that the term "dedicated" so liberally applied to all religious and lay people staffing the Catholic schools takes on a more genuine meaning when applied to the Sisters of the Blessed Sacrament who conduct five of Harlem's eight parochial schools. Nor does this congregation consider its "dedication" as a substitute for professional competence.

Yet no matter how one tries to balance the advantages and disadvantages of public and Catholic education in the archdiocese, he does not come away impressed with the efforts of the latter to make any extraordinary contribution to either the desegregation problem nor its psychological corollaries. Here as elsewhere, the initiative and leadership come from outside. The best that can be said about Catholic institutions is that they follow only where the civil rights movement has consolidated its advances. Catholic schools, in other words, will adopt bussing (or whatever other means of achieving integration eventually succeeds) when the public at large accepts it.

This facility for accommodation is further illustrated by the widespread cooperation of parishes and other Catholic institutions with government-sponsored poverty projects. The last few summers, for example, saw practically all Harlem parishes with a project of some kind in operation. Adult literacy programs are also in evidence and run on a year round basis. Teenagers have been incorporated into jobs in parish or school. While all this may signify accommodation from the sociological point of view, the end results are nonetheless all to the good: both for the individuals who benefit and for the larger society whose social problems are thereby ameliorated. Had the Federal government, however, not formulated the principles and financed the numerous projects, the number of parishes engaged would be substantially less.[1]

Employment

Catholic support for FEPC, job opportunities for minorities and more recently the Economic Opportunity Act have been strategic rather than broad and cumulative. Although priests and Catholic labor figures have spoken out for improved job opportunities, Catholic institutions and Catholic employers have not been notable for their initiation of racial change in job patterns. Indeed, there are a number of service industries in New York—the restaurant business is one—where Catholics predominate in certain chains, but where Negroes are notably absent from the work force. This has been true in white-collar fields like insurance and banking as well.

Much the same holds true for unions. Some craft unions with heavily Catholic membership have either refused to accept Negro apprentices at all or have admitted only token numbers. In the Steamfitters Union, for example, a traditional father-son apprenticeship pattern has resulted in a tight organization largely in Irish hands. In the Amalgamated Clothing Workers-Cutters Union, the hegemony is Jewish with a glaring absence of Christians and Negroes. In such ethnic unions (and there are many) the siege mentality is becoming more and more evident as efforts are made to break in and as automation consumes jobs. Whether the phenomenon be called ethnic prejudice, group solidarity, or in-group out-group rivalry, the net result is suspicion, hostility and insufficient job opportunities for Negroes.

Yet the problem has its own dynamics. The inexorable influence of education and the hard realities of political pressure and economics bring, little by little, employment and upgrading of Negroes. Insufficient as these are and costly in terms of effort or conflict, the gains are made without any noticeable contribution from the Catholic union man or employer.

1. There are several parishes operating "Head Start" and tutoring type projects on a volunteer basis, with no external financing.

Within Catholic institutions the employment pattern, while it does not usually exclude Negroes, has continued to be heavily white. There are still many white Catholics in the lower-paying job categories, and immigrant ties in parishes, hospitals and schools are still strong. The Irish immigrant housekeeper at the rectory, the Polish immigrant cook and the Italian gardener have long traditions of association with Catholic institutions; their need for employment often parallels that of the distressed Negro and still gets precedence.

Housing

Catholic spokesmen in New York have supported public housing as a means to decent dwellings for minority families. (A recently completed public housing development in Harlem was named for one of the best-loved of these spokesmen, the late Monsignor Drew.) The Catholic Interracial Council backed the first fair-housing laws in the nation in New York, and Cardinal Spellman himself spoke in favor of fair-housing legislation at a critical moment in 1957, when the pioneering Sharkey-Brown-Isaacs law against housing discrimination was being debated in the city.

Nevertheless, for the average white Catholic layman, the whole issue of residential racial change has been fraught with misunderstanding and irritation. Three factors have blunted the basically benevolent response which should be characteristic of Catholics on such a racial issue. The first has been the lingering attachment of ethnic parishes to their traditional residential pattern. Elderly parish stalwarts—and elderly priests—have accepted only very reluctantly the new ethnic and racial diversities. Second, the financial jeopardy implied by racial change causes difficulty for most parishes. When Catholic working-class families with a strong tradition of supporting their pastor are replaced by a largely Protestant or unchurched Negro population—and an economically poorer one, at that—the impact on parish revenue can be great. This worry has undoubtedly led many a pastor to look upon racial change in his neighborhood with something less than enthusiasm. Third, the social differences between the second and third-generation Catholics, with their pattern of stable family life, and the incoming Negro families, with their legacy of family problems caused by multiple privations, leads to resentment on the part of whites—and quite often to flight. In New York, with its particularly dense housing and property patterns, only a highly skillful and potent leadership campaign could be expected to overcome the accumulated misunderstanding and prejudice. The Catholic community has not been able to mount such a campaign, and while it has done no worse than other religious groups (and better than some), it has not succeeded in breaking down existing walls of segregation or preventing the erection of new ones.

Personal Status

Within the Negro population there has been, quite naturally, a constant aspiration for personal recognition and status. Catholic leaders have not been insensitive to this fact, and have on a number of occasions made efforts to accommodate it. In 1950, for example, Cardinal Spellman, in behalf of Pope Pius XII, conferred a high honor, the Pro Ecclesia et Pontifice Medal, upon three Negro laymen prominent in interracial work: Emanuel Romero, Elmo Anderson and Maceo Thomas. In the course of their official duties or in informal settings the Cardinal and his auxiliary bishops have frequently been photographed with Negroes. In many ways the attentiveness of Catholic officials to Negro causes and affairs has been evident. Cardinal Spellman has supported the United Negro College Fund, arranged a visit for the head of the NAACP with Pope John XXIII, and worked for the placement of Negro foundlings in stable homes. A special celebration in St. Patrick's Cathedral was arranged in 1962 to fete the elevation of the colored Peruvian *beatus* Martin de Porres to sainthood. Such demonstrations have played a significant part in giving the Catholic Church a "good press" in race relations.

Some Key Experiences of Catholic Interracial Contact

In evaluating any broad social confrontation like that between Negroes and the Catholic Church in New York, it is inevitable that certain events and experiences will be more timely, impressive or distinctive than others. Three of them will be evaluated here.

(1) THE HARLEM EXPERIENCE

When racial change began to occur on a large scale in Harlem, the Irish and German Catholic families there underwent the classic distress now so familiar to students of racial movement. Conflict, often violent, followed initial contact. The whites then moved from the area, and after some years of indecision the Church began gradually to develop a new life, adapted to the conditions of the Negro "ghetto." There were adjustments in finances, school administration, schedules of services, time spent on family problems and welfare matters. The pastors who directed this adjustment came to be regarded as the "experts" on racial matters. Their difficulties were unenviable, and most of their peers conceded to them a certain deference and admiration. Younger priests learned from these pastors, and a fund of hard-won knowledge about convert instruction, the orientation of the Negro Protestant churches, and the red tape of the municipal and state social welfare agencies was built up.

The pastors in the Harlem area did not always work together: often they were too hard-pressed to have time for liaison and exchange of information. But the knowledge and attachments they have accrued are bound to have an important influence upon the official endeavors of the Church to meet the social challenge of wholesale population movement. Although this experience has not been formalized in terms of an "operating procedure" or a definite body of religious sociology, it gives the local clergy a certain autonomy and status. The chancery, for example, treats gently all issues and problems affecting Harlem.

It is perhaps no exaggeration to say that representative government in the New York archdiocese came by way of Harlem.

(2) THE CATHOLIC INTERRACIAL COUNCIL

The New York Council was the first of its kind. Founded in 1934 under the leadership of the late Father LaFarge, that Council brought together white and Negro Catholics for a fourfold purpose: to spread the doctrine of the spiritual dignity of the human person, to apply this doctrine to race relations, to combat racial prejudice, and to strive for equal justice for all Americans. The magazine of the Council, *The Interracial Review,* and its news service gradually supplied more and more material about interracial justice to the growing Catholic press and also to the Negro newspapers. The Council joined with other religious and civic groups to bring about the abandonment of discrimination in New York eating places, in athletics, in defense industries. It was instrumental in stimulating Catholic colleges to drop racial bars and to take an active interest in interracial justice.

Following New York's example, and on the initiative of Father LaFarge and George Hunton, councils were formed in most of the major U.S. cities. In 1958 these councils federated in the National Catholic Conference for Interracial Justice. In 1960 the New York Council, in order to meet the metropolitan scope of racial problems, formed chapters in the outlying areas of the New York archdiocese.

The New York Interracial Council, until the national federation of its counterparts in 1958, was for years the center and chief expression of Catholic work in race relations. The long continuity of the careers of its two main personages, Father LaFarge and Mr. Hunton, endowed it with a high reputation. For almost 30 years it attracted the attention and interest of a wide variety of important people. In a city as large as New York, such a small office as the Council was able to maintain was never adequate for servicing the community in any thorough sense. The Council's major functions were strategic and symbolic, including a virtuoso use of the news media for the purposes of providing a Christian witness in interracial affairs. A speakers' bureau helped spread the gospel of interracial justice wherever its members could gain a hearing. The interreligious associations that the work of the Council entailed were a salutary exception to the habitual reserve of the great bulk of Catholics in such matters.

The Interracial Council in the late 1950's began to work directly with Catholic parishes. It had worked for years with the Catholic press, and to a lesser extent with colleges and high schools, but had not become directly involved in helping the community cope with racial change. In 1961–1962, the Council organized in various Bronx parishes workshops aimed at meeting neighborhood problems.

The work of instruction and guidance performed by the Council was far from proportionate to the needs of the Catholic community of its area. The best the program could do was to act as a stimulant within the framework of Catholic opinion and organizational life. An unstable budget prevented expansion or the mounting of large-scale programs for Catholic teachers, schools, parishes and institutions, though such educational work was definitely needed. For some years the bulk of the Council's financial needs had been met by private foundations and by well-to-do individual Catholics. By the 1960's the grants from foundations largely ceased (for reasons internal to the foundations themselves), and rising costs of maintaining an office placed the Council under considerable stress.

This situation was relieved somewhat when the chancery began, in 1963, to express increased concern over the Council and the race problem in general. Besides giving financial aid, the chancery also sought to enliven interest in the Council among pastors. The latter were encouraged to invite speakers to address parish societies and to run day-long or evening institutes on race relations. Assistance was likewise given by influential monsignori in membership drives. The archdiocesan weekly, *The Catholic News,* ran full accounts of Council forums and other activities and significant news stories from the civil rights front. A $15,000 contribution toward the 1965 budget from the chancery was, however, not followed by a donation toward the 1966 budget. Thus the erratic record of official diocesan support has led many Council members to believe that the chancery does not care whether their work continues or not.

In addition to its perpetually precarious financial position, the Council has been beset in the 1960's with several other internal problems. As the civil rights movement gained momentum and the headquarters for the newly created National Catholic Conference for Interracial Justice was established under the more sustaining aegis of Cardinal Meyer, both the goals and the leadership of the Council fell under closer scrutiny by its board of directors. For 28 years Mr. Hunton had worked small miracles in a cramped office in downtown New York, on an impossible budget. But age and failing eyesight were added to his handicaps at the precise moment acceleration was in order. Both Hunton and Father LaFarge stepped aside into consultative roles early in 1962, active leadership passing to Dennis Clark and Father Philip Hurley, S.J. But this did not solve the Council's basic financial problem. Both men were a generation younger; they were tuned to the mood and tempo of the civil rights movement with all its ramifications in the social and economic order. Clark particularly felt that he should not be burdened by fund-raising chores. This, said he, had to be undertaken by professionals which would relieve him to fulfill the more basic goal of mobilizing Catholic power in the struggle for interracial justice. After only a year's service, Clark resigned, in January, 1963, over the insistence of the board that fund raising was his basic responsibility. Two years later Father Hurley resigned, only to assume the chaplain's post with the more militant Bronx chapter.

With the succession of Arthur Wright, a sociologist, to Clark's position in late 1963, the CIC defined a new goal for itself. The new goal is action research[1] in and for select "natural" communities. Urban communities such as Inwood, Chelsea and Riv-

1. Action research is aimed solely at providing solutions to problems rather than knowledge.

erdale, where ethnic, religious and class conflict lie just below the surface, are researched to establish a bedrock of socio-economic data that will provide the clues for ameliorative programs. With the assistance of seminarians from the diocesan seminary at Dunwoodie, Inwood was surveyed. Programs are being drawn up in cooperation with its indigenous leadership groups to overcome anti-Semitism and other ethnic rivalries that threaten its peace. The hope is that success in Inwood or Chelsea will establish a reputation for a new competence and this will be followed by funds that will in turn allow the Council to expand its activities.

New York is the center for much Catholic intellectual and publishing activity. *America, Commonweal, The Catholic World, Jubilee* and many other Catholic periodicals have for years had offices in the area. Editorially, these publications have usually been in advance of general Catholic opinion, often taking controversial positions and acting as forums for the exposition of "liberal" Catholic social viewpoints. Their policies have been steadily in favor of desegregation and Catholic initiative in behalf of interracial justice.

The authors and editors associated with these publications have kept up a steady round of appearances and speaking engagements, nationwide as well as in the New York area. In their lectures and comments on current events they asserted strongly the principles of interracial justice and kept them associated with Catholicism. When television succeeded radio as a mass medium, these same Catholics were readily available for programs of debate and comment. This Catholic opinion leadership presented the true Catholic position on race relations, and helped offset the contradictions apparent in the social life of the metropolis, where Catholics often responded in very diverse fashion to racial change.

Despite the preoccupation of most Catholics with other things, these three key factors—the accumulation of pastoral experience in Harlem, the work of the Catholic Interracial Council, and the positive contribution of Catholic periodicals and their staffs

—have added to the social knowledge and capacity of the Church (in its larger sense) in race relations. Through them, the Church in New York, despite its conservative core, has managed to build a reservoir of concern and understanding about racial matters that could be readily drawn upon to develop a truly extensive campaign for overcoming the effects of racism in the metropolis.

By 1963 there were signs that the archdiocese itself was developing a more purposeful and innovating policy toward segregation. In 1960 a Cardinal's Committee on Housing and Urban Renewal was inaugurated, made up of priests and functioning under the direction of Auxiliary Bishop John Maguire. This Committee was a response to the problems of social welfare, racial change and property-transfer growing out of large-scale slum clearance and urban-renewal projects. Some of the priest-members of the committee were from Harlem parishes. One was attempting to develop a cooperative apartment project on a small scale in St. Aloysius parish. Another was busily organizing the Strykers Bay Neighborhood Council in the urban-renewal area around St. Gregory's parish on Manhattan's West Side. One monsignor became a member of the Advisory Committee to the New York State housing agency. These were all men of imagination and energy, keenly aware of the race problem as it affected housing and renewal work. The Cardinal's Committee, a very significant extension of interest and concern on the part of Church officials in the civic sphere, has organized information meetings for pastors and parish representatives on housing matters, publishes a newsletter and generally tries to keep informed about the entire process of urban renovation and reorganization.

In a period when racial restrictions and inequities in housing were conceded to be the foremost problem in urban race relations, such a committee would inevitably find itself deeply probing the effect of race upon residential—and hence, parish—life. Such an investigation could only have a good result. Catholic awareness of such issues had long been marginal, but the demonstration of highly placed official interest in them not only garnered more knowledge, but related the Church to a vital social subject. The entire urban-renewal process, coupled with the war on poverty, will have a continuing impact upon not only the racial composition, but the course of urban development itself. Catholic concern with these matters—if it grows apace—will make possible a contribution to the renewal of the world's largest metropolis.

Another sign of growing official concern over race relations was the calling of a clergy conference on race relations in 1962. This was not a special conference, but one of the regular quarterly sessions for his priests presided over by Cardinal Spellman. Every priest in the archdiocese was required to attend. The sessions were large, but valuable in demonstrating forthrightly the continued interest of the Cardinal and chancery officials in racial matters. Such policy reminders should not be underestimated; in a large archdiocese they can be a very important guide to pastoral opinion. A somewhat similar undertaking, but on a smaller and more intensive scale, was the sponsorship of a lecture series and seminar for priests at Dunwoodie Seminary. Attendance was voluntary, but the sessions drew about 50 priests from the New York area for a study of Negro life and problems. Top authorities in history, family life, civil rights and welfare were invited to address the group and answer questions afterward.

Like the city itself, the archdiocese of New York faces an uncertain future. It has shown remarkable flexibility with respect to the problems that rode in on the crest of Puerto Rican immigration, training clergy in the language customs and pathologies of the new immigrant. But it has yet to take root among the lowest classes. In the suburbs residential segregation persists. In Staten Island particularly, the John Birch Society flourishes with a membership over more than 50 per cent Catholic.

Priests and laymen both refer to "451 Madison," the chancery office, as they would to a political headquarters. It is the font of ecclesiastical favor but also an obstacle to progress. From it flow honors, promotions, funds, imprimaturs—and transfers for the "troublesome." Least of all is it a source of inspiration or spiritual leadership. No one wants it this way and no one designed it thus, but there it stands—a huge ecclesiastical bureaucracy rich with the goods of this world but poor in its ability to touch the attitudes of Westchester suburbanites or Staten Island Birchites.

Ultimately, of course, the hope of the archdiocese lies with the religious body of which it is only a part. The spiritual resources of the Catholic Church do not flow through its official channels. They seem at this time to be welling up through a restless lower clergy, young lay people and in marginal movements, some old, like the Catholic Worker and some new, like the Cursillo. As the civil rights movement engaged the Federal government in its cause, it seems likely that these movements in the Church at large will likewise enlist "451 Madison" in their spiritual tasks.

PHILADELPHIA: CITY OF BROTHERLY LOVE

The archdiocese of Philadelphia is one of the largest and most historic in the United States. Formed in 1808 and elevated to archdiocesan status in 1875, it has long been known for the energy of its prelates, the efficiency of its clergy and the solid responsibility of its lay people. Many of the qualities of the Catholic Church in Philadelphia arise out of the general social setting and distinctive characteristics of the community, which even in colonial times was a center of culture and stability; to these virtues, as the city grew, were added traditions of good citizenship and modest domesticity.

The social life of the city grew around its historical inheritance. As the nation's first capital, Philadelphia has through the decades been especially devoted to the ideals of freedom and democracy. Its patrician families formed a strong core of civic leadership, albeit one more intent upon patriotic observance and cultural pursuits than political action or daring innovation.

Even the city's neighborhoods originally grew around a cluster of colonial shrines and buildings, revolutionary battlegrounds and land holdings of families whose names were reminiscent of outstanding service to a young America. Gradually, the burgeoning industrialism of the 19th century spread the city into the hinterlands between the Delaware and Schuylkill rivers. Little outlying villages and settlements blended into the larger city by gradual annexation, but these retained a strong sense of local identity. The dominant housing for over a century was the red-brick row-house on a narrow street; trim, often drab and monotonous, but economical and productive of a tenacious sense of neighborhood kinship and solidarity. In such houses the bulk of the vast immigrant population that poured into the city in the 19th century sheltered, often in the shadow of the textile mills, foundries and commercial enterprises that were the backbone of the city's economy. The stable neighborhood life prospered as the immigrant ghettos dissolved, the shanty towns disappeared and successive waves of homebuilding added new residential areas in the 1920's and 1940's.

Although the municipal government was beset by repeated scandals, other phases of civic life retained much of the idealism and high purpose inherited from colonial times and the original benevolent rule of William Penn. Charities under religious and philanthropic auspices flourished. Stephen Girard is just one example of immensely rich men who established excellent institutions—for the white populace only—to meet social needs.[1] The Society of Friends continuously worked for civic betterment in the city, and the historical prestige and simple directness of the Quakers imparted a persistent tradition of service and concern for civic life.

The Catholic Church in Philadelphia was established under tolerant Quaker eyes long before the Revolution. Old St. Joseph's Church was founded by Jesuits in 1733, discreetly built in an alley off the public streets. Old St. Mary's was established in 1763, becoming the seat of the first bishop and the place of worship of those Catholic notables who took part

1. Interestingly enough, Girard's will also forbade the entry of Catholic priests upon his property, unless in other than clerical attire.

in the Revolutionary War and the first sessions of Congress. The ascendency of types of Protestantism more militant than Quakerism imposed difficulties upon the Catholics who were largely immigrants and laboring people in the early 19th century. Furious disputes between the legitimate Church authorities and dissident parish trustees in the 1830's marred the early Catholic expansion and marked the ecclesiastical outlook with a wariness of lay interference. In the 1840's severe anti-Catholic riots generated in part by ethnic hostility between English Protestant stock and destitute Irish immigrants resulted in another shock to the Philadelphia Catholic community. Two churches were burned and the homes of Catholics were set on fire and vandalized.

The last half of the 19th century brought an easing of the earlier tensions. New parishes were founded in rapid succession as Catholic immigration continued. Neighborhoods became strongly "Catholic" and parishes became the focus of their life. Many parishes operated camps and a variety of social services. Thus, the red-brick row-house neighborhoods became strongholds of Victorian Catholic family life, a pattern that continued largely unchanged until the new mobility of the motor car and the affluence of the years after the depression loosened the old neighborhood and parish bonds.

One of the keys to the stability and conservatism of Philadelphia is home ownership. For decades over two-thirds of the city's residents—a very high proportion in a major metropolitan center—have been homeowners. Another key to the settled atmosphere is the low density of the residential areas. High-rise apartment buildings are still the exception in Philadelphia. These factors have influenced the temper and quality of the city's Catholicism. In addition, Philadelphia has for decades had fewer immigrants who were foreign-born than cities like New York, Chicago, Pittsburgh or Detroit. The Church is much more of a native Catholic Church—and foreign influences are less noticeable—than in other areas.

In addition to the solid fabric of parish and neighborhood life, the archdiocese of Philadelphia is proud of its very extensive school system. Every parish, almost without exception, has a primary school. The first diocesan-wide secondary school, Roman Catholic High School, was built in Philadelphia. Now a strong chain of large diocesan high schools and various academies and schools serves the archdiocese. These schools provide a steady clientele for the various colleges and the one Catholic university in the area. The integrating influence of this educational system is great and enhances the sense of unity, respectability and achievement on the part of Philadelphia's Catholic community.

Because of the above factors, the Catholic community fits well and easily into the basically conservative atmosphere of Philadelphia, which has more similarities to Boston than to any other American city. The reaction of the ecclesiastics to the anti-Catholic fervors and to the trustee disputes of the last century endowed them with a rather cautious cast of mind. Two recent prelates in particular were widely noted as men of strong conservative views. Cardinal Dennis Dougherty, who presided over the archdiocese from 1918 to 1951, was a vigorous administrator whose firm and steady influence was impregnated into many diocesan institutions. Cardinal John O'Hara (1952 to 1960) was ill during much of his active period of rule in the archdiocese, but his guarded views on civic matters and his skepticism toward experiments were widely known. The attitudes engendered by these various conditions have stamped the Philadelphia archdiocese with a character notably similar to that which prevails in the city institutions of a non-religious nature. Settled but steadily growing, Philadelphia has had a settled but steadily growing Catholic life that has proceeded in peace for over a hundred years.

The demographic distribution of Philadelphia's non-white population has been one of gradual expansion of islands of Negro residence. There were Negroes in the city in colonial times, in the vicinity of Old St. Joseph's, and during the 19th century this Negro population extended itself along South Street and Bainbridge Street as these thoroughfares lost their colonial character and declined. The original Philadelphia

Negroes were free men and artisans, a few of them gained modest fortunes. After the Civil War freed slaves migrated to the city in growing numbers. Around 12th Street and Columbia Avenue in North Philadelphia a second Negro "island" grew, at first because of the importation of Negroes to work on the Reading Railroad which paralleled 10th Street. In the 19th century these two areas were colored sections that co-existed in a constellation of ethnic islands that composed the immigrant demographic pattern of the growing city. A few outlying pockets of Negroes developed in Eastwick, Roxborough, Germantown and Holmesburg in the late 19th century—small clusters of Negro families that performed traditional tasks and menial chores for the white population.

In 1890 race riots around Wilmington, North Carolina, sent hundreds of Negroes to Philadelphia as refugees, and in 1906 the major race riots in Atlanta brought several thousand more. During World War I still others came to work in the sprawling shipyard at Hog Island or at the Cramp shipyard on the Delaware. And in 1921–1922 Negroes were imported as strikebreakers during labor-management disputes at such companies as Philadelphia Electric.

Racial friction was part of the general ethnic friction during the 19th century. Independence Hall was burned down during the Civil War period when it was being used as a meeting place by the city's vigorous abolitionists. Most of the residential expansion of Negroes was tortuously slow and accompanied by occasional violence; homes to be occupied by Negroes would be burned or vandalized. But the last event that could be termed a lynching in the city occurred in the 1920's, when a Negro was killed and dragged behind an automobile in the Richmond area after he attacked a white woman.

The original pocket of Negroes in South Philadelphia moved west below the central business area and just north of a series of immigrant communities; the growth of the Italian population in the late 19th century and before World War I effectively shut off any possibility of expansion southward. This course brought Negroes from the original parishes of St. Joseph's and Old St.

Mary's through St. Theresa's to the fashionable area of Rittenhouse Square, where they shared the alley dwellings with the Irish of St. Patrick's. Later, Negroes reached St. Charles farther west.

The first archdiocesan foundation specifically for Negroes was set up in 1889, when St. Peter Claver's Church was started and placed in the care of the Holy Ghost missionary fathers. Here, in the midst of a squalid slum, the mission parish worked to bring Catholic teaching and charity to the Negro families around what had become the notorious South Street area.

In North Philadelphia the Negro area around 12th Street and Columbia Avenue expanded first northward, then westward. The northward movement began in the last century and is still in progress. It has placed Negroes in St. Malachy's, Our Lady of Mercy and St. Edward's parishes in strong numbers, so that they are now dominant there. The presence of Negroes in North Philadelphia led the archdiocese to establish, in 1910, the parish of Our Lady of the Blessed Sacrament, like St. Peter Claver's under the care of the Holy Ghost fathers.

The westward expansion of the Negroes in North Philadelphia first followed the route of Fairmount Avenue, then turned northeast along heavily traveled Ridge Avenue. From this axis, during the 1920's and 1930's, the Negro population moved back into adjacent residential areas, into the Jesuits' Gesu parish, into St. Elizabeth's, Most Precious Blood and Holy Souls, Annunciation, as well as into Cathedral parish and St. Francis Xavier. In recent years Negroes have moved slowly into St. Columba's and Corpus Christi. Today all of these parishes, with the possible exception of Cathedral parish, are predominantly Negro in the sense that most of the residents within the parish boundaries are Negroes. Movement eastward in the North Philadelphia area was hampered by the existence of strong ethnic immigrant pockets that tenaciously defended their areas against Negro penetration.

In West Philadelphia the areas around 42nd and Mantua Streets were Negro-occupied in the 1890's. From here the colored moved to other areas in an ever enlarging westward sweep. The archdiocese began a parish for Negroes (or "Colored," as it used to be designated on the diocesan map) at St. Ignatius in 1893 with diocesan priests in charge. The parishes penetrated from this locus were St. Agatha, Our Mother of Sorrows, Our Lady of Victory, St. Gregory, St. Rose and Our Lady of the Rosary. Since the 1930's the movement south of Market Street, which for years was a demarcation line, has included St. James, Transfiguration, St. Francis de Sales and Most Blessed Sacrament parishes.

These expansions of the Negro in South, North and West Philadelphia also affected a variety of ethnic foreign language parishes—German, Lithuanian, Polish, Italian—whose membership gradually eroded with the movement of immigrants to outlying areas as the second and third generation became assimilated. The influx of Negroes usually meant the end of the old immigrant communities, but the parishes persisted with small nationalist cores and ties to families who had previously lived in the neighborhood.

The small Negro pockets in outlying areas were in St. Raphael's, St. Dominic's, Holy Angels, Holy Family and St. Vincent's. (The Negroes in Holy Angels parish dated from the Civil War, when the Union army trained Negro regiments at a little hamlet called La Mott. After the war Negroes returned and settled there.) Only one of these pockets was the target of special Catholic evangelization. In 1910 the little pocket in the Pulaskitown area of Germantown was endowed with a Negro mission parish, St. Catherine of Siena, largely through the efforts of Mother Katharine Drexel. This parish is in the care of the Vincentian fathers, who have a seminary nearby.

For the last four decades, the pattern of Negro expansion has been attended by growing segregation. Negroes live with Negroes, except where there is a transition process underway and the movement is from original penetration of non-whites to total segregation or nearly so. Thus, all of the older parishes built by the Catholic immigrants have largely been occupied by Negroes, while those built since the First World War remain largely white. In some of the older outlying areas 19th-century parishes exist with tiny Negro enclaves in them, but in the central-city parishes the growing concentration of Negroes has resulted in almost total segregation after the continuous white exodus of the last 40 years.

The entry of Negroes into residential neighborhoods that were not traditionally designated and circumscribed for their occupancy has always been fraught with difficulty and resentment, despite the fact that in recent years the formal parish administration has officially accepted them. During the 19th century it was the custom to erect special parishes for any immigrant ethnic group that did not accommodate itself readily to native, English-speaking parish conditions, and until 1920 that same course was followed for Negro Catholics.

The Negro differed, though, in that he did not have a Catholic folk culture; neither did he have strong traditions of family life, a regular calendar of religious feasts or a well-formed Catholic consciousness. His attachment to Catholicism was recent, and therefore he was viewed primarily as a missionary and social-service problem. Even in the 19th-century world of relatively co-equal ethnic enclaves, therefore, the Negro was in a special category. The religious ministration to his sufferings and the preaching of the Gospel to him were viewed as being particularly difficult, and were often entrusted to those orders of priests or sisters whose special mission it was to work among colored peoples. This fact was to have the most important implication for the future: in the ecclesiastical mind it surrounded the Negro with an aura of remoteness and "difficulty" and tended to transfer his problems to specialized channels outside the orbit of regular, geographical parishes of the archdiocese.

For many years problems and services related to Negroes were handled almost exclusively through the four "colored" parishes that had been set up in various sections of the city. No matter where they lived, Negroes who were Catholics were expected to register in and attend one of these parishes, to which the work of conversion and instruction of would-be Negro converts was also allotted. Gradually, these parishes built up their own clientele and tradition. Negro school children were enrolled in their schools, to which pastors of geographical parishes transferred Negroes who applied for *their* schools. It was presumed and practically unquestioned that Negroes would affiliate and adhere to the four "colored" parishes.

In 1932, as the impact of assimilation upon national parishes became very evident, the archdiocese issued instructions that every Catholic child seeking a Catholic education was to be eligible for enrollment in his or her geographical parish. The significance of this regulation for Negroes was not immediately evident, but one by one cases of Negroes applying for geographical parishes arose. Some pastors accepted the children readily, others with misgivings; still others relied upon tradition and continued to refer them to the nearest "colored" parish. In 1938, for example, six years after the policy change, there was a case of a pastor refusing to enroll a Negro child in his school for tenuous reasons and referring the child to a distant "colored" parish. Upon being informed of this case the chancery office intervened and the child was placed in the appropriate geographical parish school. The practice of many decades was obviously not changed easily. Sometimes Negro children were accepted in the parish school, while at the same time the Negro family itself was encouraged to maintain its ties with the "colored" parish. There is very little documentary evidence about this confusing period, but Negro families attest to a wide variety of instructions received from parish priests about just where they were to affiliate and send their children to school. There is little evidence among such families, however, that they were ever definitely excluded from *some* form of parish jurisdiction.

The influx of Negroes during the period at the beginning of World War II and the movement of Negro Catholics to take jobs in rapidly emerging war industries throughout the city may have been responsible for the instruction from the chancery office late in 1945 which said that as of January 1, 1946, Negro families who chose to do so were to become parishioners of the parishes in which they resided. This clarified matters considerably, particularly for those Negro families whose employment gains of the 1940's were permitting them to obtain housing in areas heretofore all white. In the Germantown area, for example, the Negro enrollment in various parishes such as St. Vincent's, Immaculate Conception, Little Flower and St. Madeleine Sophie rose notably both as the result of conversions and because of transfers from the older downtown parishes and the old "colored" parishes.

Since 1946, it can be said, Negroes have not experienced difficulties of an administrative nature in enrolling in parishes where they resided. There have been instances of chagrin on the part of priests or parishioners, but to their credit these reactions have not deterred the persons in positions of responsibility from ensuring the admission of Negroes to parish services and functions. This has often required the most resolute stand on the part of priests. Often the entry of Negroes into the parish boundaries is viewed by the priests themselves with the utmost trepidation, unrelieved by any clear knowledge or appreciation of the causes or implications of racial change. Against traditional attitudes of suspicion and prejudice, against the ill-concealed resentment of white parishioners and against the uncertain and wavering posture of Negro families themselves, parish administrators have received Negroes into their churches. In cases where neighborhoods have been in a state of racial panic with whites moving out rapidly, the priests have maintained a clear line: whatever their personal irritations about the course and pace of the population turnover, the pastors accept the Negroes.

There have frequently been rumors, discussed in both Catholic and non-Catholic communities, that certain pastors encouraged or conspired in property-buying schemes to prevent Negro entry into their areas of the city. Since the financial affairs of parishes are largely unknown, there is no way definitely and conclusively to rebut these rumors by citing official records for the utilization of parish funds. To say the least, it would be an imprudent pastor who would use parish funds for such a purpose. It is a fact, however, that on numerous informal occasions some pastors and curates have made no secret of their distaste for racial change, expressing antipathy toward the entry of Negroes into their areas. Sometimes the opposition is stated in the crudest terms; on occasion, the personal prejudice or lack of knowledge on the part of the clergy has resulted in statements contrary both to their training and to their status as leaders of the Catholic community. In some instances police officers, civic leaders, intergroup-relations workers and interested non-Catholic clergymen have been shocked by these expressions. At times, priests have argued for the right of parishioners to exclude Negroes from an area. At least twice, priests have discoursed at length on the right of the parish to buy property if it sees fit to keep the property out of the hands of Negroes. (These latter conversations have never pertained to a specific instance of such actions, but were theoretical discussions.) If priests and laymen are willing to argue for the right of a parish, either directly or by covert encouragement and collusion, to engage in racial exclusion in the residential market, then it is little wonder that rumors circulate concerning parish responsibility for the fact that all-white neighborhoods have persisted for years adjacent to Negro-occupied areas. When priests and real-estate brokers, civic leaders and other parishioners have revealed their distaste for racial change and the entry of Negroes, the soil is fertile for the growth of the most damaging suspicions.

It must be added that there has been only one case to our knowledge in which a priest actively and overtly campaigned among parishioners for the exclusion of Negroes from the parish area, and that was in the 1920's. More often, lay leaders known to be confidants of the parish priest (frequently undertakers, real-estate brokers, contractors, judges or political figures) will frankly state their opposition to racial change and then add that the "pastor sees eye to eye with me." In the absence of any vigorous support for desegregation among local Catholics, such statements are all too readily believed and circulated.

The movement of Negroes throughout the areas of the city that are now accessible to them has placed them in a wide variety of parish situations. The four traditional "colored" parishes have continued to represent an orientation primarily missionary and benevolent. These parishes are located in rather depressed neighborhoods and the pastoral problems there are largely those of seeking to offset the severe social problems afflicting parish members: unemployment, family disorganization, lack of education, school drop outs, alcoholism, mental retardation and illness, cults of juvenile excitement and delinquency.

In addition to the four "colored" parishes, there are as of 1966 13 more wholly Negro parishes. There are 21 more with varying racial mixtures. Thus, the parishes with substantial numbers of Negroes range from the most underprivileged slum areas through the older row-house, working-class neighborhoods to the tree-shaded areas of single and semi-detached middle-class residences in several outlying areas. Basically, however, the predominantly Negro parishes are located in the older areas of the city, where slum and deteriorating areas blend with the modest working-class districts.[1]

These facts have made the integration of Negroes into parish life spotty. The most evident feature of the interracial parish is that Negroes are accepted in the full juridical sense. Secondly, as a general rule Negroes are included normally, often casually, in all those activities that are under the administration of the priests and nuns and for which they are directly responsible. Hence, the altar boys, the choir, the church ushers and the parish committees that solicit funds door to door for Catholic charities or parish functions usually include Negroes. Thirdly, in those activities and groups that are under strong influence from the lay people, and that frequently have a tradition of social intercourse and friendship attached to them, Negroes are excluded or only marginally included for some years after the initial racial change in a parish. If the parish becomes heavily Negro such organizations (the Holy Name Society, the Sodality or the Altar Society) will gradually begin to reflect this composition. The absence of Negroes from these groups apparently results from the simple

1. Six of the foreign-language parishes are also located in Negro neighborhoods. But these draw their parishioners from their respective national populations in the whole metropolitan area.

social distance that persists between parishioners of different races. Seldom does the parish priest take the initiative in introducing Negroes directly into these groups, although he may encourage the Negro parishioners personally to join.

On the whole, relations between Negroes and whites are seldom marked by resentment, enmity or agitation after the first decade of Negro penetration of a parish. The relations between parishioners of different races are characterized by that degree of social distance and vague anonymity that is common to general parish relationships in the large, busy urban parishes. Except where long residence or family ties make an exception, the parishes tend to be organizations rather than communities and contacts between parishioners are usually transitory and impersonal. Negroes become part of the parish groups on a nominal basis, just as whites do, and fuller participation is the exception rather than the rule.

Parish priests or lay leaders rarely show any demonstrable interest in civil rights issues. Their thoughts on such matters are subsumed into those broad categories of Catholic moral classification that embrace wide areas of human frailty and discipline. Innocuous Gospel commentaries and discourses on the moral virtues and the examination of conscience comprise the content of sermons; frequenting the sacraments is also stressed. It is highly unusual for priests to allude to specific and particular social issues from the pulpit. Some selected issues—indecent literature, Communism and juvenile disobedience—are singled out for constant attention and use as examples, but exposition on social issues seldom goes beyond these. Until recently, it was only occasionally that one would hear a parish sermon or exposition of any sort on the specific subject of race relations as a moral problem.

The attitude of the laity is only rarely informed about the doctrinal or social implications of racial issues. Those few persons who are aware of such implications seldom see any relevance to their parish situation, whether they live in an all-white, an interracial or a heavily Negro parish. The laity tend, in overwhelming numbers, to be subject to that tradition of pathological thinking that sets Negroes apart as a peculiar and special group to be treated with only by necessity and in the most circumspect way.

The clergy usually are conscious of a general obligation to work for improved race relations, no matter how confused their personal ideas about Negroes and their social situation may be. But their consciousness of this obligation hardly ever extends to public action in behalf of civil rights, individual Negro rights in particular local situations, or movements for desegregation. This aversion to public involvement is part of the general reserve that has characterized the Philadelphia Catholic clergy—and indeed has marked virtually the entire American Catholic priesthood—for decades. If the clergy are not cloistered, they are at least sequestered from civic affairs in the city. The most common rationale given in interviews is that they prefer to work quietly on racial attitudes, that publicity is damaging and inflammatory, that grace works silently, and above all that race relations can be improved only over a long period of time as both Negroes and whites adjust.

Although the archdiocesan newspaper, *The Catholic Standard and Times,* carries good material on racial issues (almost all of it from the wires of the NCWC and Religious News services), and although the college and high school social science teachers vigorously expound on race relations and Catholic responsibility, the parish clergy seem to lack assurance to perform a similar task. Where a young curate might preach a forthright sermon on interracial justice here and there in the diocese, the pastors as a group are silent. Yet their silence negates the message of the curate, for Philadelphia's Catholics, like those in New York, are more inclined to take their pastor seriously than the curate—particularly on "controversial" issues.

On some occasions the police or public officials have had the responsibility of going to parishes to ask their cooperation in reducing neighborhood racial tension or in counteracting states of inflamed opinion which might lead to outbreaks of street violence, juvenile combat or vandalism to property recently acquired by Negroes; such contacts have become more frequent since the city set up a Commission on Human Relations in 1950. But priests seldom cooperate openly in trying to mitigate such frictions or disorders. On one occasion in 1955 a monsignor did visit the members of his nationality parish to ask their forbearance during a period of tense demonstrations against newly arrived Negroes. In 1960 a priest responded to the plea of a police inspector to help disperse an unruly and irate crowd that was demonstrating against a Negro occupant of a house in an all-white area. Garbled news accounts of the priest's role led to sharp criticism of him in the Negro press, and his deed as peacemaker was misconstrued: he was alleged to have reassured the crowd that no Negro would enter the area. Such twisted interpretations by irresponsible news media tend to confirm the clergy in their attitude of careful reserve and reluctance to "get involved."

On several occasions of high tension pastors have flatly refused even to discuss nearby racial problems. In two cases of violent demonstrations and irate anti-Negro crowds, the houses that were the targets of the disorders were within one block of Catholic churches in heavily Catholic neighborhoods. To the unprejudiced Catholic and non-Catholic alike, a pastor's refusal to play any constructive role at all in difficult situations is a devastating example of inertia. When the refusal is abrupt, curt or even uncivil, it gives rise to the most cynical interpretations and erects psychological barriers between the pastor and these parishioners.

Despite such unhappy occurrences, Negro converts continue to enter the Catholic Church through the parishes. In 1960, when Philadelphia's Negro population topped 500,000, there were approximately 40,000 Negro Catholics in the archdiocese, the overwhelming majority of them in metropolitan Philadelphia. This is 8 per cent of the Negro population and 2 per cent of the entire Philadelphia population. A proportion of 8 per cent of the Negro population in the Catholic Church is rare in most of the major cities. This may also be a factor in inducing an outlook of complacency on the part of the local clergy. It is a common attitude among priests that conversion of Negroes and the holding of the gains made is very difficult work and cannot be expected to proceed very rapidly. Therefore, the proportion of Negro Catholics must appear substantial and encouraging. The late Cardinal O'Hara actually expressed the belief that the succession of Negroes to neighborhoods and parish facilities abandoned by whites due to racial panic was providential, for the lower economic level of Negroes would not permit them to build such parish facilities and thus, in a fashion little realized, the white population was unwittingly providing for the educational and spiritual needs of Negroes.

Diocesan-wide organizations in Philadelphia are of the traditional Catholic variety. Men and women are members of separate parish societies or chapters that are linked on an archdiocesan basis. The city-wide echelons hold intermittent functions publicized in *The Catholic Standard and Times*. The Knights of Columbus has for some years had Negro members, though usually in heavily Negro or all-Negro councils. A longtime Negro leader in the St. Vincent de Paul Society was honored before his death with special recognition for his service. The Holy Name Union and the Legion of Mary generally follow parish patterns of racial composition, as do the Catholic Youth Organization and Confraternity of Christian Doctrine. Lay apostolic organizations of a more recent origin are scarcely represented in the archdiocese. Of such groups, only The Grail is active in Philadelphia. The Christian Family Movement, the Cana Conference, the Liturgical Conference, the Young Christian Workers, the Association of Catholic Trade Unionists and other modern groups are absent. The Grail Center in the city has had several Negro and Asian staff members working with it at various periods.

The institutions of the archdiocese have historically had a rather benevolent but uneven racial policy. The Catholic Charities office serves both races without distinction. The orphanages accept children of different racial backgrounds. For most of the institutions this has not been a serious problem: their clientele was for generations largely white, and the entry of the few Negro Catholics demanding their attention was not a threat to their predominantly white character, or to their prestige or finances. As one doctor said, "St. X's hospital is so old-fashioned and representative of the immigrant neighborhoods that current concern about Negro access to equal facilities is hardly related to it. It serves Negroes with a sort of kindly, patronizing view that abstracts from civil rights." The St. Vincent de Paul Society does operate two summer camps for poor children, one white and one Negro, but though some Catholics have protested the apparent segregation, it can be said that their racial characters fairly reflect the residential pattern of the parishes from which the children come. The institutions of the archdiocese are certainly open to Negroes. The differential use of them by different racial groups is largely the result of differing social needs, the complex factors of social distance between two traditionally separated groups, and the geographical location of the institutions in relation to the segregated housing pattern.

One proof that a parish threatened by racial change can be more than a helpless victim is to be found in the example of St. Elizabeth's. It was originally a German parish, then Irish, and finally in the 1930's became more and more Negro. By 1937, when Father Edward Cunnie was appointed pastor, the parish had shrunk from the 1,000 white families to less than half that number. One of the city's first public housing projects was built within the parish and this hastened both the exodus of whites and the arrival of Negroes. The school, built for 2,200 students, had only 600 in 1937, and the enrollment eventually declined to 200. Father Cunnie began an administration of the parish that was to revive it in a most spirited fashion and to identify him till his death in 1957 with the Catholic apostolate to the Negroes of Philadelphia. With down-to-earth initiative, good humor and priestly zeal, Father Cunnie tackled the problems of his Negro parishioners and impressed the non-Catholic Negroes of the area with his keen concern for their welfare and rights.

Through a diligent attention to family life and the instruction of children, parish morale was rebuilt. The works of mercy and charity flourished. By 1955 there were 3,000 Catholics enrolled in the parish and the school enrollment had risen to 900. Father

Cunnie was made a monsignor, much to the pride and satisfaction of his parishioners, nine out of 10 of whom were converts.

Part of the secret of this revival was the warm and inventive personality of Monsignor Cunnie himself, but much of the progress was due to the program that he had devised for his parish. He arranged for hot lunches for the children of working mothers. He obtained shoes at cut rates for hard-pressed families. He made good use of willing lay workers who helped him organize a Holy Family group to strengthen family life, and a credit union to offset sharp sales practices and the exploitation of families. He arranged for health and nursing care. A survey of the parish conducted by college students gave an accurate picture of population and permitted new contacts with interested families.

Through contributions that he solicited outside the parish, Monsignor Cunnie aided the unemployed. To train young people to take advantage of better job opportunities, he was instrumental in having the Mercy Technical Institute formed and operated by the Sisters of the Blessed Sacrament. Here the young could learn carpentry, metal work, baking, dressmaking and secretarial skills.

Private instruction and counseling about marriage, vocations and the spiritual life he made especially practical, always weighing the social and financial conditions of the counselee. Cunnie's informal sermons at the children's Mass on Sundays were delightful question-answer-and-comment sessions in which the portly pastor moved among the children explaining religious teachings.

Collaborating with Monsignor Cunnie in many of the parish activities were Mrs. Anna McGarry and her friends. Monsignor Cunnie became the informal consultant of other priests involved in work in heavily Negro parishes. In addition, he became recognized in the non-Catholic community, particularly the Negro community, as a generous and able leader and he became the archdiocese's chief Catholic spokesman on Negro affairs. As chaplain he provided guidance to the Catholic Interracial Council, up until the time of his death. For two decades Monsignor

Cunnie was the most notable priest in the archdiocese connected with work among the Negro population.

Since his death St. Elizabeth's has continued to grow and to benefit from the increased steady employment that has been available to Negroes since World War II. Families from this parish have moved to other areas open to Negroes to improve their housing conditions, but invariably they remember Monsignor Cunnie with affection and respect.

Nowhere is it more true than in Philadelphia that the Church is the school system. It is estimated that over 80 per cent of the Catholic elementary school population attends parochial schools. What this means is that at this educational level, Negro and white Catholics enjoy equal opportunity. And where the parish includes a mixed population, the school does likewise. But for the most part the schools are uniracial, reflecting residential patterns. Where this is Negro, the parochial school is likely to have enrolled a good number of non-Catholic Negroes. In perhaps a dozen of these schools the non-Catholic enrollment runs between one-fifth and one-third. In one it is near the 50 per cent mark. Such schools undoubtedly serve a latent missionary function.

Under the archdiocesan superintendent of schools there are 10 Catholic regional high schools in the city of Philadelphia and 15 outside it. In addition, there are 23 private Catholic high schools in the city and its nearby suburbs. These schools, some of which have fine buildings and equipment and several thousand students, represent an outstanding achievement of school administration and are unrivalled in any diocese in the United States—perhaps the world. Students for the diocesan high schools pay no tuition directly. This cost falls to the pastors, who must raise money in the parish to pay the *per capita* cost of each student's education. Even in recent years, when the school population has risen, the city's Catholic population has not suffered any notable shortage of high school classrooms. The energetic building policies of Cardinals Dougherty and O'Hara ensured against this.

Even in its early days, the first diocesan high school, Roman Catholic, had an occasional Negro student. During the 1940's the number of Negroes in the Catholic high schools gradually increased. The archdiocesan high schools acquired Negro students largely as a result of their location. Those in outlying, all-white areas tended to have only one or two students from the rare pockets of Negroes in these areas. In the center of the city, however, the parishes that were becoming heavily Negro began to channel their grade school graduates to the Catholic high schools as a matter of course. These students tended to represent the more stable and accomplished portions of the Negro population; the very fact that they were able to remain in high school and graduate indicated that their parents did not have to force them to leave school to earn money.

The relationships between Negro and white high school students present few, if any, disciplinary problems; a prevailing air of casual teenage camaraderie seems to exist. In a number of schools Negroes have been elected class officers. Negro athletes have provided a good image of prowess and initiative when they excelled on school teams. In one school in 1961 a Negro student had the lead in a play by Shakespeare that the school drama club was presenting. The presence of Negroes in such normal extracurricular activities indicates the bland and even manner in which the teaching priests and nuns treat the problem of race. The more intimate social activities of the schools, such as dances, sometimes present problems of social adjustment, but usually they are patronized by students who almost universally choose partners of the same race as dates.

The parents of children in the private Catholic schools occasionally betray their concern about contact between the races. This concern is a large element in the social pretensions and petty snobbery so common among the Catholic families who have emerged from the working class only in the last generation and are still too insecure in their own social standing to look with equanimity upon interracial living patterns. But in no instance have the private schools given evidence that they encourage racial taboos or snobbery. Some of the private Catholic high schools have Negro students. Some have long-standing ties with

Latin America through the religious orders that conduct them, and this has meant that the daughters of dark-complexioned Latin families have matriculated at such schools from time to time.

On the whole, the administration of the Catholic high schools has made a good adjustment to the great racial changes of the last thirty years. The decrees of Vatican II and the forward-looking social encyclicals of the recent popes are strongly stressed, and the teaching about race is fully Catholic and creditable. Whether the schools are responding well enough to the task of offsetting the social disadvantage of Negro students and providing the needed vocational guidance and training for their special problems is a question that must await a full analysis of local Catholic education. Distinctive or different treatment of the needs of Negro students would probably be frowned upon by the administrators. St. Joseph's Preparatory School, conducted by the Jesuits, does have students that attend through a Martin de Porres Scholarship instituted by a prominent Catholic contractor, and one or two students benefit from it annually, but this is the only benefice specifically for Negro youngsters.

There are nine Catholic colleges, one university and two junior colleges in the archdiocese. Five of the colleges and the university have had Negroes on campus since the late 1930's, but Negro students were an intermittent phenomenon until after World War II. Their numbers are still small; a survey made in 1960 revealed that out of a total Catholic enrollment of some 11,000 students, there were only 125 Negroes. The number today is undoubtedly larger as the financial means come within the grasp of the expanding Negro middle class. Negro students testify that they do not experience any form of difficulty because of race. It is not an issue on campus. One widely experienced Negro Catholic student leader stated that while Catholic students were not racist in outlook, they rarely expressed any really Catholic view of racial problems because they were so generally inarticulate. Racial matters or issues are seldom commented upon outside of the social science classes, but there our interviews indicate that the teachers experience considerable difficulty with student attitudes on the matter of race. The students are notably reluctant to accept scientific facts or authentic Church teaching. The teaching about racial problems in the sociology courses is professional rather than dogmatic or hortatory. The same can be said of the teaching in religion and ethics. Negro faculty members, however, are almost non-existent, though a Negro heads the nursing education department at Villanova University.

On campus the students tend toward an informal self-segregation; this may be a habit pattern developed during high school years. This habit carries over to the college dances also. At one college there is an off-campus fraternity of the Negro students. All this does not, however, prevent associating in the cafeteria, library, student union and so forth. One Negro at a girls' college stated that social life for the few Negro girls in the college was nil, and that for this reason many of her Negro high school friends had elected to attend non-Catholic schools. Negro students have resided on campus in the Catholic colleges, but always in tiny numbers, and usually they room together.

Of all the levels of Catholic education in the archdiocese, it appears that the colleges have least actual contact with Negroes, with an estimated 200–300 in a total enrollment of over 11,000. In a city where one out of four residents is a Negro, the Catholic colleges can at best be said to be serving Negroes only in a marginal fashion. This accounts, at least partially, for the dearth of Negro clergy.

There are eight seminaries, both major and minor, religious and secular, in the archdiocese, and one house of studies (for the Christian Brothers). Most of these institutions have at one time or another had a Negro student, but in only the last two years were two Negro students on campus at a seminary simultaneously. The archdiocesan seminary, St. Charles Borromeo, recently had a Negro student for the priesthood, but no Negro has ever successfully completed studies and become an archdiocesan priest, although Philadelphia Negroes have been ordained outside of the archdiocese in several religious orders.

Negro Catholics in Community Life

Negro Catholics are not leaders in the Negro community. The leaders of the Negro community are grouped in three categories: civil rights, political and religious. (There is, of course, much overlapping in these categories.) Catholics have not been prominent on the boards of the NAACP, the Urban League or CORE in the Philadelphia area, though Catholics did work hard for FEPC when that was an issue in legislative battles. There is hardly a political leader of significance in the city who is a Negro and also a Catholic. Of the four municipal and Federal judgeships held by Negroes, none is a Catholic. The religious leadership in the Negro community is also often political. One Negro minister is a city councilman, another is a member of the Civil Service Commission. The Negro clergy are strongly Baptist or Methodist, although their relationship to the body of white members of these denominations is frequently negligible. To many of these ministers the Catholic Church is a direct competitor and an agency to be feared. Some allege that it is making big gains in the Negro community. Others comment that these gains are not among "the better class of Negro," but among the depressed group who need the ministrations and social aid of the Catholic parishes.

Despite such allegations, the evidence indicates stronger inroads among the middle classes than among the lower. Catholic social work and poverty programs do not match the impact of the parochial school—which is *de facto* a middle-class institution. Uncounted thousands of Negro children have benefited from educational opportunity offered by the parochial school in Philadelphia. But so far their impact as leaders in the Negro community or the civil rights movement has not been felt. The road to power apparently runs through the Negro Protestant Church, not the Catholic.

The city's Negro Catholics seem to lack a clear focus within the Church. They have at best only a few models of leadership and modest success, no distinctive groups or achievements. On

the other hand, they see little lasting racial integration in parish
fruition of its leadership potential.
life, for in the past the integrated parishes have tended to be half-way houses to totally Negro parishes. The Negro Catholics have limited contacts with whites in the parishes, through whom run channels of civic and political power. The obvious habits of avoidance, prejudice and outright discrimination among their white Catholic conferes add up to a contradiction that they reconcile with their faith as best they can. Despite the Church's strong formal ideological position against prejudice and discrimination, there is ample evidence of fumbling, passivity and slothfulness in measuring up to this position, and these things have adversely affected Negro Catholic morale, as well as the

Catholics and Civil Rights Activity

Catholics in Philadelphia have not been noted for their general participation in city-wide civic groups seeking civil rights objectives. For a number of years their efforts were centered in the Philadelphia Catholic Interracial Council. In the 1930's the issuance of Pius XI's encyclical *Quadragesimo Anno,* and the social problems connected with the depression, gave impetus to a lively interest among Catholics in social matters. There were lectures and discussions in the Catholic community on social justice. At this time Father LaFarge was organizing the Catholic interracial movement in every place where interest could be ignited. In 1938 a group of young Philadelphians, among them Miss Mary McGarry, daughter of Mrs. Anna McGarry, and Daniel Kane began holding sessions on the various college campuses with the aid of Father Gerard Murphy, S.J. After some of the interested persons had discussed the matter with Cardinal Dougherty, the Catholic Intercollegiate Interracial Council was formed. It was the view of the cardinal that the most profitable work of improving interracial attitudes and studying interracial problems could be carried out among the young people in the colleges. Gradually, this collegiate group evolved into the adult Interracial Council.

During the 1940's, as Negroes moved rapidly into the city to work in war industries, there were tensions and irritations which, in countless small situations, the Interracial Council worked to alleviate. In 1946 a transit strike arose, partly over the issue of whether Negroes would be hired to replace men who had been called to war. Feeling ran high and there was some violence. Mrs. McGarry took an active part in ameliorating this situation.

The demand for a city Fair Employment Practices Ordinance to curb flagrant job discrimination against Negroes had been pressed for a number of years during the 1940's and the Catholic Interracial Council worked side by side with non-Catholic groups to build support for its enactment. In 1948 an FEP ordinance was adopted and Judge Flood was appointed head of a commission to enforce it. Robert Callaghan replaced Judge Flood as Chairman of this Commission and became first chairman in 1952 of an enlarged agency titled the Commission on Human Relations, which made its first breakthroughs in employment patterns in department stores, factories and service industries.

Soon after its inception the FEP Commission took advantage of the skills of Mrs. McGarry and employed her full-time on its staff. She remained with the Commission on Human Relations until her retirement from the civil service in 1959. In addition to the work of supervising a staff dealing with racial tensions and conflicts throughout the city, she found time to direct and participate in a number of activities related to the Catholic Interracial Council. She and other members set up workshops and panels, filled speaking engagements, published bulletins and newsletters, collected funds and sponsored lectures on interracial topics. At one time a young Negro graduate of Xavier University was employed by the Council to share some of this activity. The Council for some years conducted a radio program weekly over station WJMJ. It offered guidance to Catholics faced by neighborhood racial change and by a wide variety of problems ranging from interracial marriage to finding scholarship aid. In recognition of this work Mrs. McGarry was awarded the Hoey Award for

Interracial Justice, and was frequently cited in the Philadelphia community for her outstanding leadership.

But the Catholic Interracial Council never received broad support from the Catholic community. It was identified with a group of gifted activists, and it was always somewhat controversial because of the nature of the problem with which it dealt. When Monsignor Cunnie died in 1957 the Council lost a chaplain with great prestige, and thereafter no successor was appointed. This may have been due to the fact that the Council displeased persons in the administration of the archdiocese.

A particular instance of the Council's work is said by some to have caused antagonism toward it. In 1957, when the first Negro family moved into the 16,000-home community of Levittown, a Philadelphia suburb, rioting broke out and was widely publicized. Several persons active with the Interracial Council went to Levittown and attempted to work with local Catholics to aid in the restoration of community peace and order. A statement was issued urging Catholics to consider objectively the issue of racial change and to uphold the forces of law and order. This action may have distressed persons in the archdiocese who would have taken a different approach to the racial flare-up.

Between 1959 and late 1963 the Interracial Council ceased to function as an entity in the city. A few years later, however, it had a successor—born of conflict. In September of 1963 a Negro family named Baker moved into the suburban village of Folcroft. Although heavily Catholic, the area's white neighbors took to the streets, stoning and vandalizing the house. After weeks of tension and impending violence, Horace Baker, the father of the family, was confined to a rest home with a nervous breakdown. Pressured into action by a group of Negro Catholic men, the archdiocese formed a Catholic Intergroup Relations Council. This was followed by a strong and eloquent statement from the chancellor addressed to the parishioners of Folcroft.

But this was the extent of official Catholic leadership. The local pastor, addressing an overflow crowd of some 300 parishioners, who moved in uninvited to a leadership meeting of some

40 selected people, brought about the collapse of the Intergroup Relations Council's efforts to restore peace to Folcroft.

In February, 1964, six months after its formation the Council began to disintegrate. Failure of Catholic officials and the Council itself to solve the Folcroft problem led to internal dissention and a drift particularly of its Negro members into CORE and the Student Non-Violent Coordinating Committee. The group that remained tried in vain to get the archbishop to bring the prestige and influence of the Church to bear on the problem. But apparently the archbishop could see only the ecclesiastical dimensions: what the Church was already doing for Negroes by way of charity and through non-discriminatory policies in schools and other Church institutions. He was also concerned about the bureaucratic problem of supporting local pastoral authority and suggested to the Council that in a clash with such authority the Council would have to give way. The bureaucratic dictum that superior officers have to "stand behind" their subordinates overruled the problem of social justice.

After this failure to implement Catholic social principles through the official Catholic institution, the Council split in two. One group opted for loyalty to the archbishop and only those operations consonant with his way of doing things; the other for independent "efforts which we believe to be just and necessary either now or in the future."[1] The "loyalists" formed a Catholic Human Relations Council; the liberals retained the original title but having lost favor at the chancery went "underground." Vitality and achievement from either have since been hardly significant.

Meanwhile the Archbishop's Commission of Human Relations was established. Interracial in make-up, it was strongly supported by several pastors from older Negro parishes—a fact that suggests they have new leverage with the archbishop. The Commission backed the 1964 Civil Rights Act; Archbishop Krol himself signed a joint statement with other bishops from the state urging its passage. *The Catholic Standard and Times*

1. Quoted from the letter the Council voted to send to the Archbishop, 43 to 30.

increased its coverage of the civil rights movement and emphasized the formal episcopal statements and the work of the Archbishop's Commission. With the inauguration of the Federal Anti-Poverty Program, the archbishop appointed another commission to devise and coordinate diocesan projects in this area.

Unlike those of New York, Chicago and Detroit, the Negro population of Philadelphia seems to be less volatile. The rate of geographical mobility seems slower, and the city itself in contrast to New York is able to keep a safe distance ahead of its problems. Such conditions offer the archdiocese a relatively better opportunity to experiment with structural reform, set new goals for itself and assume moral leadership. Yet the bureaucratic character of ecclesiastical operations weighs heavily on both clergy and laity. Folcroft seems to have been the high-water mark of the spirit of reform. The archdiocese will join the march toward a better metropolis—for example, the war on poverty—but it will be at a safe distance from the front of that march.

ROCKVILLE CENTRE: SUBURBIA

No one has ever made a count of American suburbs, much less a thorough study of them. They are whimsically believed to have been born of a union between the urban dweller's desire for more living room and the trolley car. Although there are industrial suburbs and a variety of other types of settlements satellite to large cities, the most common type is still the residential. And it is with this that we are concerned. The sociologists and demographers who have researched these areas have struck a consensus on several of their characteristics. For one thing, suburbs are, compared to the city, deficient in the number of single or unattached individuals. Suburbia is reserved for families only. The ratios of children under 14 to the total population and adults in the 34–35 age group is much higher here than in cities. So too is the proportion of middle-income people; cities have much higher percentages from the low-income groups. (Rural areas, however, exceed both in this regard.)

The single family house is the typical dwelling unit, and more important is the fact that it is owned by its occupants. (Rentals in the suburb are scarce in the middle and upper-income brackets.) From this mortgaged domicile come more youngsters than from its counterpart in the city. The residents have more years of schooling and are more likely to be regular churchgoers than the urbanite. White collar and professional workers are proportionately more numerous than in the city, while the converse is true for the unskilled laborer and the unemployed.

From these demographic characteristics develops an outlook on life or a mentality whose salient features are readily observable. Civic and political values tend to orbit around the child, the home and the immediate environment of both: the neighborhood. Problems and issues surrounding schools, public utilities, traffic, recreational facilities, parking accommodations, police and fire protection are all of paramount interest to the suburbanite. For unlike the city dweller, he has a higher degree of control over these matters. And the instruments of this control, the school board and town government, he also guards jealously from incursions by higher echelons of county and state governments. Furthermore, he demands all these domestic services at the lowest possible cost in taxes. In short, his vested interests in family and property make him a conservative.

Obviously, peace and order in the neighborhood and its larger society are of the utmost value. So too is religion. Suburban religion centers not only on its formal structure and Church properties, but a calendar of feast days and rituals for the sabbath and for the milestones of life: birth, the passage from puberty, marriage and death. There is also a religious tradition from which solace, counsel and eulogy can be fashioned on the occasion of suffering, crisis or tragedy. Religion, in other words, plays a highly functional role by making meanings available for the life of affluence. For Catholics it frequently takes on added significance by providing eight to 12 years of education. The church or synagogue generally is not expected to be relevant to social or political issues except perhaps on the abstract level; it is not expected to play a prophetic role.

Here then, in brief, is a sociological profile of the suburb and the suburban mentality. Together they constitute the cultual milieu of those dioceses located in whole or part, in the suburbs. The diocese of Rockville Centre is in the former category. And, as we asserted with respect to the Southern dioceses, we believe that the most meaningful observation and analysis can spring only from within its cultural context.[1] In the words of Kurt Lewin, a noted social psychologist, "Behavior is a function of the total situation."

The diocese of Rockville Centre was established in 1957 by cutting the two eastern counties, Nassau and Suffolk, off the Brooklyn diocese. Located on Long Island with its nearest border just 17 miles from midtown Manhattan, the diocese is an integral part of the New York metropolitan region.[2] For those New Yorkers tied by job or sentiment to the city and yet who desire a little more ground than is available in Brooklyn or Queens, "Long Island" is the goal. Much of the middle and upper-middle class overflow from the city is into contiguous Nassau County.

In Suffolk County, the more distant half of the diocese, the relationships to and dependence on New York are counterbalanced by some independent economic activity. Fishing, truck farming and aircraft manufacture are the main industries; population, while growing rapidly, is still spread rather thinly compared to Nassau and strikingly so, compared to the residential boroughs of Queens and Brooklyn in New York City.

The diocese's population is conservatively estimated at 806,472 out of a total population of about 2,000,000. It includes some of the nation's wealthiest communities: Flower Hill, Garden City and Rockville Centre. Here on the latter's most valuable and main corner stands the diocesan headquarters.

1. It is easier to follow this procedure where the features of the cultural environment have a more clear or traceable connection to the behavioral patterns of the institutions. This is the case with the South and the suburbs. It is obviously not the case with the cities.

2. See Edgar Hoover and Raymond Vernon, *Anatomy of a Metropolis,* New York, 1962.

Two modern office buildings, the tallest in the area, house the chancery, Catholic Charities and other bureaus. Nearby is the office of *The Long Island Catholic,* a rather liberal paper as far as diocesan organs go. Inaugurated four year ago, the paper cut sharply into the circulation of *The Brooklyn Tablet.*

The relative paucity of Negroes and especially Negro Catholics and the scattering of their enclaves relieve the two counties of any problem with the explosive potential of a Watts. Out of the 2,000,000 estimated total population, there are approximately 71,000 Negroes living in uniracial communities and ghettoes scattered randomly across the diocese. A closer examination of the census data, however, reveals that 76 per cent of all the Negro households in Nassau were concentrated in nine census tracts out of a total of over 200. The housing conditions of these families is (est. 42,000) classified as 25 per cent "deteriorating" or "dilapidated,"[1] compared to only 3.4 per cent of the white housing in this condition. This geographic concentration and its settlement in older and deteriorating housing suggests that the seeds of a troublesome future have been sown. Our own inspection of these census tract areas confirms the statistical evidence, that in Nassau county alone eight to 10 full-blown slums are well under way.

Meanwhile this population is growing rapidly. In the decade 1950–1960 it has increased by over 75 per cent (as compared to 45 per cent in New York City). It is, furthermore, a segment of the population with a disproportionate share of handicaps. In Nassau and Suffolk both, the sex ratio is rather low, namely, there are far more women than men. They are for the most part young single girls brought up from the South by some 40 employment agencies to work in the homes of the wealthy. In the age bracket 20–30 the ratio is three to one in favor of the female. Such a disproportion carries with it a potential for the moral, physical and mental ills attendant on the lack of oppor-

1. "Race Relations in Nassau County," *The Quorum,* May, 1963, Hofstra University, Hempstead, N.Y. The data is from the 1960 census and has been culled from official sources by a team of sociology students from Hofstra University: Stephen Rosen, Stefan Leader, *et al.*

tunity for marriage and normal heterosexual relationships. Disproportionate also is the ratio of single men to married men, vis-à-vis the white male population.

With respect to the unbroken Negro family, it will have more children than its white counterpart and, it is estimated, close to 50 per cent of them will have both parents working. Income and educational levels for Negroes as a whole are markedly lower than their white neighbors. Thus when one considers their rapid growth in this diocese and matches it with the potential for generating social problems, it is evident that intelligent social planning is in order, not only by the governmental agencies, but by any institution which professes to be concerned with such problems.

The difficulty, however, seems to be with the fact that this sort of data is not the starting point for diocesan policy or decision making. Neither the Bishop's Commission on Interracial Affairs, which has no full-time professional worker, nor the Catholic Interracial Council has any long-term plan of operations nor the data from which to make one. The Council's Executive Secretary, Mrs. Catherine Rowcroft, is on a three-day work week and operates out of a bank balance which hovers habitually around the $1,000 mark. In its present precarious state it obviously cannot be expected to be an effective agency of the diocese. The Bishop's Commission works on an *ad hoc* basis, stepping in and out of some crises and avoiding others. It meets once a month or in between times if an occasion seems to demand. Perhaps the greatest handicap to both agencies is the lack of any over-all blueprint for rendering diocesan concern effective. Also lacking is a detailed episcopal statement of policy that could be used by leaders in the field to generate support for their programs. But were both of these available, there would still be the need for a heavy financial commitment.

On the other hand, it may be the view of the diocese that its Bureau of Catholic Charities plus its recently organized Diocesan Committee for Community Interests are the principal avenues of commitment. Through both these agencies the diocese has become actively engaged in a series of projects financed for the most part by the Federal Office of Economic Opportunity or the Department of Health, Education and Welfare. Thus under diocesan sponsorship there are programs of remedial tutorial service, a pre-school child-care center, a work-training program for high school drop-outs, an incentive program for poor but talented youth and a summer tutorial and enrichment program for under-achieving junior high school students. The size of the programs might be estimated from the cost and numbers involved. Cash outlay by the diocese is in the neighborhood of $10,000 and as of 1966 some seven hundred youths were serviced. Most of the programs are less than two years old, and have an uncertain life expectancy. Since the Federal government subsidizes 90 per cent of the cost, these projects will thrive or collapse depending on the political climate in Washington.

Catholic Charities also responded in an energetic way to a call for help from the Suffolk County Welfare Department. In the summer of 1964 the living conditions of some 256 migrant workers and their families on the Hollis Warner Duck Ranch in Riverhead were revealed to the public by CORE. The pressure that resulted in the speedy relocation of these people came from a joint inspection of the destitute area by Lincoln Lynch, the Long Island president of CORE, and Monsignor Michael McLaughlin, the chairman of the Bishop's Commission on Interracial Affairs. The visit of these two, and the efforts of reporters and photographers, catalyzed several sectors of political influence. The county officials[1] were forced to evacuate the families and find new homes for them before winter set in. Catholic Charities and the Salvation Army were requested to provide social-service needs of the group. Although financial help allegedly was promised by the Long Island Fund it was not forthcoming because the public exposure in the secular and diocesan press turned this problem of destitution into a "controversy" and brought a torrent of criticism not only on the Long Island Fund

1. They had been working on the problem but were hampered by bureaucratic procedures.

but also on Monsignor McLaughlin. Fourteen social workers and two priests from Catholic Charities donated overtime hours to the project while the Bureau's budget absorbed $5,000 in costs and financial assistance to the needy families.

Bureau officials when discussing social problems of race or poverty emphasize the community orientation of their operations. Neither a person's race nor his religion is considered in administering to its clientele.

On the other sector of the official front is the diocesan paper, *The Long Island Catholic*. Here the coverage of problems of interracial relations, poverty and the slowly mounting influx of Puerto Ricans is given a prominence that often matches the more provincial news. The fact that its editor is a monsignor, Richard Hanley, who has been given a large measure of independence by the bishop, enables it to withstand the fury of the diocese's extreme right wing. When *The Long Island Catholic* carried on its front page the photograph and comments of Monsignor McLaughlin on the plight of the migrant workers on the Hollis Warner Duck Ranch, the switchboard and editor's desk were flooded with protest. The fact that many other scandalous conditions and events do not make its news columns reflects not so much on its editor and staff as it does on the hypersensitivity of the diocesan high command to criticism and on the low tolerance level of the paper's readership.

However one may regard the official stance to the social problems we are here discussing, one cannot avoid comparing it with its commitment to Catholic education. In 1963 the bishop and his diocesan school board, which even at this writing lacks lay representation, embarked on a high school building campaign. Four high schools located at strategic points of projected population growth were planned. A fund-raising corporation was hired and a $20,000,000 campaign was inaugurated. Every parish was engaged and teams of laymen canvassed every Catholic family on the parish roll. The fund was oversubscribed and brought to a more or less successful completion in late 1966. The input of time, labor and money testifies to the resources, moral and material, that the diocese can command for a cause it deems worthy.

The Parish

Long Island presents a variety of "race" problems, some only indirectly connected with racial prejudice, but all of which call for a competence in social planning not usually found in the Catholic parish. However, the response of the Catholic family and its parish clergy springs not so much from a feeling of inadequacy but from other sources ranging from fear to prejudice. Thus at the level of the parish the two problems emerge, competence and what may loosely be called a fear-prejudice continuum, neither of which seem as yet to have been functionally defined by diocesan officials, much less by the pastors. Undoubtedly, they know the existence of prejudice and suffer from the confusion of not knowing what to do. But these are states of mind to be endured; they are not regarded as problems to be solved. The experience of one parish with an urban-renewal project in its village might illustrate the point.

About eight years ago this village, one of the wealthiest on Long Island, undertook a slum-clearance project within the neighborhood of the Catholic church. The area was about 90 per cent Negro, but contained many excellent properties and sound housing units. As condemnation proceedings advanced far ahead of relocation plans, the Negro families began to move out. Since the rest of the village contained an overwhelmingly large percentage of middle and upper-class properties, the dislocated families from the urban renewal area had to move elsewhere in the county. Even the few Negro families who could afford to buy in the other sections of the village found it impossible to do so. A successful Negro doctor from Queens, for example, offered some $5,000 over the $50,000 list price of a house he had been shown by a real-estate broker (who claimed he had been tricked). But at the last minute, a quick coalition of Catholics prevented the sale of the house. The reputation of the village as a white preserve was built over the years on a number of such incidents. (A Human Rights Committee, meanwhile, started by a man of no religious affiliation and three Jewish couples, had formed and began planning for a solution to the problem of discrimination in the sale of homes in the village.)

Of 390 Negro families in the area in 1959, the number had dwindled to about 150 in 1966. By that time seven houses had been completed and occupied by former residents of the area. Two other families found houses in the blocks immediately adjacent to the project. On balance, some 240 families had left Rockville Centre.

In 1962 a Christian Family Movement group from the parish became curious as to what was going on. Their own investigation convinced them that this was a simple case of urban renewal equaling Negro removal, and forthwith decided to see what could be done to salvage homes for the remaining Negro families. Being an official parish organization which had only recently been recognized by the bishop, they decided to enter the struggle as individuals. They were well aware that the overlapping friendships between the rectory and the village government might prove embarrassing for the newly recognized and fragile CFM. Caution was in order for they soon found that there was need of alliance with the NAACP and other unpopular but involved individuals to grasp the complicated technicalities of law and architectural planning underlying the renewal process. The group developed competence in the relevant state and Federal laws, in planning and in the unchartered waters of battling a village government. They proved strong allies to the secular groups in the fight and brought in other young Catholics. Political "connections" to Albany and the Federal government were utilized and pressure brought to bear on sensitive politicians. The press was skillfully managed, picket lines organized and open board meetings used to expose the deplorable state of the Negro families. By 1964 the village board was on the defensive; changes in the architectural layout of the area were made as was some improvement in administrative practice. By early 1965 a Congregational minister, ignoring the wrath of his parishioners, had helped the remaining Negro families to organize their own Tenants Association which at this writing is carrying on a successful salvage operation against the village board.[1]

What is of significance in this experience is that the Catholics, although their inspiration sprang from their Christian formation in CFM, could not work from a parish base. They could not, so they felt, act as a Catholic organization. The legitimate ties between the clergy and the village government suggested that the existence of the CFM itself or its involvement in the urban renewal problem might be jeopardized. But real or imagined as this threat may have been, the problem seems to have been one of class bias more than anything else. What was lacking really were ties to the people in the urban-renewal area. The parish simply had no roots in the Negro community, especially in the poor sector of that community. Personal acquaintances, much less friendships, between clergy and that community were almost non-existent. The parish was solidly middle and upper-class, laity as well as clergy. By tradition and personality it was oriented toward legal procedures and suspicion or hostility toward "troublemakers." Thus the Catholics on the village board (the others too) could perceive only the bureaucratic, legal and technical dimensions of the problem. They seemed to have no sensitivity to the human dimension—the anxiety and frustration, the suffering that accompanies living in sub-standard dwellings with nothing better in sight for years to come. Parish life meanwhile continued as though the problem did not exist. With perhaps one or two exceptions, there were no pertinent sermons and no action from the Holy Name or other parish societies.

Further evidence of the insulated state of the parish came when the one curate who was very much involved (and who was also the CFM moderator) was transferred. He was selected to be a principal in one of the projected Catholic high schools and was sent off to do graduate work in education. A man with no fears, he had been a source of inspiration and support for

1. At some point, the Catholic pastor turned sympathetic to the protest movement for he allowed the Tenants Association to hold its first meeting in the rectory.

the dozen or so Catholics involved. He was also emerging as a center around which several factions among the pro-Negro forces could coalesce.

Changing Neighborhoods

All neighborhoods whether in the city or suburb are changing. Sometimes the change is rapid and blatant; but most of the time the pace is evidenced only by the unnoticed aging of houses and their transfer from one generation to another. Where the pace is quick and where it involves the entry of a group regarded as undesirable the experience is painful. In such situations emerge what is called the fear-prejudice continuum, to deal with which the Catholic parish—if not all institutions—seems powerless.

A typical case might be had in the experience of Roosevelt, Long Island, most of whose residents are in the low to middle-income category. Through the 1960's many of its neighborhoods underwent integration. Block-busting and panic selling reigned in a few places but for the most part the integration succeeded. The parish played little or no role either in fending off crises or in promoting orderly integration. The reactions of individual Catholics did, on the other hand, contribute to both the problem and its solutions.

One layman asserted: "It's bad enough I have to live with Jews—and you want to bring niggers in here." This was a man whose whole education, up to and including college, was in Catholic institutions. Another whose move out of the nighborhood led to a rash of panic sales had warned his neighbors: "I saw what happened in Jamaica [New York City]. If they come in, I move out." It is easy to classify such reactions as prejudice. It is just as plausible, on the other hand, to describe them as cliché-cloaked articulations of fear. One of the Roosevelt parishioners who optimistically faced the entry of Negroes to the neighborhood later became embittered. For next door to him a group of five or six Negro women had moved in—all single and working. Men were frequent and often overnight visitors, and week-end parties and brawls made life miserable for the whole neighborhood. In another block, a number of single men rented a house with much the same result. The street is usually littered with empty beer cans and liquor bottles.

Clearly, such fear-prejudice reactions can have solid ground under them. Living standards, norms for social and interpersonal relations and moral norms do vary from one social class to another. People whose family structures have been all but destroyed by either poverty or slavery cannot be expected to have the same attitudes and mores as those whose family lines have been intact for generations. To mix the two types in a neighborhood with no agency having the competence to manage the process is to invite conflict. Yet what alternative is there? And what can a parish do? What is the role of pastor and curate in this type of neighborhood change?

As we indicated above, the proportionately large number of single men and women in the Negro population, their high rate of geographical mobility and the low rate of home ownership contrasted with the high rate among whites are characteristics of the county-wide population over which local neighborhoods or parishes have no control. It does seem, however, that the diocese, rich as it is in financial resources and in the untapped talents of its highly educated people, could create in either its interracial council or its human rights commission an agency which could develop the competence and do the research necessary to service parishes or neighborhoods with no power to help themselves.

Bussing vs. the Neighborhood School

School segregation whether it be *de jure* or *de facto* has an adverse effect on the education of all children. This finding of the Supreme Court of the United States in 1954 underlies the educational policy of the State of New York. Many communities, therefore, are under legal obligation to end *de facto* school segregation even at the cost of bussing children out of their neighborhood. To say the obvious, this has caused bitter social conflict in countless school districts throughout the state.

One of the most notorious conflicts has been under way for over two years in Malverne, Nassau County. The apparent solution to the problem of one overwhelmingly Negro elementary school and several others almost 100 per cent white was to integrate the children via the bus. This meant, in effect, an end to the neighborhood school and to the feeling of security for parents whose children could walk to school in a matter of minutes, be home for lunch, and so forth. The *raison d'être* for the move to the suburbs by middle-class families thus came under direct attack. The reaction was as might be expected: sit-ins by white mothers in the school buildings, picketing, lobbying in the state capitol at Albany and law suits.

The most vitriolic attack on the bussing decision seems to have come from one of the most Catholic sections of the school district. However, the Catholic Interracial Council, after considerable study and discussion of the problem, came to the conclusion that bussing with all its disadvantages was the only available solution to the problem of integration and better education. One of the pastors involved, although he was willing to go along with the Council and the so-called Allen Plan,[1] believed nonetheless that it was all a political scheme to capture Negro votes. The other priests maintained a discreet silence. Attempts were made to get the Bishop's Commission to support the Allen Plan and mitigate the fury of the Catholics fighting it. But the Commission, according to one informed source, has decided that it will let the local pastors handle the problem as they see fit. At any rate, neither school officials nor the public are aware of any contribution from the Bishop's Commission.

Once a conflict of this intensity gets under way, it is an exceedingly difficult and fearful decision to join one side or the other. Facts become obscure and the fervor of the contending factions seems to generate an argumentative super-ability that puts virtue and principle on one side and villainy and evil on

1. James Allen, the State Commissioner of Education, after whom the bussing plan was named.

the other. No action or else going along with one side as inconspicuously and ambiguously as possible are the temptations of officials or groups whose support is demanded by the factions. It is for these reasons easy to sympathize with officials who find themselves in this kind of a situation. On the other hand, it seems to be an inevitable result of the *ad hoc* approach to the problem. Without a clear definition of its role the Commission seems doomed to be drawn from one fire to the other. Even the common but relatively mild crisis involving the attempt of affluent Negro families to buy homes in matching communities, where the risk of downgrading is manageable and negligible, has evoked no significant support from the Commission.

Suburbia's Moral Dilemma

In the diocese of Rockville Centre, as in many others observed during the course of this study, the articulation of the moral problem arising from interracial relations comes most frequently from secular quarters. The moral problem, in a word, is how to get "religious" (that is, church-going) people interested in the moral problem. The chairman of a human rights committee in a populous section of Nassau put the matter this way:

> Our organization is similar to many in Nassau and Westchester Counties. We want homes made available to all people, regardless of race, color or creed.
>
> We have approached many community leaders, professional people and the clergy in order to gain their encouragement and support. As a result the great majority of the Jewish and Protestant religious leaders have become sponsors or board members.
>
> The Catholic Church has persistently taken a leadership position in the protection of minority rights. Despite this we have yet to receive the active support of our local Catholic churches whose two parishes represent 55 per cent of the population of our community.

The Catholic Interracial Council has long been aware of this problem. Yet it has no authority, no mandate from the bishop in this particular matter of the parishes and no funds for research or consultation services that might provide a breakthrough. Two major attempts were made to provide inspiration, technique and contacts for pastors of parishes facing racial problems. In 1963 and 1964 the Council sponsored a workshop type conference for the 119 parishes of the diocese. In 1963 40 per cent of the parishes sent delegates, 56 per cent the following year. The delegates in most cases were those who needed the conference least: the young, informed and committed curate or layman. Having no vote or effective influence in the making of parish policy, these curates and laymen are for the most part ineffective.[1] As one curate observed: "They [the congregation] ignore me when I talk about race from the pulpit. They have the pastor on their side. If the pastor doesn't lead in this matter there can be no leadership—at least not from the parish." As this realization grows, those who take the race problem seriously tend to leave or ignore the interracial councils and move toward the more effective secular counterparts. Leaders of CORE, NAACP and local human rights committees which before 1960 had few Catholic members, today report that the Catholic percentage is rising from year to year, particularly among the college age group.

The Catholic Church of the suburbs, insofar as it might be represented by this one diocese, faces this problem: Although the evidence is by no means comprehensive or conclusive, it is sufficient enough to warrant attention. Among those Catholics oriented to change or reform, "leakage" to secular organizations seems to be growing. This can be good and bad for it includes "leakage" of college graduates to the Peace Corps, and older married people to secular human rights groups; but it means a loss to the parish. The question that must be raised and discussed is whether or not this is inevitable, and to what extent. Is this the way in which the parish should "leaven" the community?

The statistical data introduced earlier into this section indi-

1. There is at this writing one exception to this statement. St. Aidan's parish in Williston Park has just completed its own "Vatican II Council" and is about to embark on a structural reform that will give curates and lay people a voice in the governing of the parish.

cates an accelerating growth for the Negro population in the diocese of Rockville Centre (and suburbs in general). A substantial segment of that population still suffers the effects of the brutality of slavery and the caste system which followed it. Its family structure is so weak that it cannot help but be a source of social infection. The census data for Nassau and Suffolk counties, previously referred to, support this contention. As the Southern farm empties its unneeded young Negroes on city and suburb, they will inevitably cause "trouble" for any community unprepared to handle them. Whether they come singly or in fatherless families, the diocese has to define its relationship to them. The assumption that Catholic Charities has and always will be able to handle this aspect of the Church's mission is, in effect, a denial of the need for social reform. The diocesan bureau of Catholic Charities historically had its origin in an era which did not believe social reform possible or desirable. Thus the bureau has been oriented toward amelioration of the plight of individual victims of the dip in the business cycle or other personal disasters. Even today in its engagement in "poverty projects" (Head Start, tutorials, vocational guidance for drop-outs, etc.), the best results are counted in terms of individual lives improved or rescued. This leaves untouched the social order that generates the pathology, which in turn provides the clientele for Catholic Charities. And so the cycle perpetuates itself.

Another source of trouble for this diocese, as well as others with suburbs, is the growing movement of middle and upper-class Negroes toward their residential districts. Cicero, Illinois, and Folcroft, Pennsylvania, are two Catholic suburbs that could not meet the challenge, except by riot. The diocese of Rockville Centre lives on apparently oblivious of this relevant bit of history. Its Catholic Interracial Council, while burdened with this knowledge and the large residue of fear-prejudice latent in the Catholic population, feels too frustrated and hamstrung to take precautionary measures. The parish is shielded from its operations by pastoral autonomy. The point here is not to predict, but to indicate that the diocese does not (as far as we have been able to ascertain) make any effort to keep itself informed on demographic developments, and the relevant attitudes of its people. In an area where almost every community has a population more than 30 per cent Catholic and many more than 50 per cent, the first responsibility of Church authority would seem to be knowledge of its people, particularly those living in the areas adjacent to the census tracts housing the concentration of Negro population. These could be explosive areas. Since it is possible to acquire the knowledge necessary to determine this state, it would seem mandatory that it be gathered.

In a word, the challenge facing the suburban Church is the challenge to become competent. If the Church does have a social mission, if it does need scientific knowledge to operate as an effective body and to anticipate change, then it must incorporate the social scientist into its structure or train its key personnel in social studies. This it has not done; worse yet, there seems to be little evidence that there is an awareness of the problem. Playing the race problem "by ear," with the slimmest of all budgets, while the pathology of the problem is still small enough to be manageable, strikes one as an abuse of the talent and resources of white Catholic suburbia.

V.

THE MIDWEST

DATING from the 1880's and 1890's when Archbishop John Ireland of St. Paul almost uniquely in the Church and society at large struggled against segregation, the Midwest has been the locus of ferment for reform in the Church. Liturgical reform, for example, springing first from Benedictine monasteries in Minnesota, Indiana, Kentucky and Kansas, took root in neighboring dioceses a decade before it caught on elsewhere in the nation. The Christian Family Movement, the Young Christian Workers and the Young Christian Students originated and seem to thrive more vigorously in the Midwest than in the East. All three of these represent new departures from the more traditional forms of Catholic organizations. Bishop Bernard Sheil, auxiliary of Chicago in the 1930's and 1940's, was the only bishop (after Cardinal Gibbons and Archbishop John Lancaster Spalding of Peoria) to champion the labor movement publicly and consistently. Nor was it a mere coincidence that the two wings of the Catholic interracial movement shifted their headquarters from New York to Chicago: Friendship House in the 1940's and the Catholic Interracial Council in the late 1950's. Most of the reform-minded Catholic newspapers, including *The Oklahoma Courier* (Oklahoma City), *The Catholic Messenger* (Davenport), *The St. Louis Review, The Criterion* (Indianapolis) and *The National Catholic Reporter* (Kansas City) publish from the Midwest.

How or why this leaven exists is not a matter that can be

readily explained. It could perhaps be simply a time-lag in response to the same stimuli or problems. For example, Chicago had its Cicero riot in 1951; six years later Philadelphia had its Levittown—a remarkably similar affair to Cicero. On the other hand, Catholic action both by Father Sauer the local pastor in Skokie, Illinois, and John McDermott, the president of the Chicago Catholic Interracial Council, helped the situation in that suburb when a Negro couple, Lois and David Jones, moved into an all-white neighborhood. But two years later the even more Catholic suburb of Rockville Centre, New York, prevented, when faced with an identical situation, a Negro doctor from buying a $50,000 home. Are these contrary examples of Catholics' response to identical stimuli, explainable as a simple matter of individual differences? Or are they reactions springing from some regional characteristic?

The basis of the commonly held belief that the Midwest is the source of reform movements in the Church is not without evidence. Our purpose here, however, is not to settle that question but rather to examine how the Church in several of these dioceses responds to the racial issue. Because these are for the most part those discussed in relation to the dioceses treated above—bussing vs. the neighborhood school, the changing neighborhood in the inner city, the restricted white residential areas in the suburbs, Negro unemployment and job discrimination, urban renewal and others[1]—we shall omit most of the historical analysis from the present section.

DETROIT: KEEPING ABREAST OF CHANGE

The Midwestern response to these problems has been radical and energetic. Detroit, however, displayed little activity before

1. If there is any difference in the number or variety of these problems it would seem that Chicago had one extra problem: that of desegregating its Rainbow Beach, perhaps the city's most attractive area. This it did in the summer of 1961 with substantial help from the Catholic Interracial Council, the YCS, the YCW and several priests.

the winter of 1963–1964. About that time the Archbishop's Human Relations Commission began studying and planning for social change on the parish level. As a result, it became clear to the Commission that the archdiocese's roots were very weak on the lower reaches of the social scale. Detroit Catholicism was, in other words, almost exclusively middle class and there was danger of losing the lower classes completely. Negro migration to the city was increasing more rapidly than Chicago and if present trends continued it would be over more than 50 per cent Negro in less than 20 years. Archbishop Dearden's reaction was a mixture of awe for the problems the migrants would bring, and determination that the archdiocese would face up to its spiritual and social responsibilities. The Commission has for over two years now been sending in teams to the city's poorer parishes to assist in policy and structural reform that will enable them to meet the inevitable social change.

A notable parish that has undergone such a transformation is Most Holy Trinity in Corktown, a run-down neighborhood in the inner city. Here the pastor, Monsignor Clement Kern, has obliterated the old formal structure. The rectory, for example, while it does house the clergy, is also a community headquarters where social workers, youth leaders, doctors or sociologists meet to discuss and plan their activities. Dinner time will frequently find laymen, priests and Little Brothers of Jesus—whoever happens to be working there—sharing the meal. Several other parishes are likewise changing form.

In order to keep the clergy abreast of social change and keep himself informed, the archbishop convenes a diocesan meeting monthly with some 50 to 70 priests at each one. Here a sociologist, social worker or city planner discusses problems relating to the future of the archdiocese. Through the Michigan Catholic Conference of which Archbishop Dearden is chairman, all the dioceses of the state are associated with the Federal Economic Opportunity Program. Archdiocesan administrative structures and offices are heavily utilized. This undoubtedly is one reason why Michigan seems to be one of the most effective areas in the nation's war on poverty.

Detroit was also, along with St. Louis, the first to adopt Project Equality. Designed by the National Catholic Conference for Interracial Justice, this project utilizes the purchasing power of the archdiocese as a lever to prod all who sell to Catholic institutions into active efforts to recruit Negroes. It is a sophisticated operation, based on sound legal and economic principles which give it the capacity to enforce its program. The guiding hand in this and most of the diocesan policy in interracial affairs is the director of the Archbishop's Commission on Human Relations, Father James Shehan—one of the first Catholic priests to arrive at Selma. It is significant, incidentally, that neither Father Shehan nor Mr. William Sweeney, who handled the logistics for the Detroit delegation to Selma, felt any need to get episcopal approval for that operation.

Undoubtedly, the key to the future of this archdiocese and its stance toward the racial problem is to be found in the outlines for diocesan reform drawn in the spring of 1966. These outlines or suggestions grew from an eight-week discussion the archbishop held with some 100 laymen. The major decision to emerge from these talks was to hold a diocesan synod in the spring of 1967, where clergy, religious and laity will legislate for the future development of the diocese. A clue to what will probably emerge from this historic event might be had from the archbishop's observation on "the big parish": "A parish of such huge proportions has to be broken up into several areas . . . to try to deal with it as one great formless mass is foolish." The prevailing rule in pastoral appointments in Detroit, even now, is talent and ability, not seniority. From the point of view of the race problem in the inner city an equally promising item on the synod agenda is that support in dollars and personnel is to be levied on the more affluent suburban parishes for the poorer ones. The archdiocese of Detroit, therefore, inasmuch as it has faced the need for structural reform directly and proceeded with it, seems to be of all American dioceses the best equipped to face the mounting influx of Negro poor.

MILWAUKEE: CONSCIENCE VS. AUTHORITY

The salient feature of the response of this archdiocese to the problems arising from the city's Negro areas resembles those of Detroit: internal reform. Strong differences of opinion—over the wisdom of clergy participation in sit-ins and other protest tactics—between Archbishop William Cousins and his Auxiliary Bishop Roman Atkielski on the one side, and the priests and sisters of the troubled areas on the other, have led to the formation of a Civil Rights Council. The clergy in the Negro areas were authorized by the ordinary in January, 1966, to form a council "to act and to advise as a recognized religious entity." With a considerable degree of autonomy from the chancery, the new organization is designed to pool the knowledge of the clergy most intimately involved in the problems of interracial justice and to make decisions binding on all its members. While curbing what some chancery officials regarded as rash behavior by individual priests who supported boycotts against the city's public schools, the new council would still permit such action if it were the result of a majority decision. Archbishop Cousins has apparently recognized, by authorizing this council, the right of his clergy to disagree with him and to follow their collective conscience. The problem of individual conscience in conflict with the council still remains; but shortly after its formation there seemed to be widespread agreement among the priests on the feasibility of the compromise. They seemed satisfied that it removed—between themselves and the archbishop—an antagonism which, however, emerged in October, 1965, while Archbishop Cousins was in Rome for the Ecumenical Council.

It started when a local civil rights group called a boycott of public schools to protest the *de facto* segregation in the school system. "Freedom schools" were to be conducted with the cooperation of 40 priests and nuns. Marilyn Morheuser, executive coordinator of the civil rights group staging the boycott, reported that more than a dozen priests and 25 nuns had agreed to serve as "principals" and teachers. Bishop Atkielski, acting head of the diocese, forbade the use of any parish facility for this purpose, and cited an opinion by the district attorney that the boycott was illegal.

Then the clergymen and nuns personally involved in the boycott turned to an unprecedented action. They held a four-hour meeting after which they issued a statement about the bishop's order. They said they would obey it "with sorrow and regret." But, they added: "In our consciences, we do not see his direction based on a legal opinion as morally binding with the force of Christ's words." Their protest was underscored two days later when four priests led by Father James Groppi and nuns at St. Boniface parish took out an advertisement in the *Milwaukee Journal.* In part the advertisement read:

> As priests and sisters, servants of our parishes, we were faced with the choice of obeying the Bishop, in which case we feel that our Church fails to give its true Christian witness here . . .
>
> On the other hand, should we disobey the Bishop, we feel that at this time in our Church many would not be able to understand our actions because they are not yet ready to receive the full impact of Vatican II.
>
> With every protest short of direct disobedience and with the conviction that we are substantially betraying our people, but with the hope that we might be wrong, we revert to the basic training we have been given and reluctantly we have closed our parish facilities to the use of freedom schools.

This was a case illustrating one of the thorniest problems facing the Church today: the clash of conscience and legitimate authority. A few days later the bishop ordered two priests—Fathers James Groppi and William J. Whelan—who were most active in the boycott to cease participation. Shortly after this action a group of Catholic laymen picketed the chancery in protest against the bishop's order and charged that it violated not only freedom of conscience, but also abused the Church's authority over its clergy. The picket line was organized by a group called Catholics for Social Responsibility. The group's spokesman, Paul Byrne, an assistant professor in Marquette University, declared: "In every diocese there is a conservative faction that exercises the decisions. The non-conservatives usually grumble quietly to themselves. We felt it was no longer possible to grumble quietly."

The number of priests and sisters involved here gave to this conflict of conscience and authority a collective dimension lacking in the cases—which we shall review shortly—of Fathers William DuBay and John Coffield in the Los Angeles archdiocese. The idiosyncratic element was obliterated and the problem henceforth began to receive serious attention on a national scale. The Milwaukee archdiocese, furthermore, by the formation of its Civil Rights Council, has given free play to the energies of those of its clergy most directly concerned with the racial problem.

CHICAGO: FROM CICERO TO THE SOUTH SIDE

The history of race relations in Chicago has been among the stormiest in the entire country. With one of the largest Negro populations in the nation—Chicago Negroes numbered over 800,000 in 1960—penned into a narrow ghetto walled about by economic barriers and white prejudice, it could hardly have been otherwise. Chicago is, moreover, one of the most Catholic cities in the country. Time after time Negroes, in their efforts to break out of the ghetto, have encountered the resolute opposition of the city's white Catholics; it was no isolated phenomenon when during the city's widely publicized racial incident in the summer of 1966, Martin Luther King's marches into Southwest Side communities, many of the white teenagers who demonstrated against the marchers wore scapulars around their neck and sweatshirts emblazoned with the names of Catholic schools. Similarly, massive demonstrations in the summer of the preceding year, demanding the ouster of School Superintendent Benjamin Willis for allegedly not desegregating the public schools, had, like the Cicero riot of 14 years earlier, a strong Catholic flavor. These incidents represent different sectors of Catholic opinion—but nevertheless there can be no doubt as to the crucial problems they portend for the future.

In the interval btween 1951 and 1965, the leadership of the Catholic interracial movement shifted from New York to Chicago. A tracing of the relationship between the Church and the Negro in Chicago should be, therefore, particularly revealing of progress made and problems unresolved.

Though Chicago's very first resident frontiersman was a Negro Catholic—Baptiste Pointe du Sable, who arrived in 1795—it was not until the 1890's that he was followed by significant numbers who shared both his color and his creed. During those years—the last decade of the 19th century and the first decade of the 20th—Negro migrant groups were arriving to join the half-million foreign-born who had already found their way to Chicago. In providing for their spiritual welfare the ordinary, Bishop Patrick Feehan, decided to follow the same practice he had initiated for the other immigrants: he gave them a church and a pastor of their own. The church was St. Monica's, at 36th and Dearborn Streets; the priest, a Negro named Tolton "imported" from Peoria. The great migration of Southern Negroes to the North during and after World War I brought greater numbers of them to the Chicago area. Most were Methodists and Baptists (though they included a few Catholics from Louisiana), and the task of the Church was not, as with the white immigrants, one of conserving their Catholic faith; the challenge the Negro presented was one of conversion. About 1921 Archbishop—later Cardinal—George Mundelein invited a missionary order, the Divine Word Fathers, to come to Chicago and take over the apostolate to the Negro, while his diocesan priests continued their work among the white Catholics, both native and foreign-born. In 1924 Father Joseph Eckert, S.V.D., was assigned to the Church of St. Elizabeth at 41st Street and Michigan Avenue, in the heart of what had already begun to be known as "the black belt."

He made many converts over the next years, but St. Elizabeth's was, in fact if not in intention, what we would call today a "Jim Crow church"; no whites worshipped there, and Father Eckert, who considered all Catholic Negroes members of "his" flock even if moved to another section of the city, expected all to return to St. Elizabeth's to be confirmed, to be married, to have their children baptized, even to receive the final rites. In the next few years several other "Negro churches" were established, all of them in the hands of religious orders rather than the diocesan clergy. But by the late 1930's the growing Negro population had seeped into some 20 other parishes, and Cardinal Mundelein realized that turning over the care of the Catholics among them to missionary orders could not continue; instead, pastors of the parishes affected were permitted to establish their own policy. For the most part the policy they set was one of segregation, except at Mass and the administration of the sacraments: parish societies and the parochial schools were closed to the Negro.

World War II brought a new influx of Negroes to the City and a movement outward from the ghetto of those already there. The number of "white" parishes "threatened" by Negro "invasion" nearly doubled, and in some, Negroes came to predominate. And as that has occurred more and more during the war and post-war years, the problem for the Church has become acute. As Father Anthony Vader writes:

> There is a marked decline in the attendance at Sunday Mass [because so few Negroes are Catholics] and also the concomitant drop in parish revenue. School enrollment drops off, and there is less and less participation in parish activities. The Catholic families are abandoning the neighborhood, and then the parish seems on the way downward.
>
> Soon the neighborhood becomes predominantly Negro. Its whole social pattern becomes that of a Negro community. Basically, this state is realized when the family life of the neighborhood is Negro, even though segments of the white population remain, such as elderly people, single people, or an occasional white family down on its luck. At this stage, the whole course of the parish Catholic church

has been decided, for better or worse, depending on the policy established before the neighborhood changed completely.[1]

The process of change has continued, of course, for after the Korean War the Negro population again burst from its boundaries and spread out to adjoining communities. Two reasons were behind the movement. First, the Supreme Court had in 1948 declared restrictive covenants legally unenforceable. Second, after the war (in many cases with savings accumulated during it), Negroes were economically prepared to move into better areas and purchase property there. Naturally, more parishes than ever have been affected by racial change. Today 66 of the 281 parishes within the city limits—nearly one in four—have Negro families living within their boundaries. Ten of these are located in nearly 100 per cent colored communities; eighteen others, in areas more than 80 per cent Negro; seven more, in sections more than 50 per cent Negro. Within the next five years, it is estimated that 24 additional presently "white" parishes will see the entrance of Negroes.

Parishes

The pastors of the affected parishes reacted to this demographic change in one of three ways: by outright opposition—encouraging community organizations which purchased property to keep Negroes out; by apathy—often springing from indecision, from unwillingness to hurt the feelings of "old-timers," or simply from inability to oppose the participation of Negroes in the parish; or, finally, by welcoming the new families.

When a pastor made the decision actively to assist his white parishioners in their efforts to "keep them [that is, Negroes] out," he took the easiest available course. He was in sympathy with the interests of the white majority in preserving the status quo. His parishioners' desires to protect real-estate values coincided with his own desire to protect the property value of the parish plant. In a number cases it was he who had built the

1. *The Catholic Church and the Negro in Chicago,* unpublished Master's Thesis, Chicago, 1962.

parish; his parishioners were devoted to it, and its strong community ties were being threatened. The customary fears associated with racial change were rampant: fear of an increased crime rate; fear of interracial contacts, leading possibly to interracial marriage; fear of economic losses; fear on the part of white Catholics that they would become a minority, and thus lose social status.

Some priests gave active or passive support to so-called "improvement associations" designed to keep Negroes out.[1] That meant, in some cases, participating directly with the community leaders who were organizing to buy up any homes offered for sale, and then to make sure they were sold to white families. As recently as July, 1961, one of these pastors participated in such a negotiation. Though he was visiting on the West Coast at the time, he made three long-distance telephone calls to Chicago within 24 hours offering his advice. The board of the "improvement association" was stalemated, and it was the pastor's calls that somehow resulted in the sale of the home to a noncolored family. In another instance a pastor served as a character reference for teenagers who were on trial for murdering a Negro boy. And in another instance a pastor testified for gradeschool children who had tossed a Molotov cocktail on the porch of a newly arrived Negro family.

But by 1964 this type of activity had almost entirely ceased. Such men have either retired, been relocated or are silent. Some have even made complete reversals in their position. Yet passive assistance to "improvement associations" still exists in the archdiocese. Without directly participating in the operation of the organization, a pastor may lead prayers at association meetings, allow his parish facilities to be used or let it be known quietly that he agrees with the position of the association. But as chancery officials take firmer positions for racial justice, even this kind of support is dying out.

1. In local jargon, an "improvement association" is generally regarded as a group which engages in "keep them out" activity, whereas a "community council" seeks to maintain a community's standards regardless of the race of the persons within it.

Such resistance to incoming Negroes as still exists in the parochial network centers mostly in the national parish, and in a few regular diocesan parishes run by hard-core "anti-Negro" pastors.

In 1950 there were 138 national parishes in the city of Chicago. Forty-three were Polish, 27 German, 12 Italian, 10 Lithuanian, eight Bohemian and eight Slovakian. There were also five French, four Croatian, two Slovenian, two Hungarian, two Mexican and one Dutch, Belgian, Melkite, Chaldean and Chinese parishes. But during the following decade, with European immigration slowed to a trickle and the rush to the suburbs beginning, many of the established patterns of the national parishes were upset. It became increasingly difficult to hold the younger generations: the housing was getting older, the neighborhood shabbier. For the most part, therefore, it was the foreign-born and the second generation who stayed behind, and in the few national parishes where they remain in the majority the resistance to newcomers is still formidable. Often the pastor is just as concerned as his parishioners with living out his life amid the security of old friends and familiar traditions.

Many national parishes also have served another little-known function. Fathers François Houtart and Norbert Lacoste, in a study entitled "The Parishes of Chicago, 1843–1953: Historical Evolution, Geography, Population, Ecology," make the observation that it was the national parishes that formed the boundary lines for the adjoining all-Negro communities.

> We have observed that the Negroes try to settle down near the industrial areas, but that most of them [industrial areas] were occupied by national groups. Their only alternative then was to settle down in the in-between area. This is true for their penetration toward the west. The central part of the city offers an area completely devoid of any national parishes.

The study also examined other areas of the city in relation to national parishes:

> On the South Side the colored people are east of almost all the national parishes. They don't penetrate, for example, the "Back of the Yards" area.

In South Chicago, near the steel mills, there are Negroes. Their number, however, is still low. Here they have settled down exactly south of the section where the national parishes are located. Finally east of the Lake Calumet we see the colored occupying territories situated to the left or to the right of an area having 12 national parishes.

As sociologists, Fathers Houtart and Lacoste gave this explanation of national parishes and areas of Negro occupancy:

> . . . the constant correlation between the two factors: presence of national parishes and non-penetration of Negroes seems to have some meaning. When a community has strong institutions the social cohesion of the group is high. This means that the group will resist much more strongly any kind of self-disintegration . . . We may suppose that this is the case with the national parishes. They are a factor of resistance against dislocation of the group. We may suspect that as long as they have such an impact on the community the areas of resistance will continue to be the same.

There is another kind of parish in Chicago which has been the seat of racial troubles—most recently in the summer of 1966. This is the parish populated by members of two or three various first and second-generation nationalities. Unlike the national parishes, they are directly under diocesan control, but their resistance to racial change has been almost as strong as that of the old-fashioned national parish. When civil rights demonstrators marched into one such area, a priest of the local Catholic Church, St. Rita of Cacia, advised his people from the pulpit to stay loyal to their neighborhood; that if they remained united, the drive to break down racial barriers would fail. Fear of the Negro, or perhaps hatred, moved people of this and numerous other parishes to the violence that was unleashed on the marchers.

Besides the few national parishes where racial problems persist, there remain a few headed by hard-core "anti-Negro" pastors unresigned to looking upon Negroes as members of the human race. Some parishes of this kind are on the border of Negro areas, some are removed from them, and one exists within a colored neighborhood. This last is located in an upper-middle-income Negro area, and the speeches of the pastor—who has since been retired—have been responsible for a deluge of letters to the chancery office, loss of at least a dozen people to the Church, and an unpleasant view of Catholicism among this most influential segment of Chicago Negro society.

Elementary Schools

Even more than some other areas of parish life, the parochial elementary school is a good yardstick for measuring the progress of integration. Unlike membership in a parish society, attendance at some school is an essential. Furthermore, in Chicago as elsewhere, the Catholic elementary school has appealed even to non-Catholic Negro parents because they believe its discipline to be superior to that of the public school, and because they admire the total dedication of the nuns and brothers to their young charges. Negroes who might not come to Mass (because they are not Catholic or because their canonical obligation sits as lightly upon them as it does upon some of their white co-religionists), or who would not join the parish societies (because they do not want to be pioneers or because the activities of the societies simply do not interest them) may still seek to have their children enrolled in the parish school.

The elementary schools of the archdiocese are, of course, creatures of the parishes, and their policies in racial matters have been set by the pastor. Thus, if the school was connected with a national parish or one in which the pastor had anti-Negro sentiments, the school reflected this attitude. Conversely, a pastor who welcomed incoming Negroes invited them to send their children to the parochial school.

Father Vader's study showed that by 1960 in 37 territorial parishes in neighborhoods more than 50 per cent Negro, the percentage of such pupils in the schools was usually a fair reflection of the neighborhood. There were exceptions; some could be explained by the fact that the school was small and the classrooms were already filled with the children of the "original" white families. In parishes where the containing neighborhood was only slightly Negro, the record was frequently scandalous. Where there would obviously be no space problem, Negro Catholics would be referred to "their own parish." Again, the most frequent offender in this category was the national parish. The blow to discrimination on this level of Catholic education was struck at the Clergy Conference of 1960 by Cardinal Meyer when he personally nullified, one by one, the specific excuses or evasions traditionally used by pastors or principals to discriminate.

Father Vader cites several instances, up to perhaps 1964, of direct intervention by the chancery to force integration in parochial schools and concludes: "In general, we can say that today no pastor would dare refuse a Negro child in his school . . . the pastor would not contradict the archbishop." Not all pastors may be happy about the situation, but they obey.

Meanwhile the problem of *de facto* segregation in these schools is no less serious than that facing the public schools. There are an estimated 38 parochial schools whose enrollment is over 90 per cent Negro. The huge white enrollment on the other hand, reduces the number of white pupils available to offset racial imbalance in the public schools. Cooperation and compromise by the Catholic school system therefore seems mandatory if this problem is to be resolved.

Secondary Schools

In contrast to the elementary school, which is attached to a parish and draws its students from the parochial territory, most of the 92 Catholic high schools in the archdiocese have no territorial limits or boundaries. Moreover, all but a few are owned and administered either by the archdiocese or by religious orders, and are therefore much less subject to prejudice on the part of parents or pastors. There are several grounds for considering high schools the brightest area of Negro-white interrelationships in the archdiocese.

In the first place, one may consider the tuition problem, crucial to many Negro applicants. Ability to pay does not constitute a necessary stumbling block to attendance. Catholic high school tuition fees range from approximately $50 to $400 per year (exclusive of boarding schools), but many offer either full or partial scholarships, a great many of which are awarded to Negroes. Moreover, the Catholic Interracial Council has had an active scholarship program for many years; at its high point it was sending 49 students to Catholic high schools. In half the cases, the Council paid the tuition; for the others, the schools themselves donated the tuition. The Council awarded the scholarships on the basis of scholastic ability, maturity and financial need. Moreover, its purpose was partly missionary; it strove to get its Negro scholarship students admitted to schools which did not have Negro students. When one of these Negro teenage pioneers persevered, there was often a growing willingness on the part of school authorities to accept other Negroes.

Secondly, one may consider the progress made over the last nine or 10 years. In 1956 the Council conducted a high school integration survey. Seventy-five of the 81 schools then in existence responded, and the results showed that 37 had Negro students totaling 493 (exclusive of the two all-Negro high schools, which had a combined total of 603). At that time, 20 schools had no Negroes. Thirteen of these never had had any, seven did not have any in 1956, though they had had some in prior years. Since 1956 great strides have been made in the Catholic high schools—especially those for boys. One of the main reasons for the progress has been the dynamic leadership of priests in all-Negro parishes who wanted their graduates to be able to attend any high school. They have been able to convince high schools to accept sizable numbers of their Negro elementary school graduates. The priests are now trying to encourage Negro girls, too, to attend Catholic high schools, especially those where none or very few colored girls are presently enrolled. There is a great pressure being exerted by the predominantly Negro high schools to attract these girls, so the priests are in the position of holding off these schools with one hand while trying to break down segregation in other high schools.

Finally, one may consider the example set by some Catholic

high schools whose concern for interracial justice goes beyond admission policies. Two of them cancelled contracts at swimming pools because the pools would not admit their Negro students. Another, located in a changing area, expelled two girls who had distributed racist literature. Still a third school cancelled a contract with an employment agency when that agency refused to place one of its Negro graduates. And the high schools in general have had an excellent record of participation with the Catholic Interracial Council in study days, pilot-training programs for teachers, distribution of human relations literature, and so forth.

Yet when one goes beneath the surface of this record, a deeper problem becomes evident. The presence of a representative number from a minority group in a high school indicates not integration so much but simply the end of discriminatory admission policies. Integration has social and psychological dimensions that can be explored only by deeper probing. Even simple observation reveals that voluntary segregation by race prevails in clubs, informal groups, social affairs and so forth, in partically all of the 35 Catholic high schools—not rigidly and presumably not maliciously, but commonly nonetheless.

Father Vader also probed, by interview, administrative attitudes in these schools. He attempted to "rate" these 35 high schools according to the following scale: "P" indicated a positive attitude on the part of the administration, in that the school was happy to have already enrolled Negro students or would willingly and unhesitatingly enroll them; "G" indicated that the administration was "glad" to enroll Negroes, that its official attitude went beyond mere tolerance; "I" stood for an indifferent school which did not seem to care one way or another about enrolling Negro students; "U" represented a school definitely "unhappy" with the Negroes it had accepted; and "N" for "negative" was the lowest rating—schools so rated did not want Negroes enrolled at all.

Of the 21 institutions conducted by religious orders, only three received a "P" rating; all three are conducted by the same order, the Christian Brothers. Three others had a "G" rating;

one rated "I," eight rated "U," and six were definitely classified "N." The 14 diocesan schools, on the other hand, did much better: three rated "P," six rated "G," and only two were in the "negative" category.

Father Vader concluded—and his evidence is convincing—that in schools operated by the diocese, and therefore under the archbishop's control, admission policies and the general attitude of the administration toward Negroes is good and getting better; in those owned and taught by religious orders, and therefore freer to pursue an independent policy, the record is far less impressive. Many of these latter, he found had accepted their first colored children only after direct pressure by the chancery office.

A final word about the Catholic school system in this archdiocese. After the New York, Chicago, Philadelphia and perhaps Los Angeles public school systems, the parochial school system of Chicago ranks 4th or 5th largest in the nation. With an enrollment of some 365,000 pupils, its welfare is inseparable from the public welfare—and vice versa. Perhaps nowhere else in the nation is the interdependence between the Catholic and public schools—and the *de facto* segregation that faces both—so evident.

Universities and Colleges

There are two Catholic universities and four colleges in the archdiocese. The two universities—Loyola and De Paul—are co-educational, drawing their student bodies from the whole of Chicago. The four colleges are for women—Rosary, Barat, Mundelein and Xavier. All have dormitory facilities and draw students from across the country.

The colleges, while they cannot be described as well-integrated, give no evidence of discrimination. De Paul has a Negro enrollment of close to 20 per cent and Loyola also has a significant number of Negroes. There are Negro and foreign students enrolled in all four women's colleges. Some problems do exist which are not necessarily the fault of the institutions themselves.

There are still fraternities and sororities, for example, which discriminate against Negro students; these are nationally based and pose the same problem on college campuses across the country. The students can request room-mates, and no objection is raised to an interracial arrangement. Also, there are Negro teachers in the two co-educational colleges as well as in the four women's colleges. What is perhaps more important is the active participation of students and faculty in the activities of the Catholic Interracial Council and the existence of campus organizations focused on racial problems.

Seminaries

There were, in 1966, approximately 1,500 students in the archdiocesan major and minor seminaries. There are two Negroes in the major seminary, Our Lady of the Lake, at Mundelein, and between 30 and 40 at Quigley, the minor seminary. Today there are over 2,700 priests in the archdiocese (1,200 diocesan, 1,500 members of religious orders). Of these 2,700, there are less than 10 Negroes.

The fact that there are so few diocesan Negro priests is attributable to discrimination, at least so far as the past is concerned. In 1942 a Negro student in his senior year at Loyola University wanted to enter the major seminary of the diocese. He was told to wait until he heard from the seminary. No word was forthcoming, and with the draft board pressing, the student entered a religious order and today is a priest of that order. In 1945 the first Negro boy entered the minor seminary of the diocese and went on through the major seminary to become, in 1957, the first Negro priest trained by and ordained for the archdiocese. He was not the first Negro priest to attend the major seminary, however. Some years before, a brilliant Negro student at the Univesity of Chicago had been converted to the faith, entered the major seminary and was ordained in 1949. A third Negro priest has also gone through both the major and minor seminaries and was ordained in 1960.

Although there was difficulty in getting into diocesan seminaries prior to 1945, another reason there were not more Negro applicants for these seminaries was the system of separate churches for Negroes. Staffed by various religious orders and established by the archdiocese in the 1920's, these churches and their schools produced a number of vocations which, quite naturally, were siphoned off into the religious orders which had trained them. (The Negro boy who entered the minor seminary in 1945 had, in fact, planned to attend a seminary of a religious order. It was only the prompting of various priests and laymen of the diocese that induced him to apply at the diocesan seminary.) Then too one must consider that priestly vocations most likely come from the middle class rather than the low or poverty-level classes. Since the Negro family has had greater representation in the latter than in the former, it could not produce the volume of vocations expected from a middle-class group.

Hospitals and Nursing Schools

There are 23 Catholic hospitals in the archdiocese, excluding those devoted to specialized medical care. Of these, 16 are located within the city limits and seven in the suburbs. Less than 10 years ago their treatment of the Negro was scandalous. One index of their old admission policies is to be had in the statistics on Negro births. In 1956 the 16 in the city accounted for 5.3 per cent of such births in the Chicago complex of some 52 hospitals. But this average included Lewis Memorial Hospital which alone accounted for 39 per cent of Negro hospital births. Of the other 15 Catholic institutions, one had 5.5 per cent, one had 1.8 per cent and another 1.3 per cent. The rest had percentages below 1 per cent—two had zero. Discriminatory maternity policies were common, as they were in other medical categories to a somewhat lesser degree. What has happened since then is a matter of erratic improvement stemming from policy and neighborhood changes. Four of the containing neighborhoods of these hospitals became predominantly Negro and the relevant statistics indicate that the four Catholic hospitals began to assume a more proportionate share of the Negro cases.

Exactly how equitable a share they carry is a matter that would require a separate investigation.

What is true of the Catholic high schools of the archdiocese is true of the hospitals: the record of those directly under the control of the archbishop has been far better than that of the privately owned institutions. Unfortunately, there are only three diocesan hospitals, and none is a general hospital: one is for maternity cases only, the other two are "homes" for infants' care.

As long ago as 1955 the late Cardinal Samuel Stritch, addressing a conference of hospital administrators sponsored by the Catholic Interracial Council, spoke out strongly against any discrimination within Catholic hospitals. Twelve years later injustice is fading rapidly from this scene; but not its memory. Among Chicago's Negroes, Catholic hospitals have a reputation as being discriminatory, and the reputation, over the years, has been earned. It is not likely that a Negro would be refused treatment today by any of the non-diocesan hospitals; indeed, in their clinics and out-patient departments nearly all of them accept and treat colored persons in large numbers every day. And the same is true on a smaller scale with respect to in-patients. This change has come about only in the last three or four years. It was common to treat Negro emergency patients and then, if they required hospitalization, to send them to other institutions.

In their own defense the non-diocesan hospitals adduced two arguments: first, that "the doctors want it that way," and second, that most Negro patients do not pay their bills.

The first contention was probably true. But it is worth pointing out that few of these institutions made much effort to add significant numbers of Negro physicians to their staffs: the three diocesan hospitals had, in 1963, as many colored staff members as the 10 private institutions combined. The second argument was more difficult to evaluate. A disproportionate share of the Negro cases were charity cases. And since patient fees are much more important to the nondiocesan hospital, which gets no aid from the archdiocese and must pay its own way if it is to survive, they undoubtedly put limits on the number of such cases. The whole problem was (and still is) tied up with payments and subsidies from Catholic Charities and the city Welfare Department. Today little evidence can be garnered to support a charge of racial injustice against Catholic hospitals.

The Archdiocese and the Community

The major impact of the city of Chicago came through its Archdiocesan Office of Urban Affairs (AOUA), headed originally by Monsignor John Egan. In what was probably its first public appearance, the AOUA shocked the political world of Chicago by opposing one of its major urban-renewal projects on the ground that the residents would be uprooted. Equally controversial was its involvement with Saul Alinsky's Industrial Areas Foundation (IAF). The IAF strategy is oriented toward the development of economic and political power among victim groups as a means of combatting injustice and controlling neighborhood change. The IAF, like Alinsky himself, has been charged with being power-hungry, subversive, Machiavellian and Communist, and for the Church to be even remotely associated with such a group provoked the sharpest attacks. Yet, faced with uncontrolled and devastating social deterioration in once prosperous parishes, Cardinal Meyer and his AOUA chose to experiment with Alinsky methods.

In 1959 one of the Foundation's offshoots, the Organization for the Southwest Community, united about 125 neighborhood groups into a supra-civic organization. At the urging of the chancery office, pastors cooperated with the organization and gave it strong financial support. It faced the problems of the neighborhood transition, by controlling the rate of influx and exodus. It has, for example, set up a low down-payment mortgage pool which has given out over two million dollars in mortgages money to both whites and Negroes. It has been active in reducing racial tension in areas into which Negroes have moved for the first time. It has an integrated board of directors and has fought for open-occupancy legislation and equal availability of classroom facilities. In 1961 its efforts were honored by an award from the Catholic Interracial Council.

The Temporary Woodlawn Organization set up in 1960 by the Industrial Areas Foundation was also supported by the archdiocese. In its first year it challenged the policies of the Board of Education, accusing it of segregation and discrimination and objecting particularly to double-shift classroom situations. As one of its first acts, it opposed the establishment of a "South Campus" by the University of Chicago which would necessarily have entailed razing one-seventh of the Woodlawn area. It asked that the Woodlawn community be brought in on the planning of its future, and this was done. It was also active in fair-credit campaigns and housing problems. The role of the Church in this organization was not as direct as in the OSC, though the pastor of the local parish was whole-heartedly behind it and has worked diligently for the organization. Other denominations are just as active and have just as important a role as the pastor, but some priests have referred to the actions of TWO as the Church's operations.

All things considered, then, the Archdiocesan Office for Urban Affairs, in its alliance with the Alinsky organizations, has contributed to a unique democratic experiment: the development of political and economic power at the community level, independent of the ordinary political processes. In more personal terms, the thousands of individuals living in the OSC and TWO areas are far better off, better organized and capable of self-help because of the Alinsky groups and their religious allies. (Protestant and Jewish clergy were also involved.)

It came as a shock to all in the forefront of social reform in Chicago when the AOUA's director, Monsignor John Egan, was given another full-time assignment in the spring of 1965. Appointed a pastor, he retains his post with the Urban office; but the responsibilities of the latter task are secondary to the former. What is more significant, however, is that the archbishop's desire to "run a tight ship" narrows the range of action the AOUA once had. This move, combined with a similar one for Monsignor Daniel Cantwell who was engaged full-time in interracial work, seems to be consonant with the reputation of Archbishop John Cody as a Church-oriented administrator. In contrast, it is widely believed that the late Cardinal Meyer viewed the Church as serving the community. The energy and vitality of Catholic participation in the social problems of the area can be traced in substantial measure to the support given by the Cardinal to the operations of both the Egan and Cantwell offices, and to the convening in late 1963 of the Chicago Conference on Religion and Race.

The first interreligious action organization in the history of the city, the Conference fought city hall on *de facto* school segregation, and on the neighborhood level it sent in teams of clergymen to ameliorate incipient riots in racially tense areas. These and other efforts by the Conference, formed by Cardinal Meyer and other religious leaders, indicate a vitality in the formal structure of the archdiocese that can hardly be matched in any other major city.

The Catholic Interracial Council

The Catholic Interracial Council was organized in 1946 with the approval of Cardinal Stritch and enjoyed even stronger support from his immediate successor. It is financed by voluntary contributions and for the last five years has had an annual budget of between $50,000 and $80,000. It has had up to five full-time paid employees (three professionals, two clerical) and operates solely under a lay interracial board of between 40 and 50 members. Sargent Shriver was its president in the mid-1950's.

Since 1958 the Council has been moving more toward direct action rather than education. In 1961 it was the key factor in the peaceful integration of a Negro Catholic couple into suburban Skokie, lobbied for fair-housing legislation, participated in the "wade-in" at Rainbow Beach and developed a plan with the Church Federation and Board of Rabbis to have priests, ministers and rabbis on the beach during the weekends. The Council also helped resolve a very difficult block-busting operation on the west side of the city, and testified at a public hearing of the Temporary Woodlawn Organization in opposition to double-shift schools and for racial integration of the schools.

The Council also took a position critical of the policy of a Catholic hospital which was accused of racial discrimination. Much to the chagrin of the Archdiocesan Director of Catholic Hospitals, it found that there were discriminatory practices in the hospital.

In the summer of 1963 the Council, after the failure of private negotiations, established picket-lines in front of Lewis Towers which housed the Illinois Club for Catholic women. Here, for perhaps the first time in American history, a priest and several nuns walked on a picket-line. Pictures of the spectacle were run in papers all over the world. Chagrined that the cardinal would allow such conduct, the Club soon capitulated and admitted its first Negro women. And in 1966 the Council publicly differed with Archbishop Cody on the need for continuing Dr. King's marches into white neighborhoods.

The National Catholic Conference for Interracial Justice

As the Catholic interracial councils approached their 25th anniversary in 1959, an uneasy feeling grew in many minds that the loose network into which they were woven lacked the power, the dynamism that was becoming increasingly urgent. The Supreme Court desegregation decision of 1954 was failing of implementation, and worse yet, except for a few dioceses, segregation and discrimination were as rampant as ever in the Church. There were many in the Councils who felt that a closer union or federation might be the answer to greater influence.

The call for a national conference of CIC delegates went out from the Chicago Council. Lloyd Davis, Monsignor Cantwell and Sargent Shriver were the principal architects of the conference which was convened in August, 1958. Here a small group was selected to study the problem. It was from this interim committe that came the decision to organize the National Catholic Conference for Interracial Justice.

With a governing board that comprised the most experienced Catholics in the field of race relations and a variety of others with talents in related fields of politics, labor and business, the new organization was launched with an initial budget of about $5,000. Matthew Ahmann was the first executive director. While neither he nor any member of the board of directors was a professional social scientist, most of them were intellectuals with a restlessness for action. Officialdom, in politics or ecclesiastics, was neither their master nor their guide, but a power to be harnessed to reform.

Ahmann and the handful who constituted the original staff had several difficult years that tested their motivation, their family budgets and their perseverance. But in the spring of 1962 Ahmann succeeded in opening a Southern Field Service headquartered in New Orleans which was destined to play a major role in the desegregation of the Catholic institutions of that diocese. In the summer of that year Ahmann approached Rabbi Phillip Hiatt of the Synagogue Council of America and the Reverend J. Oscar Lee of the National Council of Churches with the idea for a national conference on religion and race. With encouragement and financial support from Cardinal Meyer, the rest of the funds needed for the project were raised and the historic conference met at Chicago's Edgewater Beach Hotel in January, 1963. The official conveners of the Conference—the National Council of Churches, The Synagogue Council of America and the National Catholic Welfare Conference, represented the immense political and economic power of organized religion in America. The problem facing the small group of architects who brought the conference into being (in addition to Ahmann, Lee and Hiatt the following should be included: Monsignor Daniel Cantwell, Father John Cronin, Reverend Galen Weaver, Rabbi Marc Tannenbaum and Dr. Nathan Lander) was to build a structure capable of harnessing this power to a war on racism. This was effected before the Conference adjourned. The welding of the three major faiths into a united front for the war on racism was a monumental accomplishment, particularly in view of the fact that it did not have the impact on Vatican II behind it. Yet it was a union that was doomed—paradoxically enough, for practical rather than theological reasons. The internal or bureaucratic problems peculiar to each of the three religious organizations impeded the allocation of both funds and personnel to the NCCR secretariat. It collapsed in 1965.

The Conference on Religion and Race held together long enough, however, to be a major force behind the passage of the civil rights legislation of 1964 and to aid in the establishment of Conferences on Religion and Race in 10 cities. The one in Chicago still thrives and influences the course of civil rights there.

VI.
THE WEST COAST

PERHAPS the most tragic commentary on the negligible contribution of the Catholic Church—indeed of all religious institutions—to the amelioration of the race problem in Los Angeles is to be had in the McCone Report on Watts.[1] In the concluding section, "The Need for Leadership," the Report calls on government, business, labor, the news media and Negro leaders to make specific contributions. The omission of religious leaders is indeed significant. The omission becomes more eloquent when one realizes the great numerical strength and financial resources of the archdiocese of Los Angeles. Of an urban population of some 6,488,791 ("the city proper and its thickly settled adjacent territory"),[2] Catholics comprise 20 per cent. Every 26 days a new church or school building opens up in the archdiocese.

It is not our purpose here to detail the status of segregation and discrimination in Catholic institutions on the West Coast, nor to recount the history of diocesan response to the sequential phases of the race problem as we did in the preceding chapters. For one thing, the number of Negroes on the West Coast has, until the post World War II decades, been small. The estimated number of Negro Catholics is 75,000[3]; in 1966 Los Angeles reported 40,000; and the next largest was the diocese of San

1. *A Report by the Governors Commission on the Los Angeles Riots,* December 2, 1965.

2. The figure and definition are from official UNESCO sources for 1960 and represent an area more congruent with that of the archdiocese.

3. *Our Negro and Indian Missions.*

Francisco with 11,000. This population presents no great challenge (numerically) to Catholic institutions.

With a relatively brief national history behind it and fewer traditions, the West Coast patterns of segregation and discrimination were not as rigid nor as pervasive as in other parts of the nation. The McCone Report, for example, states:

> A Negro in Los Angeles has long been able to sit where he wants in a bus or a movie house, to shop where he wishes, to vote, and to use public facilities without discrimination. The opportunity to succeed is probably unequaled in any other major American city.

In 1964 the Urban League ranked Los Angeles first among 68 cities with respect to housing, employment and income.[1] On the other hand, the growing Negro population, particularly in the Los Angeles area, and its expansion outward from the ghettos, over and above the usual obstacles of deed restrictions and other discriminatory housing practices presented the community at large with the evidence of a mounting race problem.

In the archdiocese of Los Angeles the tone of the Catholic response to the race problem has been set by one man: Cardinal McIntyre. To many he has conveyed the impression that he believes Negroes want segregation. He points out how the Irish, Italians and other ethnic groups cling together. To people who know him, his vision of the race problem is restricted to what might be called the "conspiracy theory." The riots, demonstrations, and so forth which mark the civil rights movement he tends to view as being the work of troublemakers, perhaps Communists. His personal integrity is beyond suspicion, however, and he can hardly be accused of prejudice. It is simply a matter of a very narrow and unrealistic grasp of the problem.

Until perhaps a year ago it was archdiocesan policy that no

1. The same report suggests that the ninefold increase of Negro population in Los Angeles (from 75,000 in 1940 to 650,000 in 1965) "arrived with the anticipation that this dynamic city would somehow spell the end of life's endless problems. To those who have come with high hopes and great expectations and see the success of others so close at hand, failure brings a special measure of frustration and disillusionment."

sermons be preached on the subject of race. Today many priests assert that this policy has not changed. Those who dare to violate what is now called "the unofficial policy" risk displeasure and transfer. The clearest evidence of the diocesan view of the race problem is to be had in the Proposition 14 debate.[1] The cardinal refused to take an official position on it, nor would he allow the clergy to do so. In August, 1964, just two months before the election, the cardinal did join with his fellow bishops in the state in issuing a public statement that "discrimination based solely on race, color, nationality or religion cannot be reconciled with the truth that God has created all men with equal rights and equal dignity."[2]

Nevertheless, nine of California's 14 bishops made no public comment on Proposition 14. Five opposed it: the bishops of San Francisco, Oakland, Sacramento, Stockton and Santa Rosa. They asserted that they felt a moral issue was involved. The strongest statement came from Floyd Begin, bishop of Oakland. He said the Proposition was "of such a nature as to contradict what is clear and universal Catholic teaching on the rights and duties of those who own property." He added that Proposition 14 was "a moral issue insofar as it concedes absolute rights to property owners with no reference to the rights of others."[3]

In Los Angeles startling events took place within the Church because of Proposition 14 and the racial attitudes and policies of Cardinal McIntyre. In June Father William DuBay called a press conference at which he accused Cardinal McIntyre of "gross malfeasance" in the conduct of his office and announced that he had asked Pope Paul to remove him. He was soon joined by Father Terrence Halloran who agreed that the cardinal had repressed all participation in civil rights by diocesan priests and

1. Proposition 14 was a proposed amendment to the state constitution invalidating any law which attempted to govern the right to sell one's property to whomever one pleased. Thus it would invalidate fair-housing legislation.

2. Los Angeles *Herald Examiner,* August 24, 1964.

3. San Francisco *Monitor,* June 26, 1964.

nuns. Also, he made public that the cardinal had prevented any sermons on racial matters from being given in the Los Angeles archdiocese.

The chancery office moved to hush up the incident but without success. The oppressive climate of the archdiocese heretofore known only on a small scale was now exposed to the nation's view.[1] Meanwhile, the Negro Catholics of St. Albert's parish, which was Father DuBay's post at the time of his famous conference, indicated their support for him by sending letters of petition with thousands of signatures to the chancery. Receiving no reply, they concluded that the Church's position on civil rights was fundamentally hypocritical. Moreover, the passage of Proposition 14 (with notorious support from Catholic election districts), was cited by the McCone Commission as one of the aggravating events leading to the first riot in Watts.

What has happened in the archdiocese since that calamity offers little ground for believing that matters have changed. For one thing, the riot did not alter the clergy's point of view. Pastors of the four or five parishes in and around Watts share for the most part the cardinal's attitude toward the race problem. All trouble, they believe, stems from outside agitators or "troublemakers." Said one: "Our people are content . . . this is all the work of troublemakers. Parishioners who do have problems come to the Church. And we always help. If we can't, why we send them to someone who can." Shortly after the riot another pastor insisted: "There's no race problem in Los Angeles. What happened here was the work of a bunch of hoodlums." One pastor, however, Father George Ingrisano, O.Carm., stated in an interview that his parishioners were "angry . . . the clergy has not said nor done what has to be done"—with one exception.

In the summer of 1963 Father Coffield, pastor of Ascension

1. The incredibly naïve policy of suppressing all liberal thought in the archdiocese is further illustrated by the chancery's attempt to prevent Father Hans Küng from speaking at UCLA in 1962 and again in 1964, and in refusing permission to Archbishop Thomas Roberts, S.J., to keep several speaking engagements in the diocese.

parish, which takes in a section of Watts, had recruited 12 seminarians (six from Maryknoll and the others from the archdiocese) to work on neighborhood improvement projects. When white parishioners went to the chancery complaining that the seminarians were working with the NAACP, an organization viewed by right-wing elements as suspicious or subversive, the archdiocesan seminarians withdrew from the project. The following summer, three from Maryknoll returned, and in the tragic summer of 1965 only two were working there. Father Coffield himself had in the meanwhile run afoul of the cardinal for his work in civil rights and in the CFM and YCW. Forbidden by the cardinal to speak on the race problem, he gave one of the most blistering sermons on the rampant racism in Los Angeles ever heard in the archdiocese and called for public penance for the insult inherent in the passage of Proposition 14. In November, 1964, two days after the sermon, he was granted an indefinite leave of absence from the archdiocese. Watts thus lost its most vigorous white Catholic citizen.

One indication that official policy may be changing is the formation of the Archdiocesan Job Finding Bureau. The Bureau cooperates with the Urban League and the State Department of Employment in the task of matching job opportunities to the unemployed. The pastors of the 300 parishes in Los Angeles ask their parishioners to report to them all job openings that they as employers might have. These are then forwarded, with wage and other relevant data, to the Job Finding Bureau.

Monsignor William Johnson, director of the Catholic Welfare Bureau, in referring to the tragedy in Watts also indicated that the official view was becoming more realistic. He observed in an interview with the press on the occasion of the formation of the Job Finding Bureau:

> . . . it is not sufficient for us to confine our reaction to denunciation of violence and mob rule. . . . It is apparent that our minority groups have suffered from serious social and educational handicaps which have their roots in history. These handicaps become most burdensome and frustrating on persons newly arrived in an urban

environment which today demands an ever rising standard of education and skill as a prerequisite for steady and regarding employment.

What effect this project will have on a Catholic population which has long been deprived of a vision of the Church's social responsibilities is questionable. It is not at all likely that Los Angeles Catholics will change their attitudes any more than New Orleans Catholics did when Archbishop Rummel exhorted them to cease discrimination and segregation in his pastoral letter of 1953. The fact that the chancery may now have a more enlightened view of the necessity to cooperate in alleviating unemployment does not imply that it has been enlightened on other related and essential points—institutional reform, neighborhood change, the nature of prejudice—to mention only a few.

The Los Angeles "underground," as all liberal movements and people in the diocese label themselves, is still underground. Their guerrilla warfare with the chancery deserves a special study, and their unsanctioned existence testifies not only to the vitality of Catholicism but to the dimensions of the problem of ecclesiastical reform in the archdiocese. The Catholic Human Relations Council, Catholics United for Racial Equality, the Catholic Civil Liberty Council, plus numberless priests, sisters, brothers and laymen, fight a war on two fronts: one for the reform of their own ecclesiastical bureaucracy and one for civil rights. One of the most vigorous forces in the campaign against Proposition 14 was the liberal Catholic groups just mentioned. The Christian Brothers in particular risked their status in the archdiocese by their participation in that campaign.

NORTHERN CALIFORNIA AND SEATTLE

There is a touch of irony in a confidential government report on the cities most likely to erupt into violence in the summer of 1966, that Oakland is listed as one of them. Not that the contribution of the Church in this area to the civil rights movement has been outstanding, but there are more "deserving" dioceses.

Oakland's Bishop Floyd Begin is undoubtedly one of the most liberal on the West Coast. While ordinary of the Cleveland diocese in 1954 he publicly took the Knights of Columbus to task for the racial discrimination evident in their admissions practices. The Oakland Catholic Interracial Council is one of the most active on the coast and has his firm support. In 1964 Bishop Begin was instrumental in the formation of the city's Conference on Religion and Race; and in the spring of 1966 he was among the four of California's 14 Bishops who gave moral and financial support to the unionization of migrant farm workers.

It is worth noting in passing that the struggle of the migrant farm workers for recognition of their union has exposed the "Achilles' Heel" of several California dioceses. In the Monterey-Fresno diocese particularly, where the labor struggle was centered, the wealth is largely in the hands of the fruit growers, many of whom are Catholic. Reliable informants in the diocese assert that their contributions to the building of churches, schools and other facilities are such that the threat of losing this financial support would be serious. The public and financial support given to César Chavez, the prime mover in the organizing effort, by Archbishop McGucken and Bishops Donohoe, Begin and Bell has scandalized the conservative growers. Their Catholicism is a tenuously held belief and it takes little imagination to anticipate the fading of their financial support of the Church. Bishop Aloysius Willinger's silence, then, on the issue of collective bargaining for the long-suffering farm workers is, to say the least, open to critical interpretation.

In Seattle the diocese seems to havc contributed effectively to the civil rights movement—probably more so than any other diocese on the coast. Archbishop Thomas A. Connolly has set the tone. In a public letter dated August 1, 1965, to Mr. Walter Hubbard, president of the Catholic Interracial Council, he said: "It is my purpose to emphasize again that the Church's involvement in and commitment to the civil rights issue is a matter of moral obligation. We desire to assure you and your associates of our constant and continuing cooperation in the struggle for the full and complete exercise of their human and civil rights by our colored brothers in Christ."

In March, 1965, a Mass and March of Reparation for the injustices in Selma was held in St. James Cathedral. The archbishop presided at the Mass, and the moderator of the Local Catholic Interracial Council, Father John Lynch, gave the sermon. Just prior to the Mass, 400 persons, including many from other faiths, marched from the Federal Courthouse to the cathedral.

The archbishop by his statements and actions has endorsed all Catholic participation in peaceful civil rights demonstrations. He insists the Church is committed completely to "total involvement" in civil rights. He has supported the efforts of an energetic CIC and St. Peter Claver Center in their tutoring program to help all children identified as potential drop-outs from a public or Catholic school. The chancery, as part of clergy education on civil rights, assisted actively in organizing an institute on "Interracial Justice and the Catholic Conscience" for religious and laity.

These activities are only a few of many that could be cited. We mention them merely to indicate the "official" climate of the diocese. They cannot, on the other hand, be construed as representative of Catholic attitudes. Nor are they indicative of internal structural reform or of any substantial effort to bridge the racial gap between white Catholics and the Negro population. Seattle and its suburbs do not differ substantially from other American cities in this regard.

In short, the dioceses of the West Coast resemble the variety on the East Coast. As far as the data for our survey show, there is no diocese in the West Coast so progressively involved in the civil rights movements as are, for example, the archdioceses of St. Louis, Detroit or Chicago.

CONCLUSION: THE MORAL POWER OF THE CHURCH

THE questions which prompted this study can now be answered. All Catholic institutions North and South are now accessible to Negroes, not only Catholics but non-Catholics too. Color bars and quotas are a thing of the past. Prejudice and the more elusive forms of discrimination still, of course, persist, but without anything smacking of official sanctions. The forces bringing about this change have been, for the most part, external to the individual dioceses. The climate in the nation at large on matters racial—plus the civil rights movement—are undoubtedly the underlying causes.

Yet all is not well. There seems to be more *de facto* segregation in Catholic parishes than ever before. Population growth and the huge migration of Southern Negroes from farm to city explain much of this new phenomenon. From the point of view of the Federal Government, prodded by civil rights organizations and forward-looking social scientists, this *de facto* segregation in the cities is the new problem. The Federal aid to schools and hospitals which Catholics have been demanding as their right now unwittingly binds these Catholic institutions to the nationwide problem. The U.S. Office of Education Decision made in 1966, that the diocesan schools of Lafayette and Alexandria, Louisiana, are not in compliance with the Civil Rights Act of 1964, illustrates the point. The same is true of the Department of Health, Education and Welfare dictum on St. Francis Hospital in Monroe, Louisiana. It is evident, in other words, that now the national and the ecclesiastical problem are one. At stake is the future of American cities.

The positive finding of our study that in the last 10 years the Catholic Church has solved the desegregation problem gives rise to a new question: How well prepared is the Church to carry its share of the burden of integrating the educational institutions of American cities? It goes without saying that in places like New York, Philadelphia, Chicago, New Orleans, the task will not be accomplished without the Catholic contribution. For in such cities the school population runs between 30 and 40 per cent Catholic. And the concomitant problem of easing the way into the suburbs for the emerging Negro middle class will not be resolved without the active assistance of the middle and upper-class Catholic. Much the same can be said on the economic front. The problem of Negro unemployment and unemployability, poverty and the broken family of the poor depend to a significant degree on the total budget of the 138 Catholic diocesan institutions across the nation. If an adequate amount of these hundreds of millions of dollars is allocated to the deep-rooted problems of the inner city and these funds are effectively utilized, a significant dent can be made in the over-all problem. Thus the enormous wealth and the political and economic power of the Catholic Church have brought with them an equally enormous responsibility. How well prepared, then, is the Church vis-à-vis this burden which it now only dimly sees?

The position of the Catholic Church on discrimination in employment, housing and access to public accommodations is clear and convincing. But this is the policy statement of an organization: it is not to be mistaken for the response of the Catholic people, nor even of the bishops or clergy. As this study reveals, there are still several large dioceses where these problems receive only marginal attention, if any at all.

Our study of the race problem, for example in New Orleans, has given rise to questions concerning the nature of the Church's moral power. For almost 10 years, the ecclesiastical authority in that city faced a dead end in its drive to desegregate its own institutions. In a region of the country where Catholicism and its traditions are the dominant cultural force, it could not generate the power to solve a moral problem. Fear of violence, retaliation, heresy, or mass defection admittedly were well grounded: reluctance to desegregate was understandable. But the problem runs deeper than the administrative one suggested here. What is the nature of the power the Church wields over the minds of its members? In New Orleans the power seemed non-existent for almost a decade. When the Church says one thing with respect to segregation and the members believe another, what is it that holds them together? The fact that the New Orleans impasse was finally resolved in 1962 suggests not that Catholics had decided to believe, but that they had concluded they had better not disobey. This suggests that the power of the Church is external or disciplinary. But what of its moral power, the force of its doctrine to generate assent in the heart?

For the Christian, moral power is based on his belief in Jesus Christ. Since the Catholic believes that the Church exists to carry on the work of Christ, it should be able to elicit self-sacrifice, suffering and even martyrdom for the sake of some cause declared sacred. The demand can be initiated by a charismatic leader or, as in the case of the Crusades, by the ecclesiastical organization. Charismatic leadership in the American Catholic church being absent,[1] the question arises as to the ability of the diocese or the bishops to exercise real moral power. Assuming that the solution to the race problem in all of its aspects—employment, housing, education—is going to require not merely self-abnegation but self-sacrifice, perhaps even on a heroic scale, the question is whether or not the bishops singly or together can inspire it.

Certainly the opportunities have presented themselves. But the whole non-violent resistance movement, the preëminent embodiment of such an opportunity, has progressed with only

1. The Cursillo Movement, as we have observed it, seems to possess this power. But where the Movement does exist it is incongruous with existing structures and thereby dissipates itself.

spotty Catholic support. No doubt the fact that it originates outside the Church had something to do with it. Yet Catholic priests and laymen read the same Gospel and know Mahatma Gandhi, the inspirational sources of American non-violence. Obviously we have to go deeper to ascertain the likelihood of, or the conditions for, the exercise of moral power by American Catholicism.

The fact that *the nation* possesses tremendous reserves of moral power casts some doubt on the possibility that the Church can simultaneously possess it. As American history demonstrates, the nation can command from its citizenry an endurance of the rigors of war, even "the supreme sacrifice," because of the supreme loyalty which it elicits—whether war is imperialistic or, as in both World Wars, relatively unselfish. The reluctance, or seeming inability, of the Church in the U.S. even to raise the question of the morality of nuclear war suggests that if it did, the results might be too painful or chaotic for both the individual Christian and the nation. If the Church had the moral power the nation has, the nation might no longer have the ability to wage war.

If such analysis is correct, it seems that the problem facing the Church is the locus of the ultimate loyalty of its people. For it would seem that the Church, as the Divine surrogate, cannot continue to allow the nation (or in a Southern context, the state) to hold the ultimate loyalty without forfeiting its own integrity. It is, after all, a somewhat fortuitous circumstance for the Church that the burden of responsibility for "the nation's number one moral problem" rests on the Federal Government. But would it not have been a most embarrassing situation if in the election of 1964, there had been a shift of political power to the right and disengagement of the Federal Government? Would the Church have had the moral power to engage its own huge membership in the self-sacrifice and heroism that the problem would then, even more than now, have required? Given the state of mind of Catholics and the bureaucratic structure of diocese and parish, the answer would have to be No. It is simply incongruous to expect the members of the typical parish Rosary or Holy Name Society even to discuss non-violent resistance, much less join a picket line. Catholics, by and large, simply do not seem to comprehend, or perhaps they are reluctant to acknowledge, the Christian dimension of non-violent resistance. Even the diocesan press has rarely, and only subtly, adverted to it.[1]

Never having experienced it himself, the layman might be ignorant of moral power. In a sense man can know only what he experiences. The only Church-connected power the American Catholic has experienced is that which prelates and prominent laymen have exercised on the several levels of government. He has also seen the exercise of some economic power in the occasional use of the boycott of movies, books, or magazines; the power of pronouncements, based on the fear of hell, in the area of sexual morality; and the financial power to promote Church welfare. The paucity of comment from the Catholic press and from the pulpit on the Negro display of moral power might very well stem from ignorance of it.

While there is no doubt, theologically speaking, that the Church as the people of God has such power because it is founded on the Gospel, yet it is a power that can atrophy. In the industrial revolution, the rise of the national state, the spread of imperialism and the emergence of total war—in the influences, in short, which shaped Western civilization—the Church did not, because it could not, exercise its moral power. Solutions to basic questions on the morality of war, of slavery, of segregation and of the living wage have fallen into the hands of secular agencies: the nation, the corporation or the state government. Even the initiative for educating the young has, in modern times, come from outside the Church. If the reality of any power depends on its exercise, then the moral power of the people of God remains, for the historical reasons already discussed, in a state of atrophy.

In both its Protestant and its Catholic forms, this power has suffered from the process of bureaucratization. Necessary as this

1. The *National Catholic Reporter* and the *Catholic Messenger* are notable exceptions.

process seems to have been, it is a delicate one that at all times poses a threat to the genuinely religious spirit. The need to maintain a social structure that can mobilize resources to bring the Gospel to all peoples on a permanent basis can easily seem more important than the self-sacrificing, altruistic demands of the Gospel. It should not therefore be surprising, if indeed it is a fact, that moral power seems to arise among those removed in spirit from the bureaucratic Church. The Los Angeles "underground," the priests, sisters and laymen who marched into Chicago's Southwest Side in the summer of 1966—these and many others—seem to possess the moral power indigenous to Christianity. Yet among those against whom they demonstrate there are Catholics whose loyalty to the Church is beyond question. Such a paradox, again, suggests the existence of a schism.

It is also relevant to note that in the American experience the Church has lately shaped an image of the ideal Catholic which takes more of its ideals and values from a secularized culture than from the Gospel. The 1963 statement of the hierarchy, *Bonds of Union,* as a matter of fact, asserts that this is what ails American society in general. What the statement fails to acknowledge is the contribution of organized religion to the problem and the prevalence of materialism and secularism in the Catholic Church itself. The reluctance of rank-and-file Catholics—particularly younger people in Catholic high schools and colleges—to support, much less to participate on the freedom rides, the sit-ins and picket lines poses a problem for the bishops themselves, not society. Society is merely the dough to be leavened. If, as the bishops assert, "We must renew the saving habits of grateful humility, purposeful self-sacrifice and courage to take the risks which remain the price of truly human progress," then it would seem that the most appropriate sector in which to develop these virtues is in the Church itself.

But since there is scanty evidence that this is being done except outside the formal parish and school structure, it might be well to continue our search for the reasons. Moral power, the ability of the Church to elicit (again in the words of the bishops) "purposeful self-sacrifice and courage to take the risks" is, as we have noted, barely understood by white Christians, though it remains operative nonetheless in the service of patriotism. We must then look to our contemporary situation for the reasons why the deficiency continues to exist.

The existence of a Martin Luther King immediately suggests the absence of inspirational or charismatic leadership among the Catholic bishops. Why this should be so is partly explained by the institutional nature and administrative demands of religion. The development of the original charismatic cult into a sect, a denomination and, later, a universal Church is at once the process of growth and the encasement of the free religious spirit. The Reverend Dr. King, for example, had no rules or rulers to contend with in Montgomery. No PR image inhibited his behavior. He had no organization whose welfare distracted him. Therefore he could act as a charismatic leader. Such freedom is not characteristic of the more developed ecclesiastical organization. With its rules and rulers, patterns of acceptable behavior, and culturally derived definitions of respectability and dignity, the Catholic organization seriously hedges in whatever charismatic potential may exist, at least within the main body.

With the hierarchy, however, there is a difference. Answerable to no human authority, bishops are in a sense free of organizational restriction. They are not, on the other hand, free of responsibility for it. Many no doubt have made a total but latent commitment to advance its welfare as their mode of commitment to the Gospel. While such bishops may by their works and words inspire "loyalty and devotion to the Church," they cannot command the moral power necessary for the resolution of the moral problems in society at large. (Their impotence vis-à-vis the Peace Movement is a case in point.)

But there are more subtle restrictions on the charismatic potential of the bishops. Like all men in authority, their behavior is affected by cultural norms, current values and subliminal patterns of "expected behavior." These do not seem to us to be congruent with what the Gospel expects of its disciples. The limousine with its chauffeur and two-digit license plate, the obeisance of priests and laity, the ermine, the friendships and public association with the affluent and the powerful of the world—all these unwittingly describe a conception of the episcopal office in terms of lofty dignity, organizational power and prestige. It would seem also that such a culturally defined position narrows the range of spiritual leadership and inspiration. If so, then the liberation of the bishop for inspirational leadership would seem to depend on his disengagement from the servicing of latent cultural and psychological needs of the people. The use of the episcopal office to lend quasi-religious coloration to fund-raising socials, cornerstone-laying, commencement exercises, patriotic and civic affairs may be culturally à la mode, but it does not serve the basic spiritual needs of this age. Worse, it draws in the public mind an image of this high office as largely symbolic and pietistic. It defines its dignity more in cultural than Gospel terms.

At least by implication, episcopal association with socially acceptable organizations, their dignitaries, and their social functions, furthermore, restricts the blessing of the Church to the more conservative elements of society.[1] The presence of the bishop among these elements and his commendations of their works amount to some degree of psychological reinforcement of the status quo.

If all were well in the social order, such latent support by the bishops would be a national service. But the elements which need such support at this moment in history are those working for change. On the racial front, for example, the sponsoring of a dinner for the Reverend Martin Luther King by Archbishop Paul Hallinan to honor him for the winning of the Nobel Peace Prize in 1964, illustrates such support. As of the fall of 1963, the main line of communication between the episcopacy and the dynamic elements working for interracial justice was the NCCIJ. Here and there, there are a few other connections such as that of Auxiliary Bishop Brunini of Natchez-Jackson with the Southern Regional Council. But by and large one can say

1. The Archdiocese of New York, for example, has never to our knowledge made public reference to the heroic devotion of the Catholic Worker to society's outcasts and the poor.

that, while the annual statements of the hierarchy call for change in the social order, and while their diocesan committees have been authorized to cooperate with certain of the civil rights organizations, the image of their personal involvement in the cause is lacking. Their public associations, as reflected in the press, are still largely with the established, the dignified and the "respectable" men and institutions of American society. There are exceptions, of course, but the over-all impression of the bishops' involvement is rather ambivalent. This no doubt detracts from their moral force; certainly it vitiates their potential for charismatic leadership.

On the parish level, similar factors work against the pastor's ability to give moral leadership. Promotion to the pastorate in most dioceses is geared to what might be called organizational welfare. Seniority plays a major role, as does ability to "run a parish"—that is, to administer an organization. Legitimate as these criteria may be, they allow little room for the type of leadership which will carry the Gospel beyond the organization and in to the community. If, as the late Cardinal Suhard claimed, the mission of the parish is to all who live within its boundaries, then it follows that a pastor with a centrifugal orientation, a sense of mission, is more appropriate than one whose mentality and loyalty are those of an ecclesiastical man.

Obviously, the matter can be oversimplified, but knowledge of or experience with urban renewal or slum clearance programs, residential segregation, problems of mental health and contemporary marriage, and the like, do not seem to be among the criteria for appointing pastors. There are, furthermore, few energetic, in-service training programs for pastors. Why a Sister Formation program and a similar one for chancery officials should be encouraged (here and there), while none exists for pastors and curates, suggests a certain lack of clarity as to the mission of the parish.

We have also learned in the course of this study that the Catholic school is as much a part of the problem as the public school. If some dioceses desegregated before the local public school, there were others still waiting for the public school to lead the way. It is therefore unrealistic to expect Catholic students at any level to act distinctively in this matter. Their educational institution is too closely geared to accepted cultural values and norms to generate distinction. One has only to look at the people on whom bishops and Catholic universities bestow ecclesiastical honors and honorary degrees to realize that the organization respects mainly its friends. On the other hand, the lack of ecclesiastical honors for a Dr. Tom Dooley or a Dorothy Day seems to indicate that the Church has no living saints it wishes its youth to emulate.[1] The fact that it does honor prominent generals, judges, diplomats and businessmen in effect merges the image of the ideal Catholic with that of the ideal American. The Church, in other words, while it has and always will produce a Dr. Dooley or a Dorothy Day, fails to conceptualize the type as an ideal. Catholic youth are left with no living heroes. They are not, in effect, inspired to form themselves by the Gospel. Christian character, which is the foundation of future leadership in the Church, seems to be far down on the list of priorities in diocesan education offices, if indeed it is on the list at all. This perhaps is the inevitable result of having an organization which has no avenue of expression or influence for the Catholic mother (unless she can write a book).

Whatever the ultimate solutions, there can be no doubt that they must evoke wholehearted, even painful, commitment. The body social must be cut into deeply. Organized religion, again by its own credo, must take the first reforming cuts. For the Catholic Church in particular has unwittingly permitted the growth of what Bernard Murchland has described as the danger facing all historical institutions: "the danger that a given level of achievement be considered sufficient and become so structured that all further development be blocked off." Although he was addressing himself to another problem, Murchland's words strike a strong note of relevancy here. He speaks also of a second dan-

1. A textbook in Religion, examined for possible use in the New Orleans parochial school system, was rejected in February, 1967, because it pictured Martin Luther King as Christ-like.

ger: "the temptation of pharisaism, that is, the danger that external forms become more important than the inner spirit."

The temptation of the moment is to believe that Selma represents a mobilization of Catholic manpower standing ready for the next crisis; or that it signifies an increase in the size and nature of the Catholic contribution to the civil rights movement. But the facts do not seem to warrant either view. It is true that Cardinal Spellman's release of the New York clergy to the dictates of their own consciences in this moral crisis is a significant departure from the usual organization way of doing things. On the other hand, it is important to recognize that practically all who went to Selma went with official approval or at least got away before it was rescinded. That this approval was a precarious matter is clear from the story of how the contingent was mobilized.

The request for participation by Catholic clergy and religious was channeled through Matthew Ahmann, of the NCCIJ. He and his staff of two laymen and two sisters took to the telephones for a stretch of some 30 hours, calling religious superiors, chancery officials, Catholic interracial councils and human rights commissions. While some of the religious superiors responded affirmatively to the plea for volunteers, most of them procrastinated, waiting for some sort of approval or clearance from their local bishop or provincial superior. It went without saying that all the priests had to have approval, implicit at least. The manner in which this was achieved varied from one diocese to another. But the NCCIJ staff was hamstrung without some sort of a green light from either the NCWC, a prominent cardinal or archbishop, or the ordinary of the Mobile-Birmingham diocese itself. This break came when Archbishop O'Boyle's approval for a Washington delegation was secured. The response curve quickly took an upward swing. The fact that Archbishop O'Boyle later felt constrained to rescind his approval, after his auxiliary contacted Archbishop Toolen of Mobile, had little effect. "A delegation from Washington" was in fact enroute —a simple fact that apparently induced other officials to approve the sending of a delegation or allowing one to be formed. From this precarious beginning the Catholic contingent at Selma was built up.

It was a force of volunteers. When contrasted with the nature of the Catholic contribution to the struggle heretofore, it became clear that Selma represented a shift from official and organizational support to an individual type. All previous Catholic commitments came from NCWC, the NCCIJ, Catholic interracial councils or human rights commissions, bishop's committees or religious orders. But, at Selma, the commitment, even though officially sanctioned, was nonetheless personal, spontaneous—and for this reason religious.[1]

Yet the problem of ambivalence still remains. The centrifugal forces (or personnel) in the Church still must run the gauntlet of permissions and approvals before they can, figuratively speaking, go to Selma. Church authority, in its turn, is burdened by its responsibilities to and for the organization. As the moral obligation to contribute to the solution of civil rights and other moral problems becomes more clear and compelling, to individual priests and religious particularly, conflict with ecclesiastical authority becomes and more inevitable.

Bishops and other ecclesiastical officials hold their posts, as we noted earlier, not usually because of their prophetic or spiritual qualities, but generally because of desirable and necessary abilities for the effective command of a complex organization. No matter how lofty their vision, the "organization," its personnel, its mentality, its habits and traditions, work unwittingly to emasculate that vision. The auxiliary bishop who persuaded his ordinary not to allow his priests to go to Selma because of Archbishop Toolen's opposition is a case in point. The natural tendency of any organization is toward "prudence," routine, the maintenance of authority and internal loyalties. This explains why the NCWC, the official organization of the Ameri-

1. The teams from St. Louis and Oklahoma City were official delegations. Thus we have an exception to the point we are making. In these two cases the response was both bureaucratic and "personal, spontaneous and religious."

can hierarchy, can play only minimal or obscure roles in a united Church effort to further civil rights. It took that body four years after the Supreme Court decision of 1954 to make an unambiguous pronouncement on the moral nature of segregation and discrimination. It is likewise significant that the machinery for mobilizing the clergy at Selma was the peripheral NCCIJ and not the NCWC. To expect, therefore, that this historic event could alter the natural tendencies of ecclesiastical structures seems to us highly unrealistic.

This is particularly true in matters the chancery regards as controversial. The two priests who canvassed the farm workers in San Joaquin Valley in the fall of 1965, urging them to support the strike of the National Farm Workers Association against the Council of California Growers, is one illustration. Scheduled to address the students of Sacramento State College, Father Kenny, one of the priests involved in the strike, was forced by his chancery to cancel the engagement at the last minute. Monsignor James Cullerton, chancellor of the Monterey-Fresno diocese which embraces the strike area, confirmed that he had asked Father Kenny's chancellor to keep out of the strike area. "We don't want outside clergy making trouble in the area," he said. "The diocese is doing what it can to bring the dispute to a just and peaceful solution."[1] Six weeks earlier in Milwaukee, a group of priests and sisters ran into the same sort of difficulty with their bishop. Again it was a question of the orders of a bishop conflicting with what priests and sisters regarded as their "Christian responsibility." In New Orleans the clergy faced the problem in 1963–1964. The archdiocese had a $28,000,000 fund-raising campaign under way. Its success depended, according to well-informed sources, on keeping the civil rights issue "under control." Here the Church dared not allow itself to be identified in any way with the civil rights groups in the area. In only carefully screened and qualified situations could priests or religious participate in local civil rights demonstrations. That turned out to be one, a memorial service for the Reverend Reeb who had been slain in Selma. (Although the memorial was

1. *National Catholic Reporter,* December 1, 1965.

something more than a "service," the permission was given only for that.) In 1965 and 1966, the same conflict between authority and conscience spread to Catholic college campuses, and even to seminaries.

These considerations lead us to believe that while moral power is now stirring in the ranks of religious orders, clergy and laity, its effective use depends on an authority which is not yet sufficiently aware of its urgency. This power grows from a sensitized conscience that is becoming more intolerant, not only of injustice, but of "prudent" or gradualist solutions. As the moral power of the Church grows, therefore, a clash with authority enamored of obedience and order is almost inevitable.

In other words, as the demands of a priest's conscience pull him toward involvement in peace or racial crisis, he will also feel the tug of his vow of obedience to his bishop. Given the subconscious dimension of the human mind, resentment of that authority is the likely development. This was quite evident in several Southern dioceses, especially New Orleans. On the other hand, if the bishops give *carte blanche* to their priests to follow the dictates of their consciences, the Church will increasingly become identified with civil rights organizations, and with the even less popular peace movement. This will bring the right wing into the fray, thus polarizing the two extremes, already quite dynamic.

What this means, in effect, is that the theological problem raised earlier in this analysis remains fundamental, the root of the other two problems. Archbishop Toolen unwittingly indicated that problem when he observed that those priests and religious "intruding" in his diocese should be back home "doing God's work." Yet those who were there knew that God's work was precisely what they were doing.[1]

One cannot help but feel that the American bishops have a theological problem of which they seem only dimly aware but

1. The same theological problem (that is, differences between liberal and conservative views of the meaning of Christianity and the nature of the Church) was a basic cause of the faculty-administration conflict at St. John's University in the 1965–1966 school year.

which is, nonetheless, gathering an explosive momentum. The mild clash of opinion which appeared in a March, 1965, issue of *The Brooklyn Tablet* over the pros and cons of clerical participation in Selma is, in Jefferson's ominous phrase, "a fire bell in the night." Although some 40 years elapsed before Jefferson's fears of conflict materialized, the rapid pace of change in the 1960's promises to accelerate this theological issue to painful state much sooner than is commonly expected.

INDEX